FOCUS ON BIOLOGY

# GENETICS AND EVOLUTION

*Michael Carter*

Hodder & Stoughton
LONDON SYDNEY AUCKLAND

# Acknowledgements

We are grateful to the following companies, institutions and individuals who have given permission to reproduce photographs in this book. Every effort has been made to trace and acknowledge ownership of copyright. The publishers will be glad to make suitable arrangements with any copyright holders whom it has not been possible to contact.

Biophoto Associates (page 76); Dr R L Bringster/*Principles of Gene Manipulation*, Old et al 1985, Blackwell Scientific Publications Ltd (151); Dr Jeremy Burgess/Science Photo Library (156); D A Clayton and J Vinograd/Nature 216, 652/1967 MacMillan Magazines Ltd (28); Sally and Richard Greenhill (8, 40 top right); the crew of HMS Sultan (50); E B Lewis/Nature 276, 565/1978 MacMillan Magazines Ltd (120 two photos); J Meyer/Biozentrum, University of Basel/Science Photo Library (22); MRC Radiobiology Unit (40 top left and bottom left); Dr Gopal Murti/Science Photo Library (26); Omikron/Science Photo Library (97 two photos); J R Paulson and UK Haemmli/Cell Press (27 two photos); Photo Researchers/Science Photo Library (118); Alex Rich (107); Dr Lee D Simon/Science Photo Library (12 bottom); Gunther S Stent and Richard Calender/*Molecular Genetics: An Introductory Narrative, second edition* W H Freeman and Co 1971 and 1978 (13); D C Tiermeier/Cell Press (103); M Wurtz/Biozentrum, University of Basel/Science Photo Library (12 top).

*British Library Cataloguing in Publication Data*

Carter, Michael
   Genetics and evolution. – (Focus on biology)
   I. Title      II. Series
   575

   ISBN 0-340-53266-1

First published 1992

Typeset by Litho Link Ltd, Welshpool, Powys, Wales.
Printed in Great Britain for the educational publishing division of Hodder and Stoughton Ltd, Mill Road, Dunton Green, Sevenoaks, Kent by Thomson Litho Ltd.

# ERRATUM SLIP

**Table 1** on page 96 should appear as below.

**Table 1**   *Amino acids commonly found in proteins*

| TYPE | AMINO ACID AND ABBREVIATION | | | |
|---|---|---|---|---|
| Small polar | glycine | gly | serine | ser |
| | aspartate* | asp | asparagine | asp |
| Large polar | glutamate* | glu | glutamine | gln |
| | lysine⁺ | lys | arginine⁺ | arg |
| Intermediate polarity | tyrosine | tyr | histidine⁺ | his |
| | tryptophan | trp | | |
| Small non-polar | alanine | ala | threonine | thr |
| | proline | pro | cysteine | cys |
| Large non-polar | valine | val | isoleucine | ile |
| | leucine | leu | methionine | met |
| | phenylalanine | phe | | |

NOTE   Amino acids marked * have acid side chains.
Those marked · have basic side chains.

**Table 3** on page 102 should appear as below.

**Table 3**   *The codon dictionary of the mRNA genetic code*

| FIRST BASE | | SECOND BASE | | | | THIRD BASE |
|---|---|---|---|---|---|---|
| | | U | C | A | G | |
| U | | UUU } phe<br>UUC<br>UUA<br>UUG | UCU<br>UCC } ser<br>UCC<br>UCA | UAU } tyr<br>UAC<br>UAA stop<br>UAG stop | UGU } cys<br>UGC<br>UGA stop<br>UGG trp | U<br>C<br>A<br>G |
| | | CUU } leu<br>CUC<br>CUA<br>CUG | CCU<br>CCC } pro<br>CCA<br>CCG | CAU } his<br>CAC<br>CAA } gln<br>CAG | CGU<br>CGC } arg<br>CGA<br>CGG | U<br>C<br>A<br>G |
| A | | AUU } ileu<br>AUC<br>AUA<br>AUG met | ACU<br>ACC } thr<br>ACA<br>ACG | AAU } asn<br>AAC<br>AAA } lys<br>AAG | AGU } ser<br>AGC<br>AGA } arg<br>AGG | U<br>C<br>A<br>G |
| G | | GUU<br>GUC } val<br>GUA<br>GUG | GCU<br>GCC } ala<br>GCA<br>GCG | GAU } asp<br>GAC<br>GAA } glu<br>GAG | GGU<br>GGC } gly<br>GGA<br>GGG | U<br>C<br>A<br>G |

U = uracil (in RNA replaces thymine (T) found in DNA)
C = cytosine
A = adenine
G = guanine
The explanation of the three letter amino acid symbols is given in table 1. Stop codons stop translation and release the completed protein from the ribosome

For Lucy and Andrew

# CONTENTS

# PREFACE

A Level biology syllabuses have recently undergone extensive restructuring with increasing emphasis being placed on genetics. Genetics now occupies a central place in core courses and, in some syllabuses, there are also genetics options. Students require a fairly detailed understanding of what a gene is and how it functions. This book aims to bring together the idea of genes as molecules and our understanding of genes as units of inheritance.

The book is intended to demonstrate the fascination of modern genetics as well as provide the necessary information for A Level students. Perhaps some readers will be encouraged to look into the subject further. Genetics has been a very exciting part of biology over the last 30 years and there have been many interesting discoveries. However, there are a great many things yet to be understood.

The currently accepted ideas on the nature of genes, and on how they function, are only as good as the evidence that supports them. Science advances when scientists question existing ideas and develop new ones. These advances depend on the design and execution of experiments to test current and new ideas. For these reasons, the main threads running through this book are accompanied by at least an indication of the types of experiment, or the kinds of evidence, that support them. I am well aware that too much evidence can distract the reader from the main thrust and excitement of the subject. I hope that I have achieved a reasonable balance.

I should like to thank the series editor Chris James for his encouragement and critical advice throughout the period that I was writing the book. If you feel that some of the more difficult ideas come across reasonably clearly, then you have Chris to thank for that. I should also like to thank my friends and colleagues, Richard Arnold, Douglas Eaton and particularly Julian Mitchell. They generously gave their time to go through various drafts. The book in its final form is, to my mind, much improved by their suggestions. I am indebted to Kevin Purdy for his excellent photography. My thanks too to Vicki Smith of Hodder and Stoughton for her considerable help in converting the manuscript into the finished book.

---

The following titles are also available in the *FOCUS ON BIOLOGY* series:

*Habitats and the Environment*
   ISBN 0 340 53267X

*Habitats and the Environment Investigations* (pack)
   ISBN 0 340 554339

*Micro-organisms in Action*
   ISBN 0 340 532688

*Micro-organisms in Action Investigations* (pack)
   ISBN 0 340 539224

# INTRODUCTION

## DIVERSITY OF ORGANISMS

A striking thing about living organisms is their diversity. No two humans are exactly alike (with the exception of identical twins) yet all humans belong to a single species. In general, a species is a group of individuals which can interbreed in nature and produce fertile offspring. The variation *within* a species is quite small compared to the differences *between* species, compare, for example the differences between humans with those between humans and house mice. Individuals from different species do not normally interbreed. This reproductive isolation helps to explain the differences between them. Variation between species encompasses an enormous spectrum from the simplest virus to the mightiest tree.

## UNITY OF GENETICS

Genetics is young science. Its founder was Gregor Mendel, who was the first to demonstrate that one character in an organism is determined by a single heritable unit. We now call this unit a **gene**. He showed that different characters are determined by different genes. Over the last 50 years, genetics has developed to take a central place in biology. It aims to explain:

   (i)  how genes determine the characters of organisms;
 (ii)  how differences between genes arise;
(iii)  how genes are transmitted between generations;
(iv)  how inheritance of genes can explain differences between species.

Studies designed to answer these questions have shown a great similarity in the genetic systems of organisms as diverse as bacteria and man. Genetics is therefore a unifying science. Although there may be large differences between species, their genetic systems are variations on the same main themes rather than a vast array of completely different basic mechanisms. There are two major reasons for this unity.

   (i)  One of the most important discoveries in biology has been that molecules, called nucleic acids, form the genetic material of organisms, and deoxyribonucleic acid (DNA) is the genetic material in the very great majority of them. DNA controls the organism because it controls the structure of proteins which are the main components of all cells. DNA carries a genetic code which is decoded into the various proteins which make up a cell. The genetic code is practically universal and the decoding systems of all living organisms are very similar. The DNA is copied into ribonucleic acids (messenger or mRNAs) which are transported to the sites of protein synthesis. At these sites, the mRNAs determine the exact sequence in which amino acids are built into proteins. The decoding system can be summarised as:

$$DNA \rightarrow mRNAs \rightarrow PROTEINS$$

 (ii)  In 1858, Charles Darwin and Alfred Wallace produced the theory of evolution by natural selection. This has now been given a genetic basis and it is generally accepted as the explanation for the diversity of organisms and the unity of their genetic systems. This theory suggests that organisms have diverged over a very long period of time from a common ancestry.

# ORGANISMS AND LIFE HISTORIES

Genes can only be investigated through the **characters** they control. These characters may be **behavioural** (like courtship displays) **morphological** (like plant height), or **biochemical** (like the activity of enzymes). Therefore we need to know something about the biology of organisms before we can understand their genetics. This chapter begins by making the distinction between **environmental** and **genetic variation**. The major groups of organisms are introduced and the differences between them are outlined. **Life histories** of the different groups are summarised. Life histories must be understood before we can set up breeding experiments and interpret patterns of inheritance correctly.

## The nature of variation

### Variation due to differences in the environment

Some differences between individuals of the same

*The difference in skin pigmentation between human beings has a genetic cause*

species are brought about by variations in the **environment**. For example, the coats of several mammals, including the arctic hare and the lynx, change colour from flecked brown (agouti) to white in the winter. The environment induces changes in the activity of the genes controlling coat colour, but the actual genes present are the same in both agouti and white individuals.

### Genetic variation

Genetically different individuals maintain their different characters whatever the environmental conditions. The photograph shows Negroid and Caucasian humans. Their skins all contain the pigment **melanin** which gives protection from the Sun. The degree of pigmentation varies in both types of people according to their exposure to the Sun. However, even in the same environment, there is always pigmentation difference between them. This is because the combinations of genes controlling the distribution of melanin are different. This is one example of genetic difference.

## Types of organisms

Similar and related organisms can be grouped into a **species**. There are many millions of different species. One of the main aims of early biologists was to make sense of biological diversity so they collected, described, and named living things. An important milestone in the eighteenth century was the system of binomial classification devised by Carl von Linnaeus in about 1758. Each organism was identified as belonging to a species which was given a binomial (two part) latinised name. For example, the human species is *Homo sapiens*. Species were arranged into a hierarchy of ever larger and more general groups. Using this system, it became possible to name and classify all living organisms according to their similarities and differences. New species are still being discovered and fitted into this scheme today.

Linnaeus could place any species into one of two large groups, called **kingdoms**: the **Plantae** (plants) or the **Animalia** (animals). This distinction is based on the two very different ways that organisms get the raw materials (organic molecules based on carbon) needed to stay alive, to grow and to reproduce.

Plants are **autotrophs**: they use energy (from sunlight) to make the organic molecules they need from simpler chemicals present in the environment. Animals are **heterotrophs**: they feed on other organisms, breaking them down into their component molecules. Animals use these molecules as a source of energy and raw materials.

During the last 100 years, biologists have discovered that there are more kingdoms than Linnaeus recognised. These kingdoms rest on the discovery of **cells**. We now know that every living organism is made up of cells. Some very small organisms are made of only *one* cell. Larger organisms may be made of tens, thousands or millions or cells. Investigations of the internal structure of cells, using the electron microscope, have shown that many of the smaller organisms are made up of a structurally simpler cell than other living things (Figure 1). The genetic material in these cells is not contained within a nucleus. Such cells are called **prokaryote** ('*before a nucleus*') and we now recognise a kingdom of organisms called the **Prokaryotae** (previously **Monera**) whose cell structure is of this type.

Four other kingdoms are now recognised in addition to the Prokaryotae. The organisms in these kingdoms all have larger, **eukaryote** ('*true nucleus*') cells (Figure 2). The genetic material in these cells is contained within a membrane-bound nucleus. The cytoplasm also contains several other membranous organelles which perform different functions. Many of the organelles are about the size of a prokaryote cell. There is some evidence that eukaryote cells may have formed originally by the amalgamation of different types of prokaryote cells. Two of the four eukaryote kingdoms are those recognised by Linnaeus.

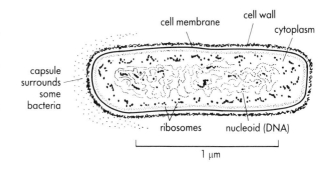

**Figure 1   A bacterial cell (prokaryote)**

The main features of the five kingdoms and examples are given in the following list.

**Prokaryotae**: Bacteria including the Cyanobacteria (blue-green algae). All are constructed from a simple prokaryote cells. Most are **unicellular**, i.e. each organism consists of a single cell. A few are **multicellular**, formed from chains of cells. Some prokaryotae are autotrophic, others are heterotrophic.

**Protoctista**: Most algae and protozoa. They are constructed from a larger, more complex eukaryote cell. Many protoctists are unicellular; some are multicellular. Some species are autotrophic, others are heterotrophic. Some species have cells walls, others do not. Some move about, others do not.

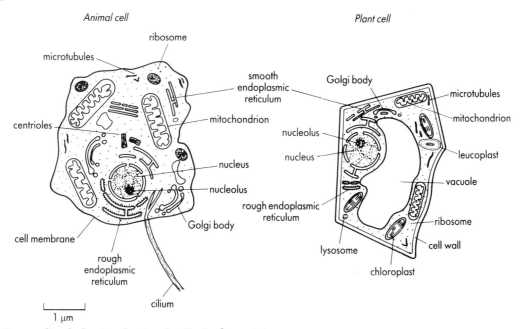

**Figure 2   Generalised plant and animal cells (eukaryote)**

The members of the other three kingdoms are also eukaryote but almost all are multicellular. Most consist of many millions of cells.

**Fungi:** All types of fungi. These are mostly non-motile organisms. Most have a cell wall containing **chitin**. All are heterotrophic.

**Plantae:** Liverworts, mosses, ferns and seed plants. All have cellulose cell walls and are non-motile. They are all autotrophic.

**Animalia:** Sponges, coelenterates, flatworms, annelids, molluscs, arthropods, echinoderms and chordates, as well as many smaller groups. Their cells have a limiting membrane but lack cell walls. All are heterotrophic. Most move about in search of food, or a mate, etc.

In addition to these five kingdoms, there are a group of subcellular organisms called **viruses**. They can only survive and reproduce as **parasites** inside the cells of members of the five cellular kingdoms. There are many different sorts of virus but none of them can reproduce or increase in number *outside* their host cell.

# Life histories

A **life history** is a summary of the types of individuals found in one generation and indicates the way in which these individuals reproduce. There are two types of reproduction: **asexual** and **sexual**.

## Asexual reproduction
A single parent copies its genes and passes the copies to its offspring by division. Parent and offspring therefore carry the same genes.

## Sexual reproduction
This is most easily explained by reference to eukaryotes. In eukaryote sexual reproduction, cell *fusion* alternates with a special type of cell *division*. The cells which fuse are male and female reproductive cells. In general, each of these cells contains a single set of genes, but they may contain alternative forms of some genes. For example, for brown or blue eyes, and dark or blond hair. Cell fusion adds the genetic information of male and female reproductive cells together, so the resulting cell (the **zygote**) contains both the maternal and the paternal information. The special cell division produces single sets of genes from the double set, but the new sets may contain a mix of maternal and paternal alternatives. This mixing is called **recombination**, and it is a very important source of **genetic variation**.

## Prokaryote life histories
Prokaryote species reproduce **asexually**. In single-celled prokaryotes, asexual reproduction can be very rapid. Under optimum conditions a bacterium may divide into two 'daughter' cells every 20 minutes (chapter 9).

Many prokaryote organisms can also pick up a few genes from other individuals by temporary cell contact (**conjugation**), or by other means (see chapter 6). The introduced genes may be added to the individual's genetic information or used to replace some of it. The replacement of some genes as a result of temporary cell contact is a form of sexual reproduction.

## Eukaryote reproduction
Eukaryotes that reproduce asexually do so by cell division. The nucleus divides first and then the cell divides. This basic type of nuclear division is called **mitosis** (chapter 9). In eukaryotes consisting of one cell, a mitosis and cell division leads to two separated daughter cells. This is asexual reproduction. Multicellular eukaryotes increase in size by mitotic cell divisions and reproduce asexually in the same way.

Most eukaryotes reproduce sexually. After cell fusion, the double set of genetic information is divided into single sets by the special nuclear division called **meiosis** (chapter 5), followed by cell division.

Mitosis produces two daughter nuclei which are exact copies of the parent nucleus. Mitosis can occur in cells with *one* set of genetic information carried on *one* set of **chromosomes**. These are called **haploid** or 'n' cells. It can also occur in cells with a *double* set of information carried on two sets of chromosomes. Thes are called **diploid** '2n' cells. The cells of some species contain more than two sets of chromosomes. They are **polyploid**, for example 3n or 4n. Mitosis can also occur in these cells. Meiosis, which halves the amount of genetic information, never occurs in haploid cells. It regularly occurs in diploid and polyploid cells, but it is often ineffective in the latter. In summary, the following nuclear divisions are possible:

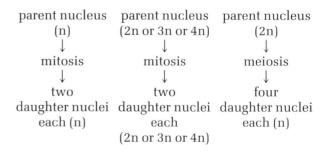

## Eukaryote life histories
There are many millions of different eukaryotes, but there are broadly *three* types of life history.

**Type (i) HAPLONTICS: Mitosis in haploid cells only**

Some protoctists e.g. *Chlamydomonas*
and fungi e.g. *Neurospora* (bread mould)

*ASEXUAL REPRODUCTION and/or GROWTH*

ORGANISM (n) → MITOSIS (n) → ORGANISM (n)

*SEXUAL REPRODUCTION*

MITOSIS (n) → male gamete (n) / female gamete (n) → FUSION → zygote (2n) → MEIOSIS → ORGANISM (n) (one cell) → MITOSIS → ORGANISM (n) (many cells)

**Type (ii) DIPLONTICS: Mitosis in diploid cells only**

Some protoctists e.g. *Amoeba*
All Animalia e.g. *Drosophila* (fruit fly)

*ASEXUAL REPRODUCTION and/or GROWTH*

ORGANISM (2n) → MITOSIS (2n) → ORGANISM (2n)

*SEXUAL REPRODUCTION*

MEIOSIS → male gamete (n) / female gamete (n) → FUSION → ORGANISM (2n) (one cell) → MITOSIS (2n) GROWTH → ORGANISM (2n) (many cells)

**Type (iii) HAPLO-DIPLONTICS: Mitosis in haploid and diploid cells**

Some protoctists e.g. some seaweeds. Fungi e.g. *Agaricus* (edible mushroom)
All Plantae e.g. mosses, ferns, flowering plants

*ASEXUAL REPRODUCTION and GROWTH*

SPOROPHYTE* ORGANISM (2n) → MITOSIS → SPOROPHYTE ORGANISM (2n)

GAMETOPHYTES* → MITOSIS (n) → GAMETOPHYTE ORGANISM (n)

*SEXUAL REPRODUCTION*

MEIOSIS → spores (n) → male (n) / female (n) → MITOSIS (n) → gametes (n) → FUSION → zygote (2n) → (2n) MITOSIS → SPOROPHYTE ORGANISM (2n)

* Sporophytes (2n) and gametophytes (n) grow and may reproduce asexually by mitosis

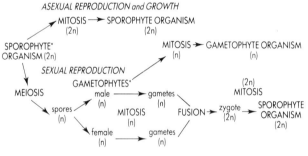

***Figure 3** The three types of life history found in eukaryote organisms*

Each eukaryote species repeats its life history in each generation; they are therefore sometimes called **life cycles**. The three types of life history can include both sexual *and* asexual reproduction. They are defined by whether the organisms have haploid mitoses, diploid mitoses, or both (Figure 3).

(i) In **haplontic life histories**, the individual organism is haploid (Figure 4). The diploid zygote is often a resistant, thick-walled unit for dispersal of the species to other habitats. There are no diploid mitoses in this group

(ii) All animals are **diplontic**. The individual is diploid and the haploid gametes are relatively short-lived (Figure 5). There are no haploid mitoses.

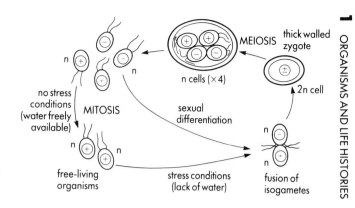

***Figure 4** The life history of a haplontic organism,* Chlamydomonas reinhardtii. *This is a single celled autotrophic protoctist. The species has two mating types: + and −*

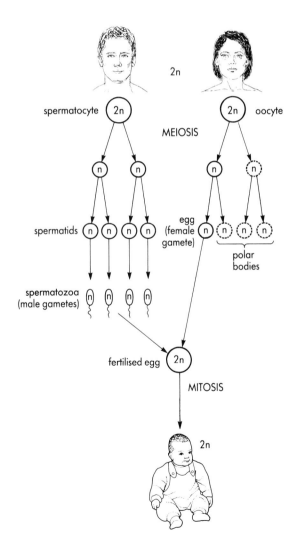

***Figure 5** The life history of a diplont species,* Homo sapiens

(iii) The third group are **haplo-diplontic**. Both haploid and diploid organisms may be well developed and there are both haploid and diploid mitoses. However, among the Plantae there is a trend for the diploid **sporophyte** plant to become the dominant form. The haploid **gametophyte** forms an adult plant in simpler groups like liverworts and mosses and the sporophyte is relatively inconspicuous. In contrast, an adult flowering plant is a sporophyte; the gametophyte stages are reduced to pollen (male gametophyte) and embryo sac (female gametophyte) as in Figure 6. There are few haploid mitoses. Possible reasons why animals and flowering plants are diploid are discussed in chapter 10.

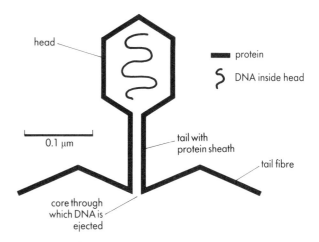

**Figure 7    The T4 virus which infects the bacterium Escherichia coli**

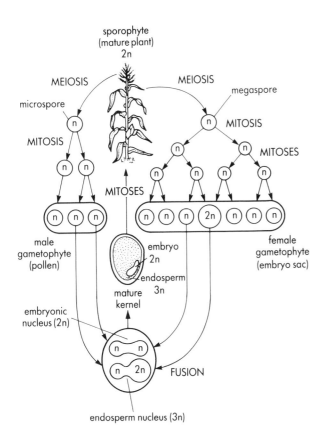

**Figure 6    The life history of a haplodiplontic species, Zea mays (maize)**

**The T4 virus, which attacks the Escherichia coli bacterium. Its structure is shown in Figure 7**

## Viral life histories

Viruses can only reproduce inside a host cell. They are very small (Figure 7) and most consist of only two types of molecule: a **nucleic acid** (e.g. deoxyribonucleic acid, DNA), surrounded by various **proteins**. In a viral infection, the nucleic acid of free viruses enters a host cell. Sometimes several virus individuals infect the same host cell

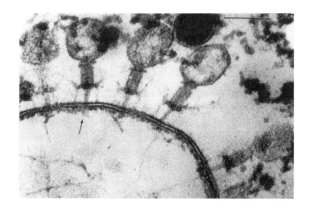

**The T4 virus adsorbs to the surface of the E. coli cell. A number of viruses can infect the same bacterial host cell and inject their DNA (see arrow)**

(Figure 7). If they are genetically different then recombination inside the host cell can produce viral offspring with different combinations of parental characters. Multiple infections of a cell by viruses can therefore be considered as a form of sexual reproduction. Once a virus has entered a host cell there are two possible life histories.

(i) **In the virulent life history** (Figure 8), the virus genes take over the synthesising system of the cell and make many copies of the viral molecules. These form viral offspring inside the host cell. They are then released. Some viruses burst the host cell (**lysis**) and release about 100 viral offspring at a time. Other viruses release individual offspring one after another, through the cell membrane, and do not kill the cell for some time. A virulent infection is the only life history open to many types of virus.

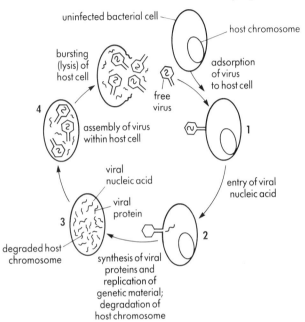

*Figure 8   The virulent life cycle of a bacterial virus,  e.g. T4*

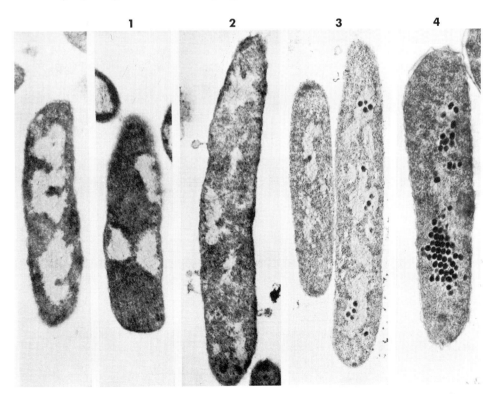

*These photographs show the virulent life cycle of the T4 bacterial virus. The number above each photograph refers to the corresponding stage in Figure 8*

(ii) **In the temperate life history** (Figure 9), the viral nucleic acid is inserted into the chromosomes of the host cell. The virus becomes **inactive** in this state. When the cell divides, the viral genes are copied along with all the host cell genes and one copy of the viral chromosome is passed to each daughter cell. This can continue for many generations of cell division. Occasionally the virus is activated and moves into a virulent life cycle.

These life cycles were originally discovered among the viruses which infect bacteria. However they are also essentially true of viruses which infect eukaryote cells, although the life histories of many of these viruses do have additional features.

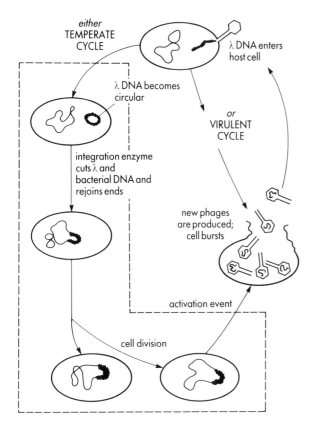

**Figure 9    The infective cycles of the temperate virus lambda (λ) which infects the bacterium Escherichia coli**

# BIBLIOGRAPHY

## Organisms and life histories

Green, N P O, Sout, G W and Taylor, D J (1990). *Biological Sciences Vol 1: Organisms, energy and environment* 2nd Edn. Cambridge University Press.

Margulis, L and Schwartz, K V (1987) *Five Kingdoms* 2nd Edn. W H Freeman.

# QUESTIONS

1 Define a species.

2 What are the differences between autotrophs and heterotrophs?

3 What are the main differences between prokaryote cells and eukaryote cells?

4 What are the differences between asexual reproduction and sexual reproduction?

5 How do viral life histories differ from those of cellular organisms?

# DNA AND THE GENETIC MATERIAL

This chapter introduces molecules called **nucleic acids**. There are two types of nucleic acid: **deoxyribonucleic acid (DNA)** and **ribonucleic acid (RNA)**. DNA is important because the genes in almost all organisms are made of it. The exceptions are some viruses in which the genes are made of RNA.

This chapter introduces experiments that first suggested that DNA is the genetic material. At first these experiments were not generally accepted because many biologists felt that nucleic acids could not have the sort of structure that would allow them to carry genetic information. The interest at that time was mostly in **proteins**. However, when the structure of DNA was discovered it was realised that this structure gave the molecule the right properties to be the genetic material. The structure of DNA and its biological significance is the second major topic considered in this chapter.

DNA has been extracted from many organisms (see box) and we now have good estimates of the amount of DNA per cell. DNA is packaged into chromosomes. The organisation of DNA in chromosomes is the third major topic dealt with in this chapter.

information. The chapter ends with a discussion of techniques being used to discover the molecular organisation of complete DNA molecules. This is called **nucleotide sequence analysis**.

## 2.1 MOLECULES IN LIVING ORGANISMS

The most abundant chemical in a living organism is water. This usually forms about 80–90% of cell material. Most of the rest is organic material. This is made of various molecules based on **carbon**. They are called **organic molecules**. Table 1 is a summary of the types of organic molecule found in a typical bacterial cell. It is relatively easy to

---

**Table 1    The organic molecules most often found in a cell (E. coli)**

| CELL COMPONENT | PER CENT DRY WEIGHT OF CELL | APPROX. No. OF MOLECULES PER CELL |
|---|---|---|
| Carbohydrates and proteins in cell wall | 10 | many |
| Lipids and proteins in cell membrane | 10 | many |
| Deoxyribonucleic acid, DNA | 2 | 1 |
| Total ribonucleic acid, RNA | 26 | |
| (transfer RNA, tRNA) | (3) | 160 000 |
| (messenger RNA, mRNA) | (2) | 2 500 |
| (ribosomal RNA, rRNA) | (21) | 20 000 ribosomes |
| Ribosomal proteins | 9 | 20 000 ribosomes |
| soluble protein | 42 | $10^6$ |
| small metabolites (including sugars, fatty acids, amino acids, ATP, NAD, NADPH, etc.) | 1 | $6.5 \times 10^6$ |

---

**Isolation of DNA from an organism**
Tissue or cells in aqueous (water) solution are broken open by chemical methods (e.g. using the enzyme lysozyme to split open bacterial cells) or physical ones (e.g. grinding). This disrupts the cell membranes and releases the cell contents which consist largely of proteins and nucleic acids. RNA is removed by enzyme degradation. Proteins are removed by extraction with phenol. The phenol is mixed with an aqueous cell extract and the water and phenol layers separate. The phenol contains the cell proteins, and the DNA remains in solution in the upper aqueous layer. This layer can be removed and the DNA concentrated by precipitating it with ethanol.

DNA is a very long and thin molecule. Different sections along the molecule carry different genetic

culture a bacterium such as *Escherichia coli* in large quantities. This gives enough material to analyse.

Some plant and animal cells can now be cultured. The overall proportions of the organic molecules in these cells are similar to those in bacteria. Table 1 shows that a group of molecules, called **proteins**, form the major cell constituent. The cells also contain various nucleic acids, smaller quantities of **carbohydrates** and **lipids** and a vast array of other small molecules.

# 2.2 DNA AS THE GENETIC MATERIAL

Until 50 years ago, biologists thought that proteins were the only molecules sufficiently variable to be carriers of biological information and hence it must have been these that were the genetic material. However, two experiments that were not generally accepted until the 1950s demonstrated that DNA must be the information-carrying molecule of the cell: the 'genetic molecule'.

**Experiment 1:** *The transforming principle*
Frederick Griffith (1928) showed that living bacteria must be able to pick up genetic information from dead individuals of a different strain. When they do this, the recipients take on the character of the donor strain and pass it to their offspring. The living bacteria have become **transformed** by some material from the dead individuals.

The bacterium used was *Streptococcus pneumoniae*, a bacterium which causes pneumonia in humans. The disease-causing strain is covered by a polysaccharide capsule (Chapter 1, Figure 2) and therefore appears smooth (S) under the microscope. Bacteria reproduce by cell division, a parent cell forming two daughter cells. In *S. pneumoniae*, daughter cells are usually smooth like their parent. Very rarely, bacteria which have lost the capsule arise from strains with capsules. These non-capsular individuals appear rough (R) under the microscope. They pass this rough character to their daughters when they divide.

Griffith discovered that S bacteria reproduced when injected into the blood stream of mice.

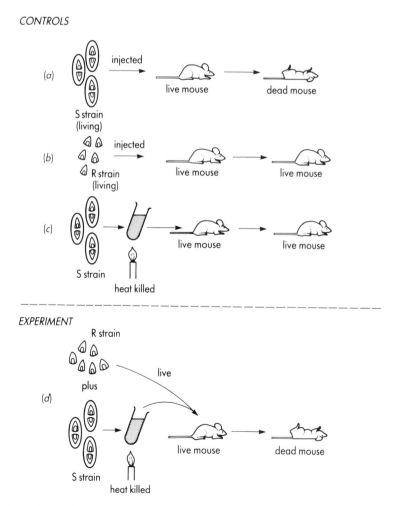

**Figure 1    Griffith's transformation experiment**

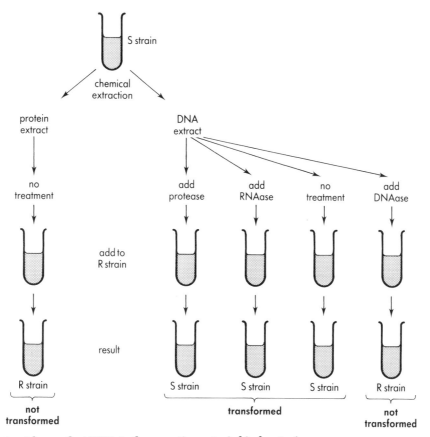

*Figure 2    The first evidence that DNA is the genetic material in bacteria, and that protein is not the genetic material*

Within 24 hours the mice died (Figure 1a). R bacteria also reproduced in a mouse's blood but did not kill it (Figure 1b). Heat-killed bacteria did not reproduce (Figure 1c). Injection of live R cells plus heat-killed S killed the mouse (Figure 1d). This suggests that living R bacteria can acquire the information to make a capsule from heat-killed S individuals and thus become virulent. The rough–smooth transformation would also occur in bacterial cells grown in laboratory culture, so mice were not essential.

**Experiment 2:** *DNA is the transforming molecule*
By 1946, Oswold Avery, Colin MacLeod and Maclyn McCarty were able to extract nucleic acids and proteins from *S. pneumoniae* and separate them. They discovered that the only cell fraction collected from smooth cells which would transform a rough strain, was the fraction containing DNA. However, if this fraction was treated with an enzyme which degraded DNA (**DNAase**), then transformation was prevented. As a control experiment, the DNA fraction was treated with enzymes which degraded RNA (**RNAase**) or protein (**protease**). There was no effect on its transforming ability (Figure 2). It was shown later that a recipient strain could be transformed for *two* different characters (smooth capsule *and* resistance to an antibiotic).

Therefore DNA was not merely a catalyst for the synthesis of a capsule. It must be the genetic material carrying *all* the information necessary to make up each bacterial cell. The transformed cells must have taken up donor DNA and somehow exchanged donor genes in this DNA for their own.

The results of many other experiments confirm that DNA is genetic material in most organisms.

## 2.3 THE COMPOSITION OF NUCLEIC ACIDS

Nucleic acids were first discovered in 1869 when Fredrich Miescher, a young Swiss doctor, showed that nuclei of human pus cells contained molecules which gave an acidic reaction. During the first 50 years of this century, the chemical components of these nucleic acids were discovered.

It became clear that there were two types of nucleic acid: **DNA** (deoxyribonucleic acid), and **RNA** (ribonucleic acid). DNA and RNA molecules are both chains. Each link in a chain is built up from three types of molecule:

    (i)  a pentose **sugar**,
    (ii)  a purine or a pyrimidine **base**,
    (iii)  phosphoric **acid**.

In DNA, the sugar is **deoxyribose** (Figure 3). Note that the carbon atoms have been numbered. Deoxyribose is named because the 2′ carbon has been deoxygenated and carries two '−H' atoms. In most DNA molecules there are two kinds of purine, and they both have a double ring structure: **adenine** (**A**) and **guanine** (**G**). There are also two kinds of pyrimidine and each of these has one six-membered ring: **cytosine** (**C**) and **thymine** (**T**). Notice the numbering of the positions in the rings of the sugar and bases. In the sugar, each number is prime (′): 1′, 2′ etc. In the base, the number is non-prime: 1, 2, etc. This numbering is used to identify the positions at which changes are made between different sugars and different bases.

In RNA, the sugar is **ribose**. It is almost identical to deoxyribose except that the 2′ carbon carries an −H and an −OH (Figure 3). In RNA, thymine is replaced by **uracil** (**U**) but the other bases are the same as in DNA. Note that thymine is also called 5-methyl-uracil because a methyl ($CH_3$) group replaces a hydride (H) attached to the '5' position of the ring. A few other bases (e.g. inosine) are found in small quantities in some RNA molecules.

Both DNA and RNA chains consist of repeated, similar units called **nucleotides**. A nucleotide is always formed from one sugar, one base and a phosphoric acid molecule. A chain is called a **polynucleotide**. A sugar and one base combined is called a **nucleoside**. Hence, a nucleotide is a nucleoside with a single phosphoric acid attached to the 5′C of the sugar (it is a nucleoside 5′ monophosphate).

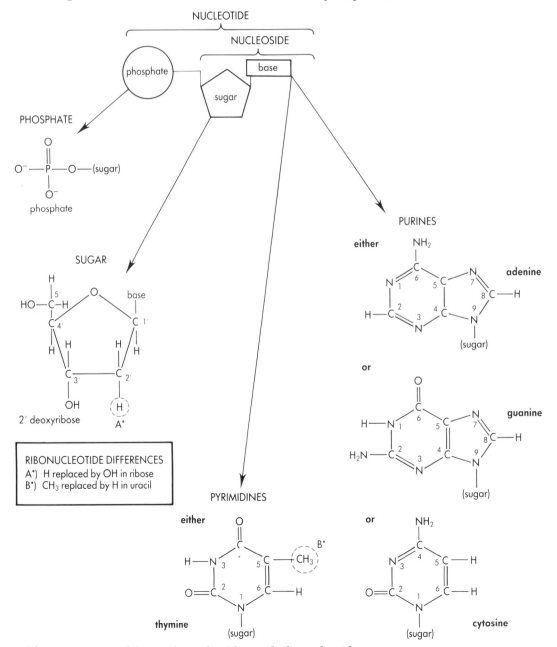

*Figure 3   The components of deoxyribonucleotides and ribonucleotides*

Nucleotides are the repeating units in nucleic acids. However, the polynucleotide chains are actually synthesised from **nucleoside 5′ triphosphates (dNTPs)**. Figure 4 shows one of the four dNTPs for DNA. This is 2′ deoxyadenosine 5′ triphosphate. The other three dNTPs substitute guanine, cytosine, or thymine for adenine.

The three phosphorus atoms are labelled α, β and γ, Radiolabelling studies (see box on page 24) have shown that the β and γ phosphates are removed when a DNA chain is formed. The two high energy phosphate bonds are broken, providing the energy to drive the attachment of the α phosphate of the next 5′ nucleotide to the 3′ carbon of the last sugar of the growing chain. This is a **condensation reaction** (Figure 5). Notice that each α phosphate binds to the 3′ carbon of one sugar which loses an OH. The α phosphate also remains attached to the 5′ carbon of its own nucleotide, so this is a 3′ − 5′ bond between adjacent sugars.

*Figure 4    2′ deoxyadenosine 5′ triphosphate. This is one of four nucleoside 5′ triphosphates which are used in the synthesis of a DNA molecule*

*Table 1    Proportions (%) of bases in DNA from different organisms*

| ORGANISM | A | T | G | C |
|---|---|---|---|---|
| *E. coli* | 26 | 24 | 25 | 25 |
| *S. cerevisiae* | 31 | 33 | 19 | 17 |
| *H. sapiens* | 30 | 30 | 20 | 20 |

## The structure of DNA

In the early 1950s, Erwin Chargaff showed that DNA from a number of different species had equal amounts of A and T (A = T), within experimental error, *and* equal amounts of G and C (G = C). However the ratio of (A + T) : (G + C) was usually not 1. i.e. the DNA from some species had more (A + T), as shown in table 2; others had more (G + C). This suggested that A paired with T, and G paired with C, but the A—T pairs must be quite independent of G—C pairs.

1953 marked a turning point in biology when James Watson and Francis Crick showed how nucleotide polymers were arranged in DNA. The structure of RNA was worked out at about the same time. Watson and Crick built a model of DNA using Chargaff's evidence, plus evidence from the X-ray diffraction patterns of DNA fibres obtained by Maurice Wilkins and Rosalind Franklin. Chargaff's evidence suggested that the bases were paired in the DNA molecule; the X-ray data suggested the molecule was a regular helical fibre.

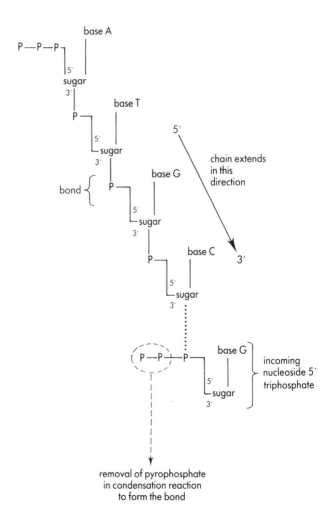

*Figure 5    The extension of the DNA polynucleotide chain. This chain is formed by a series of condensation reactions to form an ester*

Watson and Crick looked for the simplest model of DNA structure that would be consistent with this evidence. This was a molecule of two polynucleotide chains, the bases projecting in towards each other at right angles to the long axis of the molecule so that A paired with T, and G with C (Figure 6). By carefully constructing model nucleotides with all the correct bond angles, they saw that adenine was the right shape to link across to thymine by two hydrogen bonds, and guanine could form three hydrogen bonds with cytosine within the double stranded molecule.

So a DNA molecule must consist of two *complementary* polynucleotide chains, hydrogen bonded to each other by four possible **nucleotide pairs** (A==T, T==A, G≡≡C, C≡≡G) and arranged in a helix (Figure 7). Watson and Crick's model is now known to be the usual form of DNA, the **B form**. The two chains run in opposite directions, wound in a right-handed helix with bases stacked at right angles to the long axis of the chain.

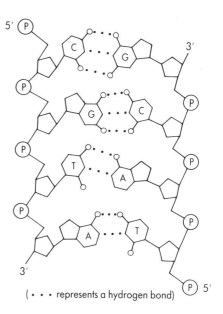

( • • • represents a hydrogen bond)

**Figure 6** *'Ladder diagram' of a DNA molecule to show four possible base pairs and oppositely polarised polynucleotides*

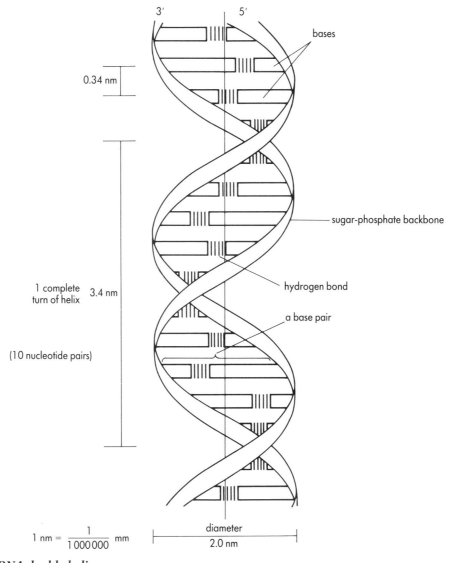

**Figure 7** *The DNA double helix*

## The genetic material

Watson and Crick realised that the structure of DNA accounted for the three main features of the genetic material:

(i) **Genetic information**: many different sequences of the four nucleotide pairs are possible along different parts of a DNA molecule (Figure 8a). The different pair sequences could be a **code** for the synthesis of all other molecules in the cell.

(ii) **Variation**: if any nucleotide pair is altered (e.g. A==T becomes G≡≡C) then that part of the code is altered (Figure 8b). This change or **mutation** may then alter the character coded by that DNA sequence (an altered **gene**).

(iii) **Inheritance**: if the two polynucleotide chains unwind and separate, each one can act as a template for the synthesis of a new complementary strand because A will only pair with T, and G with C. In this way the nucleotide pair sequence in one DNA molecule can be exactly copied into two daughter molecules (Figure 8c) so both molecules would inherit the same genetic information.

# The structure of RNA

There are several different sorts of RNA molecule in a cell. They are all synthesised by polymerisation of ribonucleoside 5′ triphosphates and are therefore similar to DNA (except for the structure of the sugar and some base differences). Unlike DNA, they are all *single* chain molecules but they differ in the length of the chain and the sequence of bases along it. All RNA molecules are much shorter than DNA. The most abundant RNAs are **ribosomal RNAs (rRNA)**, but **messenger RNAs (mRNA)** and **transfer RNAs (tRNA)** also occur (table 1). Several very small RNA molecules have recently been discovered in eukaryote cell nuclei, called **small nuclear RNA (snRNA)**.

(a) *Genetic information*

Four different nucleotide pairs give $4^n$ possible sequences of n nucleotide pairs, (n = number of nucleotide pairs in the sequence). With four consecutive nucleotide pairs, there are $4^4 = 256$ possible sequences. Here are 8 of the 256 possible sequences of four nucleotide pairs.

```
A A A A      G G G G      T T T T      C C C C
T T T T      C C C C      A A A A      G G G G

A A T T      G G C C      T T A A      C C G G
T T A A      C C G G      A A T T      G G C C
```

(b) *Genetic variation*

Alteration of the nucleotide pair sequence ( ↯ ) will alter the genetic information carried by that sequence.

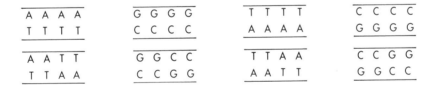

(c) *Inheritance*

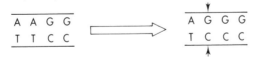

original molecule → two polynucleotide chains separate and act as templates for new DNA synthesis → two identical copies (A must pair with T, and G with C)

**Figure 8** *Three essential features of the genetic material which can be accounted for by the DNA double helix*

All these RNA molecules are important in **protein synthesis** (Chapter 8). Many RNA molecules fold back on themselves because different parts of the single strand have complementary base sequences which pair up. Thus the sequence of nucleotides in an RNA chain helps to determine the shape of the molecule (Figure 9). The shape of a molecule is very important in determining the function it performs.

(a) *tRNA molecule*

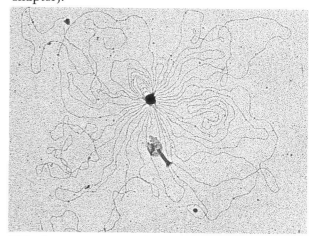

**Figure 9** *The RNA single strand folds back on itself and is held together by base pairs*

## RNA in viruses

RNA is the only nucleic acid in some viruses. Tobacco Mosaic Virus (TMV) is a virus consisting of RNA surrounded by proteins. TMV reproduces in leaf cells of tobacco plants and damages the leaves, forming brown blisters (**lesions**). Different strains of the virus cause different lesions.

In 1954, Heinz Fraenkel Conrat and Bea Williams showed that RNA is the genetic material in this virus. They extracted RNA from one strain and protein from a different strain. When these RNA and protein molecules were mixed in a test tube, they combined to form infective viruses. The progeny reproduced by these 'hybrid' viruses produced lesions like the parent which provided the *RNA*. Since then, many viruses have been found to have *DNA* as their genetic material, e.g. T4 which parasitizes *E. coli* and SV40 which infects monkey cells. However, there are a number of important RNA viruses. These include human influenza virus, and the retroviruses such as human immunodeficiency virus (HIV) which causes AIDS (Acquired Immune Deficiency Syndrome).

## The amount of DNA per cell

The photo shows that a huge length of DNA is packed inside a virus. This virus has very few genes. Cells contain larger amounts of DNA and many more genes. Figure 10 shows the range in amounts of DNA making up one set of genetic information (a **haploid genome**) among various organisms. More complex organisms tend to contain more DNA per genome than less complex ones, but there is a wide variation in genome sizes within some groups. All mammals have rather similar amounts of DNA, much less than some amphibia and some plants. The variation in amounts of DNA in cells of related animals has made geneticists wonder if all DNA carries genetic information (see last section of this chapter).

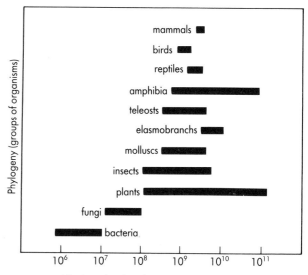

*This electron micrograph shows a bacterial virus burst to release a single very long molecule of DNA (its genetic material). The molecule is very long compared to its thickness (2 nm). The virus head is very small (85 × 110 nm)*

**Figure 10** *The variation in amount of DNA measured as number of nucleotide pairs per haploid genome in various groups of organisms. Note the wide range in quantity of DNA within some groups*

# 2.4 LOCATION OF THE GENETIC MATERIAL

Eukaryote cells contain a **nucleus** (Chapter 1, Figure 2). It is separated from the rest of the cell by a **nuclear envelope** made up of two lipoprotein membranes, one on either side of a fluid-filled **perinuclear space**. The outer membrane is continuous with the **rough endoplasmic reticulum (RER)** so the periplasmic space is continuous with the lumen of the RER, which may allow for transport of molecules. The nuclear envelope is punctured by 3000–4000 **nuclear pores** which are just big enough to allow molecules up to the size of small proteins to pass freely between the nucleus and cytoplasm. In prokaryotes, there is a distinct region of the cytoplasm called the **nucleoid** (Chapter 1, Figure 2) but it is not separated from the rest of the cytoplasm by any membrane.

Almost all genetic information is contained within the nucleus or nucleoid. This was first shown by Hammerling who grafted cell material between *Acetabularia* species. *Acetabularia* is a single cell protoctist (chapter 1), the different species having different shaped caps. In Hammerling's experiments (Figure 11) the hybrid cells always grew the cap of the parent which had donated the *nucleus*.

DNA is the genetic material in cellular organisms, and Hammerling demonstrated that the genetic information is carried in the nucleus. Hence it is not surprising that most DNA in a eukaryote cell is found in the nucleus, and most bacterial DNA is located in the nucleoid. The DNA is synthesised within the nucleus and remains there. This can be shown by providing radioactively-labelled precursors (dNTPs) in the medium surrounding the cells – these nucleotides are incorporated into newly synthesised DNA which is located by autoradiography (see box).

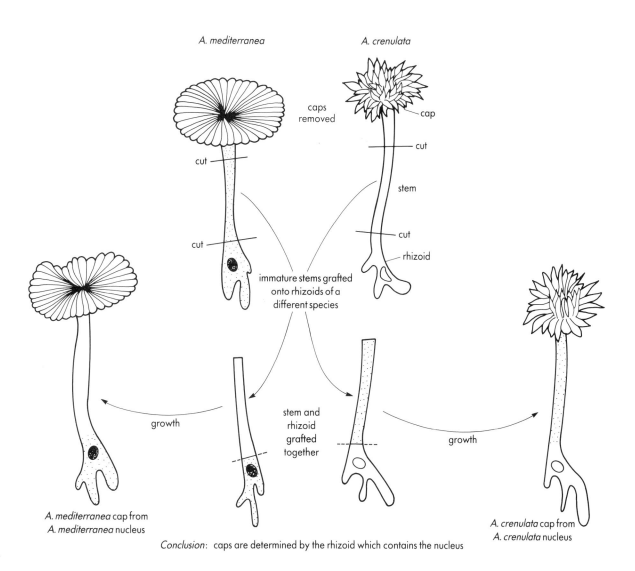

**Figure 11**   *Grafting experiments with* Acetabularia *species with different caps*

### Radioisotopes, radiolabelling and autoradiography

Atoms consist of a nucleus surrounded by one or more negatively charged electrons. The nucleus contains positively charged protons and non-charged neutrons. The number of electrons and protons for a particular atom are constant, but the number of neutrons can vary. The various forms of an atom, with different numbers of neutrons, are called **isotopes**. All isotopes of a particular atom have the same number of electrons so they all take part in chemical reactions in the same way and form the same molecules. The three different atoms in the table below have isotopes which are often used to trace biological molecules.

Isotopes with an excess of neutrons over protons are unstable. Some break down quickly, others more slowly. The **half life** is the time taken by half the quantity of the unstable isotope to decay into its product.

In decay the extra neutron splits into an electron and a proton. The electron is released as a high energy emission and the proton is retained in the nucleus, e.g. $^{14}C$ (6p+8n) $\rightarrow$ $^{14}N$ (7p+7n).

A cell or an organism cultured in a medium containing an isotope will incorporate it into an appropriate molecule. Thus $^{32}P$ can be incorporated into DNA because DNA contains phosphorus. Some of these $^{32}P$ atoms decay, releasing electrons. The electrons can be used to detect the position of the DNA molecule. One method of detection is to cover the object of interest with a photographic film which is sensitive to the high energy electrons. This technique is often used to detect the position of a molecule in a thin section of a cell, or on a gel which has been used to separate molecules by electrophoresis (see box on page 29).

| ATOM | ELECTRONS/ PROTONS | STABLE ISOTOPE | UNSTABLE ISOTOPE | PRODUCT ATOM |
|---|---|---|---|---|
| Hydrogen | 1e and 1p | 0 or 1n | 2n | Helium |
| Carbon | 6e and 6p | 6n | 8n | Nitrogen |
| Phosphorus | 15e and 15p | 15n | 17n | Sulphur |

where e are electrons, p are protons and n are neutrons

The half lives of the three unstable isotopes above are:

| | | | | HALF LIFE |
|---|---|---|---|---|
| Hydrogen | $^{3}H$ (1p + 2n) | $\rightarrow$ | Helium (2p + 1n) | 12.1 years |
| Carbon | $^{14}C$ (6p + 8n) | $\rightarrow$ | Nitrogen (7p + 7n) | 5700.0 years |
| Phosphorus | $^{32}P$ (15p + 17n) | $\rightarrow$ | Sulphur (16p + 16n) | 14.3 days |

**Chromosomes** are the most conspicuous objects within a nucleus. They are stained uniformly along their length by Feulgen's reagent which reacts specifically with DNA. After staining, they can be observed under the light microscope. Chromosomes carry most of a cell's DNA and therefore most of its genetic information. The cell nuclei of each species contains a characteristic number of chromosomes. There are 23 different human chromosomes (n = 23) but most cells in the human body contain two copies of each chromosome. This is the diploid number, 2n = 46. Human and other mammalian chromosomes are somewhat unusual. When they are stained by Acid Giemsa stain they are banded (Figure 12). Different human chromosomes have different band patterns and can therefore be individually recognised. This ability to recognise particular chromosomes is a key feature which helps geneticists to locate particular human genes on specific chromosomes.

Chromosomes are usually only visible just before a cell divides. The nucleus prepares to divide (by mitosis, see chapter 9 or meiosis, see chapter 5) and the chromosomes become highly condensed. Colchicine is a chemical which arrests nuclei in division. If colchicine is added to cells in culture, a number of them arrest in mitosis and the visible chromosomes can be studied in detail. Figure 12 shows that mitotic chromosomes prepared in this way have copied their DNA and **replicated** so they appear split down their length. Each chromosome consists of two identical **chromatids** held together at a **centromere**. Normally, each chromatid would later separate from its partner and become a chromosome in a daughter cell. Methods for studying human chromosomes are very important in medical genetics. They can be applied to a sample of human cells and the chromosomes screened for

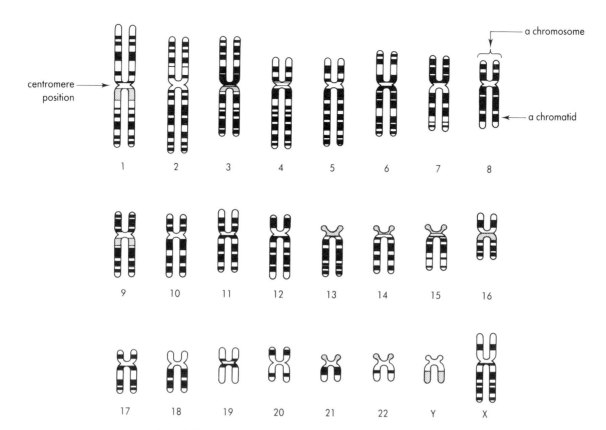

In most cells, each chromosome 1 – 22 is represented twice; plus one X and one Y chromosome for males.
In sperm, the chromosome number is halved and a sperm contains either an X or a Y chromosome.

*Figure 12   Drawings of the band patterns of human  male chromosomes seen under the light microscope*

alterations (mutations, see chapter 5).

In a few species, some *non-dividing* cells
contain visible chromosomes in their nuclei.
These chromosomes are often huge, making them
easy to study. e.g. **polytene chromosomes** in the
salivary gland cells of *Drosophila melanogaster*.
Figure 13 shows the large size of these
chromosomes compared with the chromosomes of
mitotic cells in *Drosophila*. The chromosomes are
much longer than mitotic chromosomes because
they have uncoiled. They are also much thicker
because they have gone through 10 replications
without separating. Thus there are probably $2^{10}$
(= 1024) uncoiled mitotic chromosomes lying
side by side in each polytene chromosome.
Polytene chromosomes are banded when stained
by Feulgen's method, and each different polytene
chromosome has a unique pattern of bands. Both
human and fruit fly patterns are very important in
working out the position of genes on
chromosomes.

*Drosophila melanogaster* has four different
chromosomes (n = 4), but, as in humans, each
somatic cell contains two copies of the
chromosomes. The two copies of each polytene
chromosome lie so close that they usually appear
to be a single structure. Like mitotic
chromosomes, every polytene chromosome has a

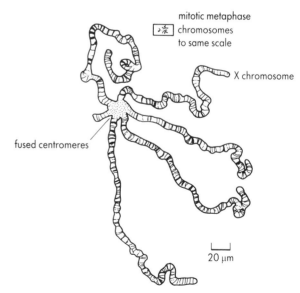

*Figure 13   The polytene chromsomes from the
salivary gland cells of the fruit fly* **Drosophila
melanogaster**

centromere. However, in the salivary gland cells
of *Drosophila*, all the polytene chromosomes are
joined at their centromeres. This contrasts with
normal mitotic cells where the chromosomes are
separate and the centromeres are not fused.

# DNA in chromosomes

A chromosome contains a single nucleic acid molecule. This was first shown for viruses and bacteria. A T4 virus chromosome consists of a linear DNA molecule with two free ends. Other viruses, including SV40, and many bacteria, have a chromosome consisting of a circular molecule of DNA. The autoradiograph of the chromosome of *E. coli* was first prepared in 1961. Cairns labelled the bacterial DNA with $^3$H-labelled thymidine and then layered the chromosome on a grid for electron microscopy. Notice that the DNA molecule in this chromosome is replicating to form two copies one for each daughter cell (Figure 14).

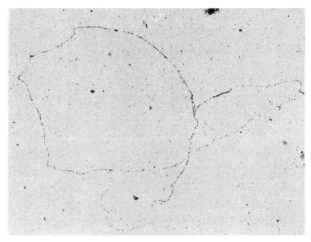

*This autoradiograph shows the circular chromosome of the* Escherichia coli *bacterium. Its structure is shown in Figure 14*

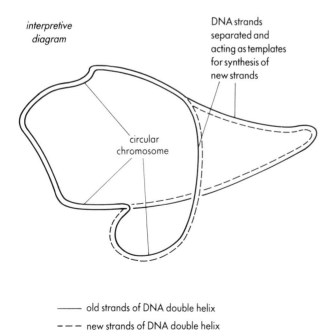

*interpretive diagram*

DNA strands separated and acting as templates for synthesis of new strands

circular chromosome

—— old strands of DNA double helix

– – – new strands of DNA double helix

**Figure 14   The circular chromosome in** Escherichia coli *(see photograph)*

It has recently become possible to separate very large DNA molecules of different sizes by one type of **electrophoresis** (see box on page 29). When this technique is applied to DNA very gently extracted from yeast (*Saccharomyces cerevisiae*), 16 different linear molecules can be separated. Linkage mapping (see chapter 5) suggests that yeast has 16 chromosomes. This correlation suggests that each yeast chromosome contains a single very long DNA molecule. This is probably true of all eukaryote species.

The longest human chromosome measured in mitosis is a cylinder 10 μm long and 0.5 μm wide. It contains about $2.5 \times 10^8$ base pairs or 8.5 cm of DNA. To get some idea of the packaging problem, scale it up and imagine trying to fit 85 km of string into a 10 m × ½ m tube. Packing a very long DNA molecule into a very small chromosome volume is a problem for all organisms. The photograph illustrates this problem for *E. coli*.

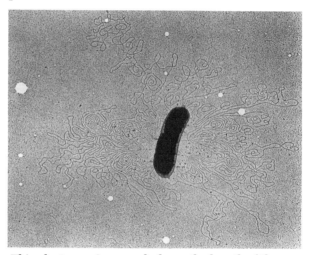

*This electron micrograph shows the length of the* E. coli *chromosome (1500 μm long) compared with the size of the bacterium (1 μm long). The nucleoid has spilled out of the lysed* E. coli *cell releasing the chromosome*

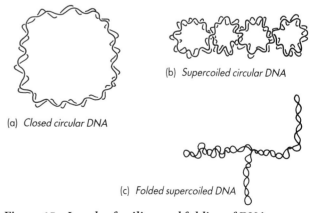

(a) *Closed circular DNA*

(b) *Supercoiled circular DNA*

(c) *Folded supercoiled DNA*

**Figure 15   Levels of coiling and folding of DNA double helix when it is a closed circle. This occurs in prokaryote chromosomes and in extrachromosomal DNA**

## Chromosome packaging

The prokaryote chromosome consists mostly of DNA, but with a much smaller amount of protein which is important in packaging. The circular DNA of *E. coli* is twisted into a single thread (Figure 15). As the DNA double helix is a coil, this extra twisting of the DNA molecule is called **supercoiling** and it helps the bacterial chromosome to fit inside the bacterium.

In eukaryote chromosomes, the single DNA molecule of each chromosome is linear, and each chromosome contains about equal amounts of proteins and DNA. Protein plus DNA is called **chromatin**. Basic (positively charged) proteins called **histones** are the most abundant chromosomal proteins. Five different histones (H1, H2A, H2B, H3 and H4) can be isolated from chromosomes. These and other proteins are used to pack an enormous length of DNA into a chromosome as follows (Figure 16):

(i) Four histones (not H1) form a protein core around which 140 nucleotide pairs of DNA

are wound (Figure 17a). This structure is called a **nucleosome**.

(ii) Nucleosomes joined by 60 nucleotide pair lengths of 'spacer' DNA form a 'beads on a string' fibre (Figure 16). This has been observed under the electron microscope. The chromatin fibre is about 6 times shorter than pure DNA.

(iii) H1 histones help the nucleosomes to pack together into a tightly coiled, flexible tube called the 30nm filament (Figure 16 and

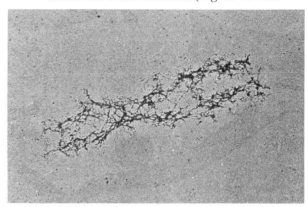

*Electron micrograph of a human metaphase chromosome with histones removed, showing the protein scaffold surrounded by loops of DNA*

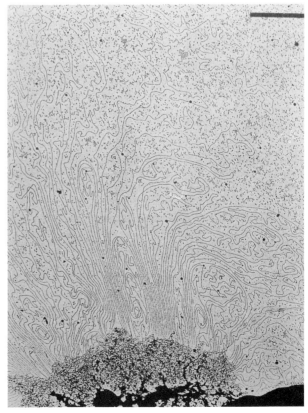

*Electron micrograph of a human metaphase chromosome with histones removed. This higher magnification shows the attachment of loops to scaffold protein*

*Stage (i) to (vi) of chromosome formation*

(i) DNA double helix

↕ 2 nm

(ii) 'beads on a string' chromatin

↕ 11 nm

(iii) packed nucleosome chromatin

↕ 30 nm

(iv) looped chromatin

↕ 300 nm

(v) condensed loop chromatin

700 nm

(vi) metaphase chromosome

↕ 1400 nm

*Figure 16   DNA is combined with histones into chromatin, which is condensed and formed into chromosomes*

(a) *Nucleosome*

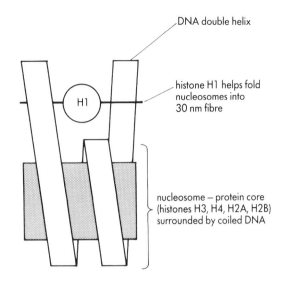

(b) *The 30 nm fibre*

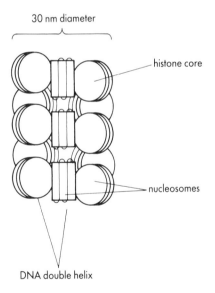

**Figure 17   From DNA to chromosome. The details of chromatin structure**

Figure 17b). This filament is about 60 times shorter than the DNA it contains. 8.5 cm DNA in the longest human chromosome is reduced to a filament about 1.5 mm long still 150 times as long as the human chromosome!

(iv)  Length is further reduced by looping the 30 nm filament (Figure 16). Each loop,

which contains one or a few genes, is held at its base onto a chromosome scaffold made of non-histone protein. This is shown in the electron micrographs. The loops reduce the length of the chromatin to a few hundred micrometres and the interphase chromosome probably has this structure. Chromosomes in dividing nuclei are about 10 times shorter than this, so there must be even further condensation (Figure 16).

# Non-chromosomal DNA

Prokaryote *and* eukaryote cells carry a small amount of genetic information in smaller DNA molecules outside their chromosomes. In prokaryotes, these small DNA molecules are called **plasmids**. They usually lie free in the bacterial cytoplasm. In eukaryote cells, the extrachromosomal DNA molecules are carried in various organelles in the cytoplasm, particularly mitochondria, chloroplasts and basal bodies of cilia. Cytoplasmic DNA molecules are usually circular, although linear molecules have been described in bacteria and yeasts. Most cytoplasmic DNA molecules can replicate independently of the chromosomal DNA. This means that some plasmids are present as several copies in a bacterial cell. Similarly, each mitochondrion may carry several copies of mitochondrial DNA, as shown in the photograph.

One way to demonstrate the existence of extrachromosomal DNA is by **density gradient centrifugation** (see box). If DNA is extracted from mammalian cells and centrifuged through a density gradient, the chromosomal DNA forms a band at one position in the gradient and the mitochondrial DNA (which has a different base pair composition) forms a subsidiary band at a slightly different position. If the mitochondria are removed from the cell extract before the DNA is collected, the subsidiary band is not present on the gradient.

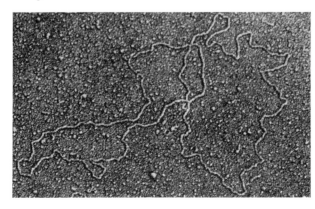

*This electron micrograph shows two interlocked circular DNA molecules extracted from a mitochondrion*

# Electrophoresis

Electrophoresis is one of the most important techniques in molecular biology. It is used to separate different proteins and also DNA molecules of different sizes. Both types of molecule are charged. A gel of starch, agarose or polyacrylamide forms a mesh with small pores through which other molecules can move. Small molecules can move through the pores easily, larger ones find it more difficult. The pores are filled with an electrically conducting buffer as shown below.

A mixture containing many copies of each of the molecules to be separated, is placed in a slit in the gel. A large potential difference is applied along the gel length. Positively charged molecules move towards the negative end of the gel (cathode), negatively charged ones move towards the positive end (anode). The exact position which a molecule reaches in the gel depends on its charge, its size and its shape.

All DNA molecules have the same negative charge per unit length due to their phosphoric acid components. However DNA molecules of different lengths can be separated by electrophoresis. The mixture is loaded on the gel near the cathode. All the copies of the shortest DNA molecules move quite easily through the pores of the gel and end up in a band towards the anode. The longest molecules remain nearer the cathode. The intermediate length molecules line up in between (as shown below). Once the current is switched off, the separated molecules can be stained, or shown up by autoradiography. A single band on the gel shown in the diagram contains all DNA molecules of the same length, i.e. different bands represent different sized molecules. they can be purified by cutting up the gel and redissolving each band separately.

(a) *Electrophoresis apparatus*

(b) *Surface view of gel*

In this example, samples from the same organism were loaded into all sample wells — each lane gives the same result

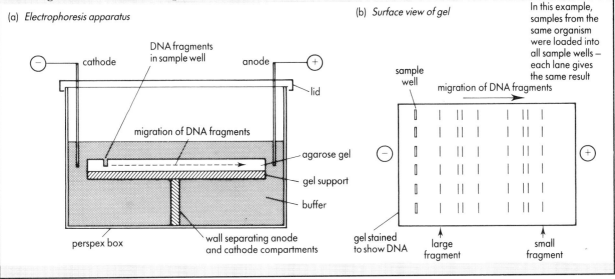

# Density gradient centrifugation

Caesium chloride ($CsCl_2$) molecules in water form a concentration gradient if spun at high speed in an ultracentrifuge. There are more molecules at the bottom of the tube than at the top. This means that the density of the liquid in the tube increases from the top to the bottom. If other molecules are added to the tube, they migrate downwards under the centrifugal force until they reach a position where their density is the same as that of the surrounding $CsCl_2$ molecules. Molecules with different densities form bands at different positions down the tube. They can therefore be separated.

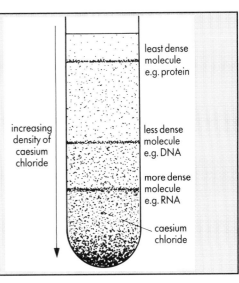

# 2.5 THE NUCLEOTIDE PAIR SEQUENCE

Molecular geneticists can now determine the exact **sequence** of thousands of nucleotide pairs along a DNA molecule. This is important because it shows the position and structure of genes and allows geneticists to investigate how they work. The main features of the present methods are outlined here (Figure 18). A viral example is then considered in more detail.

(i) Very long DNA molecules ($10^4$–$10^6$ nucleotide pairs) are too big to deal with all at once. They have to be cut into manageable lengths of a few thousand nucleotide pairs.

(ii) Many millions of copies of one of these shorter DNA molecules are produced to provide enough material to work with.

(iii) All these DNA copies are then cut at the same positions to produce several shorter fragments. At present it is only possible to sequence a few hundred nucleotide pairs at a time.

(iv) The different fragment are separated from each other.

(v) The position of each fragment in the longer chain is worked out.

(vi) The nucleotide pair sequence in each small fragment is then determined.

## The complete nucleotide sequence of a simple organism

Complete nucleotide sequences were first established for the smaller DNA viruses, e.g. SV40. Viruses like this have two advantages: they contain only a few thousand base pairs in their whole chromosome, and many million copies of SV40 DNA (or any other viral DNA) can be produced by infecting host cells in culture. It is therefore fairly easy to get enough viral DNA to work with.

To sequence a viral chromosome, the DNA is first purified from the viral culture. Samples of the DNA are then cut with different **restriction endonucleases** (see box on page 32). DNA from any organism is likely, by chance, to contain one or more recognition sites for a particular restriction endonuclease. The number of SV40 recognition sites for three restriction endonucleases is shown in Table 2.

DNA molecules from different SV40 viruses are the same, so they are all cut at the same sites by a particular endonuclease. The enzyme EcoRI cuts

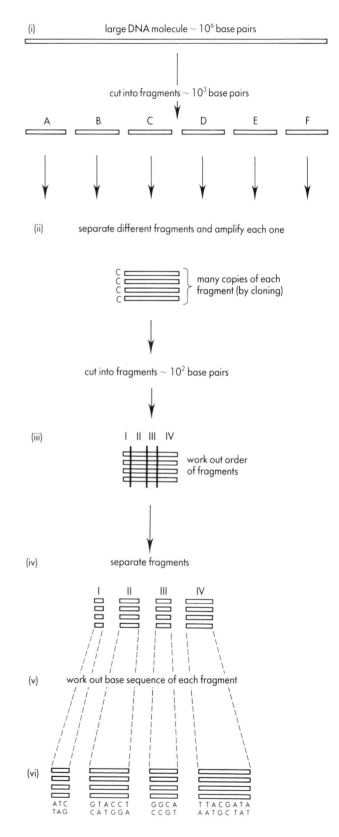

**Figure 18    The main steps needed to analyse the base sequence of a DNA molecule**

all SV40 chromosomes at one site with the nucleotide pair sequence:
5′ G A A T T C 3′
3′ C T T A A G 5′

**Table 2    Site-specific restriction endonucleases**

| BACTERIUM | ENZYME | SEQUENCE | No. of SV40 SITES |
|---|---|---|---|
| *Escherichia coli* | EcoRI | G ↓ AATCC | 1 |
| *Haemophilus aegyptus* | HaeIII | GG ↓ CC | 18 |
| *Haemophilus influenzae* | HindIII | A ↓ AGCTT | 6 |

↓ marks the site at which the sequence is cut

If an experiment starts with many SV40 chromosomes, detectable amounts of every fragment are produced. Recognition sites for several restriction enzymes are scattered along the DNA molecule at random. Therefore, enzyme digestion produces fragments of different sizes. These can be separated from each other by electrophoresis and their position in the whole molecule can be worked out. A simple generalised example is given below.

## A restriction map

Figure 19 shows DNA fragments on a gel after three different digestions of a viral chromosome. EcoRI digestion produces a single large molecule (lane 1). Digestion by a different enzyme, HindII, produces two smaller fragments (lane 2). Digestion by EcoRI *and* HindII produces three fragments (lane 3). When added together, these three fragments form a molecule the same size as the single fragment in the EcoRI digest. The same is true for the 2 fragments produced by the HindII digestion.

From the results on the gel, if the DNA molecule had been linear then EcoRI could not have cut it because EcoRI digestion produces a single band. If EcoRI did not cut the DNA, the double digest should show only the two HindII fragments. This cannot be the right explanation because the double digest produces *three* fragments.

The simplest interpretation is that EcoRI cuts at one site, making a circular DNA molecule linear. HindII cuts at two sites, one closer to the EcoRI site than the other. The positions of the three fragments must be as shown on the diagram in Figure 19. The positions of the three sites cut by each restriction enzyme, and the positions of the three different fragments in the chromosome are shown. This sort of diagram is a **restriction map**. It shows that this viral chromosome is circular, and it shows the location of each fragment in the

(a)  *Digestion of three samples of viral DNA*

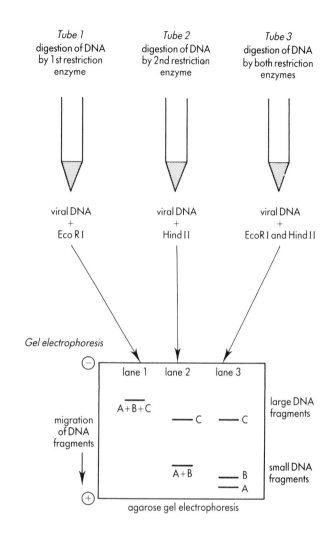

(b)  *Restriction map of the virus*

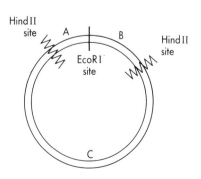

**Figure 19    (a) Digestion of three samples of viral DNA followed by gel electrophoresis, and (b) restriction map of the virus**

chromosome. If the sequence of nucleotide pairs in each fragment can be worked out, then the complete sequence of the chromosome can be established. Maps of real organisms, including SV40, contain many more fragments than shown in Figure 19.

---

**Restriction endonucleases in bacteria**

Many species of bacteria protect themselves against invasion. They produce a **restriction endonuclease** that cuts DNA between adjacent nucleotides. Their main role in bacteria is to cut up the DNA (genetic material) of invading organisms, such as viruses, to kill them. Restriction endonucleases recognise short sequences of nucleotide pairs in the DNA. Different strains of bacteria have their own enzyme and they recognise different nucleotide pair sequences:

| SPECIES | ENZYME | SEQUENCE RECOGNISED |
|---|---|---|
| | | ↓ |
| *Escherichia coli* | EcoRI | 5′G A A T T C3′ <br> 3′C T T A A G5′ <br> ↑ |
| *Arthrobacter luteus* | AluI | 5′A G C T3′ <br> 3′T C G A5′ <br> ↑ |

Notice that the recognition sequence often reads the same in both directions (5′ → 3′ on each strand). Arrows show the positions at which the recognition sequence is cut. Some enzymes make staggered cuts in the DNA (e.g. EcoRI), others make symmetric cuts (e.g. AluI). Any DNA molecule is likely to contain one or more of these short sequences, including the bacterium's own DNA. This 'own' DNA is protected by the bacterium's **modifying enzyme** which matches the particular restriction enzyme. It alters one of the bases in the recognition sequence (e.g. by adding a methyl group or a sugar); the restriction enzyme does not recognise the modified sequence and cannot cut it. Viral DNA which has not entered this bacterial host before is unlikely to be modified and therefore it is cut up.

Many different restriction enzymes have now been purified. They are crucial tools in molecular genetics and biotechnology.

---

# Nucleotide sequence analysis

There are two methods of working out the sequence of nucleotide pairs in a DNA fragment several hundred pairs long. Walter Gilbert and a colleague developed the '**chemical method**' for

sequencing DNA. Gilbert shared a Nobel Prize with Frederick Sanger who invented an alternative method called the '**enzymic method**'.

The chemical method will be summarised here as it was used to establish the sequence of the 5243 base pairs in the SV40 chromosome (Figure 20):

(i)   Many copies of a particular fragment of DNA are produced. The two strands of these DNA fragments are labelled at the 3′ end with $^{32}$P.

(ii)  The strands are separated from each other and all the copies of one strand are collected.

(iii) The single strands are distributed into four test tubes. Each tube will be used to establish the positions of one of the four different nucleotides in the strands. The tubes are labelled 'G', 'A and G', 'C and T', and 'C'.

(iv)  Chemical reagents are added to each tube. These cut a single strand of DNA at a particular kind of nucleotide, e.g. the reagents added to the 'G' tube cut the strand at a guanosine (G), the reagents added to the 'A and G' tube cut a strand at either an adenosine (A) or a guanosine (G), etc. Just enough reagents are added to cut each strand *once*. After chemical treatment, each test tube contains several fragments of different length.

(v)   The fragments from the four tubes are loaded into separate wells in a polyacrylamide gel. The gel is then put through electrophoresis. The DNA fragments in each sample separate according to their length. After electrophoresis, the gel is covered by a photographic film for autoradiography. The fragments labelled with $^{32}$P appear as dark bands over their position on the gel.

(vi)  The complete nucleotide sequence of the fragment can be read off the autoradiograph of the gel starting from the positive pole. The shortest fragment was cut nearest the 3′ end of the strand. This fragment, which migrated furthest during electrophoresis, is from the 'C and T' tube in this example. It does not appear on the 'C' track of the gel. Hence the base nearest the 3′ end of the strand is T ((C and T) − C). The next shortest fragment appears in the 'A and G' tracks on the gel, but not in the 'G' track so the next base in the series is A, and so on.

In 1976, the complete sequence of nucleotide pairs in the SV40 chromosome was worked out using restriction mapping and the Maxam and Gilbert method. The positions of the viral genes in the nucleotide sequence have also been established (Figure 21).

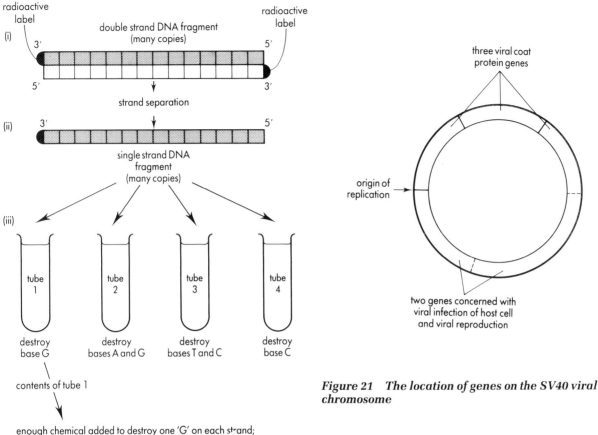

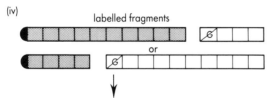

**Figure 21   The location of genes on the SV40 viral chromosome**

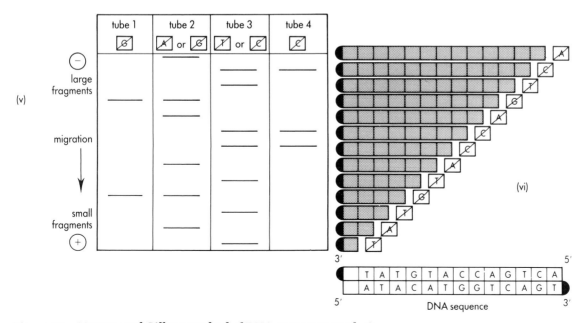

*Figure 20   Maxam and Gilbert method of DNA sequence analysis*

No cellular organism's genome has been completely sequenced yet. However, tens of thousands of bases have been sequenced round particular genes from various organisms, including humans. This has given valuable insight into the structure of genes and the way in which they function. These topics are discussed in chapters 7 and 8.

# 2 .6 DNA SEQUENCES THAT LACK GENETIC INFORMATION

In eukaryotes, there are wide differences in the amount of DNA in genomes of closely related species, and in the amount of DNA between different groups (Figure 10). About $10^8$ base pairs of the $3 \times 10^9$ total base pairs in human DNA actually code for human characters. The rest of the DNA does not code for protein. Much of this DNA consists of millions of repeats of similar short sequences of base pairs. This repetitive DNA can be isolated from the rest of the DNA in various ways, including density gradient centrifugation.

In *Drosophila*, there are three slightly different seven nucleotide pair sequences, each one repeated millions of times along the DNA. One of them is:

5′ A C A A A C T 3′
3′ T G T T T G A 5′

It has been shown that many of these repeated sequences are located close to centromeres in chromosomes. It is not known if they have a function, but they are not translated into protein and therefore do not code for the structure of the organism. In contrast to eukaryotes, almost all of the DNA in a prokaryote genome carries genetic information and is transcribed into RNA and translated into proteins.

# BIBLIOGRAPHY

Brown, T A (1989) *Genetics, a Molecular Approach* Van Nostrand Reinhold
Williams, J G and Patient, R K (1988) *Genetic Engineering* IRL Press, Oxford

# QUESTIONS

1 The following diagram represents the basic chemical unit which makes up DNA.

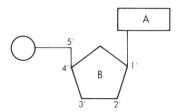

What is the name of:
a) this unit,
b) the component labelled A,
c) the component labelled B?

2 How does the structure of RNA differ from the structure of DNA?

3 If adenine (A) forms 30% of the bases in a DNA molecule, what proportion are cytosines (C)?

4 Explain how nucleotides are attached together to make a DNA strand (polynucleotide).

5 Which are the three fundamental properties of living things that can be explained by the structure of the DNA molecule?

6 How does a human chromosome differ from a bacterial chromosome?

7 How does a polytene chromosome differ from a chromosome in mitosis?

8 a) Explain the DNA packaging problem for human chromosomes.
 b) What roles do histones play in chromosome organisation?

9 What is a restriction map?

10 The nucleotide sequence in a polynucleotide is found to be:
5′ A T C G T G T T A C C G A A A 3′
Can you predict the sequence in the complementary polynucleotide? What pattern on a polyacrylamide gel, produced by the Maxam and Gilbert method, would confirm your prediction?

# PATTERNS OF INHERITANCE

This chapter considers the relationship between a **character** and a **gene**. It shows that **controlled breeding experiments**, invented by Gregor Mendel in the 1850s, can be used to prove that genes exist. Mendel used the garden pea (*Pisum sativum*) in his experiments, but his experimental design can be applied to many different organisms. In later sections of the chapter, the results of experiments carried out over the last 100 years are summarised to show that Mendel's ideas are widely applicable. These experiments have also extended Mendel's original ideas.

It is not ethical to do experiments with humans, but the ideas behind controlled breeding experiments can be used to interpret human family data. This is called **pedigree analysis** and the basic methods are introduced in this chapter.

## 3.1 MENDEL AND GENETICS

Gregor Mendel was the first person to demonstrate that genes exist. He published his work in 1865, but his ideas were ahead of their time and it was 40 years before his genius was appreciated. A gene has three features:
  (i) it controls a particular **character**,
  (ii) it can alter or **mutate** and produce different forms of the character,
  (iii) it is **inherited**, so that the character is passed from parents to their offspring.
Mendel made use of (i) and (ii) but his proof that genes exist rests on (iii). He carried out a series of controlled breeding experiments in which he selected particular plants as parents and knew the pedigree of every plant he produced. Analysis of the pattern of inheritance of various characters showed that genes, which controlled those characters, must exist. The modern term **'gene'** was coined after Mendel but it is used throughout this book.

## Mendel's experimental organism

Mendel chose the garden pea *Pisum sativum* for two main reasons.

(i) Pea plants show alternative forms for several well defined characters. Mendel used seven different characters, but concentrated in particular on seed colour and seed shape (Table 1).

(ii) Garden peas can be cross-fertilised as well as self-fertilised. The pea plant is normally self-fertile; the anthers shed pollen onto the style before the flowers open. However, a plant can easily be artificially cross-fertilised. Self-fertilisation is prevented if anthers are removed from immature flowers. In this way the flowers are made female. Pollen is then transferred by paint brush from another (male) plant. Unwanted fertilisations can be prevented by tying muslin bags round the 'female' flowers.

*Table 1 Alternative forms of the garden pea characters used by Mendel*

| CHARACTER | ALTERNATIVES |
| --- | --- |
| Plant height | Tall or short |
| Seed endosperm colour | Yellow or green |
| Seed shape | Round or wrinkled |
| Flower colour | Violet or white |
| Pod form | Uniformly inflated or constricted between seeds |
| Flower position | Axial or terminal |
| Pod colour | Green or yellow |

## Mendel's experimental designs

Mendel almost certainly designed his experiments to test hypotheses he had already formed. His experiments had the following sequence:

(i) Mendel self-fertilised plants and established that each form of the different characters was stable (inherited without change). This meant there would be no unexplainable variation when he crossed individuals with different characters.

(ii) He then cross-fertilised strains contrasted for one or more characters. He called these plants the **parental**, or $P_0$, generation. In some crosses he used a strain with one alternative of a character as a *female* parent; in a **reciprocal** cross, this strain was the *male* parent (Figure 1a).

(iii) He counted all the offspring of this cross for the parental alternative characters. These offspring were the **first filial**, or $F_1$, generation. A sample of these $F_1$ individuals were self-fertilised to produce a large number of offspring called the **second filial**, or $F_2$, generation. Each $F_2$ individual was also scored for the parental alternatives.

This experimental design meant that the original parents ($P_0$) were the only possible source of variation in the later generations.

# Mendel's single gene hypothesis

Mendel used the experiment above to obtain the results for seed colour given in Figure 1a. He concluded that seed colour was determined by a single gene with two alternative forms, one giving yellow seeds, the other given green seeds. We can explain this conclusion in modern terms:

(i) The $F_2$ green seeds must have inherited the character from their green seed grandparent ($P_0$) as this is the only source. However, their parent ($F_1$) had yellow seeds. This suggests that a determinant for green seed colour passed between the generations but was not always expressed. The green pigment in the seed must be distinct from its determinant. The determinant is now called a **gene**.

(ii) The $F_1$ plants, which all grew from yellow seeds, are the only connection between the parents ($P_0$) and their grandchildren ($F_2$). The $F_1$ must have carried a gene for green colour *as well as* one for yellow. These are alternative forms of the seed colour gene. Alternative forms of a gene are now called **alleles**. Although yellow *and* green seed colour alleles are present in the $F_1$ seed, only the yellow character is expressed. Characters which are expressed in an $F_1$ are **dominant** over the alternative which is not expressed. The latter is the **recessive** characteristic.

(iii) If the $F_1$ seeds carry a minimum of two alleles for seed colour (1 green, 1 yellow) then all other seeds are likely to carry two alleles for this character as well. The parental strains which breed true when self-fertilised carry a pair of identical seed colour alleles.

(iv) If the $F_1$ yellow seeds carry an allele for green which is masked, then the $F_2$ green seeds cannot contain an allele for yellow

(a) *Mendel's breeding results*

Seed colour (yellow seed colour determined by allele **A**; green seed colour determined by allele **a**)

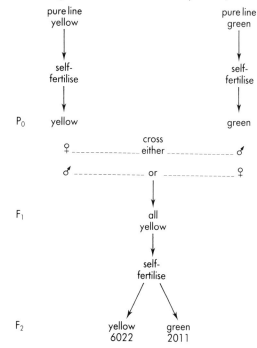

(b) *Genetic model*

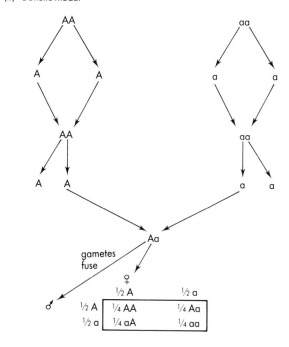

genotypes ¼ AA : ½ Aa : ¼ aa
phenotypes ¾ A– : ¼ aa

**Figure 1    Single character inheritance**

seed colour. The $F_1$ individual's yellow and green seed colour alleles must have separated from each other before the plant reproduced by self-fertilisation. Mendel suggested that this **segregation of alleles** might have occurred during the formation of ovules ('female gametes') and pollen ('male gametes'). Each ovule would contain only one allele and each type should be equally frequent. The same would be true of pollen. $P_0$ individuals differ from the $F_1$ only in that *identical* alleles segregate into their gametes.

This analysis is summarised in Figure 1b. Note the use of upper and lower case letters **A** and **a** to represent the different alleles. This step was first taken by Mendel and it emphasises the distinction between a gene and the character it controls. Johannsen later coined the terms **genotype** (for the genetics of an organism) and **phenotype** for its physical characteristics. **AA** and **aa** individuals, containing only *one* sort of allele, are called **homozygotes**. An **Aa** individual is a **heterozygote**.

The essential feature of Mendel's analysis is that individuals contain two genes for each character. Therefore a heterozygote **Aa** will segregate $\frac{1}{2}$**A** and $\frac{1}{2}$**a** female gametes. Male gametes will segregate in the same way. Mendel predicted that if any male gamete could fuse with any female gamete, the $F_2$ generation should include three genotypes in the proportion $\frac{1}{4}$**AA** : $\frac{1}{2}$**Aa** : $\frac{1}{4}$**aa** (see Figure 1b, and the box on this page).

These 1 : 2 : 1 proportions of the $F_2$ genotypes are examples of expected results. It is common experience (and also predicted by probability theory) that large deviations from expectation are less likely in large samples. This is why Mendel counted large numbers of $F_2$ seed. The two $F_2$ phenotypes for seed colour, and for the other six pea characters tested in separate experiments, were very close to the expected ratio of $\frac{3}{4}$ (**AA** plus **Aa**) : $\frac{1}{4}$ **aa**.

Mendel designed a separate experiment to give more direct evidence of the $\frac{1}{2}$**A** : $\frac{1}{2}$**a** segregation of alleles into gametes. This was a **test cross** between an **$F_1$ heterozygote (Aa)** and a **recessive homozygote (aa)**. The latter individual can give only one type of gamete carrying the recessive allele **a**. this means that the progeny phenotypes are direct expression of the genes contributed by the heterozygote's gametes (**A** or **a**) and the progeny numbers reflect their numbers ($\frac{1}{2}$**A** : $\frac{1}{2}$**a**). The results of this cross for seed colour are summarised in Figure 2.

---

**Rules for combining probabilities.**

A coin has two flat surfaces, head (H) and tail (T). If two unbiased coins are tossed, there are four possible combinations:

HH or HT or TH or TT.

**Rule of addition:** first consider one of the coins. When this is tossed it is certain to give *either* H *or* T. Thus the probability of getting *either* one result *or* another result is obtained by *adding* their independent probabilities. In this case the probability of getting H is $\frac{1}{2}$, and the probability of getting T is also $\frac{1}{2}$. Thus the probability of getting one or the other is

$\frac{1}{2} + \frac{1}{2} = 1$, or 100%, or certainty.

**Rule of multiplication:** now consider both coins. The probability that there will be H on *both* the first *and* the second coin is obtained by *multiplying* the two independent probabilities. In this case the probability of getting H on the first coin is $\frac{1}{2}$, and the probability of getting H on the second coin is also $\frac{1}{2}$. The probability of HH is therefore

$$\frac{1}{2} \times \frac{1}{2} = \frac{1}{4}.$$

These two rules are used a great deal for predicting genetic results. The first example in this book is in the calculation of the expected proportions of the three genotypes **AA**, **Aa** and **aa** in Mendel's $F_2$ generation.

---

(a) *Predicted result of a heterozygote-recessive homozygote cross*

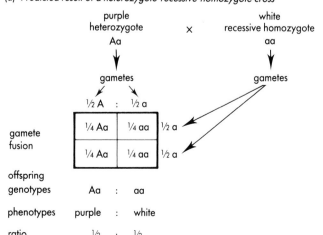

(b) *Actual test cross results*

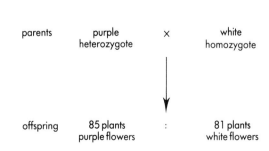

**Figure 2    A test cross experiment. The genetic composition of a heterozygote is tested by back crossing to a recessive homozygote**

# 3.2 OBSERVED AND EXPECTED RESULTS

## The Chi-squared Test

Mendelian genetics, like coin tossing, is all about making predictions. For example, you could do an experiment to test whether a tossed coin is evenly weighted. In 20 throws, you predict a ratio of 10 heads (H):10 tails (T). Your actual result is 5H : 15T. So was the idea behind the prediction (i.e. the coin was evenly weighted) wrong, or do the actual results differ from those expected merely by chance? The *larger* the differences between observed and expected results, the *less likely* they are to be due to chance. If an observed result is very different from that expected, there is a real possibility that the expected result is not the correct one.

Scientists reject the prediction behind an experiment if the differences between observed and expected numbers are so large that they are likely to occur, by chance, in only 5 experiments in 100, or less. If the experiment produces small differences which are likely to occur in more than 5 experiments in 100, then the observed and expected results **do not differ significantly** and the prediction can be accepted.

A useful test for estimating the probability that differences between observed and expected results are due to chance is based on the **Chi-squared ($\chi^2$) statistic**. The formula used is as follows:

$$\chi^2 \text{ (d. f.)} = \Sigma \frac{(\text{observed number} - \text{expected})^2}{\text{expected number}}$$

To explain this formula:

(i) Differences are **squared** to make all numbers positive. Some numbers are smaller than expected e.g. 5H instead of 10, others are larger, e.g. 15T instead of 10. If added, these two differences between observed and expected would cancel out because of their sign.

(ii) Dividing each squared difference by its expected number takes into account the number of things counted (e.g. whether a coin was tossed 20 times or 200) because larger differences are expected by chance in smaller samples.

(iii) The **degrees of freedom (d.f.)** take into account the number of comparisons made (e.g. one coin gives two observed results, H or T; two coins tossed simultaneously give four, HH : HT : TH : TT). Two large differences may give the same $\chi^2$ value as four small ones, but the latter are much more likely to be due to chance.

Using a Chi-squared comparison (see box) Mendel's data for seed colour would be tested as follows:

| Table 1 | SEED COLOURS IN F$_2$ GENERATION | | |
|---|---|---|---|
| | YELLOW | GREEN | TOTAL |
| Observed numbers | 6022 | 2011 | 8033 |
| Expected fractions | ¾ | ¼ | |
| Expected numbers | 6024.75 | 2008.25 | 8033 |
| Obs. − exp. nos. | −2.75 | 2.75 | |
| (obs. − exp.)²/exp. | 0.0013 | 0.0038 | |

$$\chi^2 = \Sigma \frac{(\text{observed number} - \text{expected number})^2}{\text{expected number}}$$

$$\chi^2 = 0.0013 + 0.0038 = 0.0051$$

The expected numbers of each seed type are obtained by multiplying their expected fraction by the total number of seeds counted. e.g. expected yellow seeds = ¾ × 8003 = 6024.75. Degrees of freedom for breeding data are calculated as: (total number of comparisons − 1). There are (2 − 1) = 1 degree of freedom.

The Chi-squared can therefore be expressed as: $\chi^2_{(1)} = 0.005$ where the subscript gives the number of degrees of freedom. The possibility of obtaining a particular value of $\chi^2$ by chance for a number of different degrees of freedom is given in Table 2. The table shows that the probability of obtaining $\chi^2_{(1)} = 0.005$ is between 0.95 and 0.98. This means that small deviations of the size of those between Mendel's observed and expected results will occur by chance in 95–98 experiments out of 100. There is obviously no need to reject his explanation on these data. Only if the $\chi^2_{(1)}$ had exceeded 3.84 would the model have been rejected. In that case the deviations would have been so large that they were likely to occur by chance, in only 5 experiments in 100.

**Table 2** Table of Chi-squared, $\chi^2$ (values taken from a larger table by Fisher and Yates)

| d. f. | PROBABILITY | | | | | | | |
|---|---|---|---|---|---|---|---|---|
| | 0.90 | 0.70 | 0.50 | 0.30 | 0.10 | 0.05 | 0.01 | 0.001 |
| 1 | 0.02 | 0.15 | 0.46 | 1.07 | 2.71 | 3.84 | 6.64 | 10.8 |
| 2 | 0.21 | 0.71 | 1.39 | 2.41 | 4.61 | 5.99 | 9.21 | 13.8 |
| 3 | 0.58 | 1.42 | 2.37 | 3.67 | 6.25 | 7.82 | 11.3 | 16.3 |
| 4 | 1.06 | 2.20 | 3.36 | 4.88 | 7.78 | 9.49 | 13.2 | 18.5 |
| 5 | 1.61 | 3.00 | 4.35 | 6.06 | 9.24 | 11.1 | 15.1 | 20.5 |

For a more complete table of $\chi^2$ values, a set of statistical tables should be consulted.

# 3.3 INTERACTIONS OF ALLELES

Characters in many other organisms exhibit dominance and recessiveness. e.g. the pigmented phenotype is dominant to the albino (with no melanin) in rodents and in humans (see photographs). With dominance, the phenotype of the heterozygote and one homozygote is the same. The alternative form of the character is only shown by the other homozygote.

However, dominance is not a universal phenomenon. In the snapdragon, *Antirrhinum majus*, there are several different flower colours. If a strain with red flowers is crossed to one with white flowers, the $F_1$ heterozygotes have a phenotype with *pink* flowers. The $F_2$ has all three flower colours in the proportions 1:2:1. In this case, heterozgotes have a *different* phenotype from either of the homozygotes. Characters determined by a pair of alleles with an intermediate heterozygote are said to be **incompletely dominant**.

In other examples, heterozygotes show *both* the alternatives shown by the separate homozygotes for example, most adult humans have spherical red blood cells containing the oxygen-carrying molecule **haemoglobin A**. These people are homozygous for the $Hb^A$ gene. People with **sickle cell disease**, have abnormal sickle-shaped red cells that contain a modified haemoglobin (chapter 8). These individuals are homozygous for an $Hb^S$ allele. Heterozygotes, $Hb^AHb^S$, show both cell types and both haemoglobins. Characters in which *both* alleles are expressed in the heterozygote are called **co-dominant**.

# 3.4 AN EXPLANATION OF DOMINANCE

Most genes determine the structure of proteins (chapter 8). It has been discovered that some alleles are 'faulty', and code for non-functional proteins. For example, people suffering from **Duchenne muscular dystrophy** (**DMD**) carry only the faulty allele 'd'. They lack normal dystrophin, a protein necessary for the maintenance of muscle. Individuals who are heterozygous (**Dd**) for the dystrophin allele have one functional gene (**D**) and produce enough normal protein to be superficially indistinguishable from non-DMD homozygotes (**DD**). So dominance can be attributed to the presence of one functional allele which covers the effect of the non-functional allele. However, there are other examples which do not fit this simple pattern, and the molecular mechanisms which determine whether or not a character shows dominance are not yet fully understood.

# 3.5 PEDIGREE ANALYSIS

Humans are difficult for the geneticist to study because controlled breeding experiments are not possible. Until recently, the only way to establish whether a human character was genetic was to look for evidence of a pattern of inheritance in family trees, and then to see if this pattern could be explained by Mendelian genetics. This approach is called **pedigree analysis** but there are a number of problems.

  (i) The size of the family is often small.

  (ii) There can be no control of who marries whom.

  (iii) Family trees are often incomplete, with no certainty that a particular character was noted down for every member of the family in earlier generations.

Patterns of inherited diseases have figured very largely in human genetic analysis. The genetics of some diseases are now quite well understood because data have been accumulated for several different families. In these cases, all the data point in the same direction. Hereditary diseases due to an alteration in a *single* gene are easiest to understand because they show simple patterns of inheritance. In some cases, the *molecular* biology of the disease is beginning to be understood. This would allow a disease to be alleviated (see chapter 8), but at present it is not possible to make a permanent cure of any genetic disease. In the future, replacement of an affected gene by its normal allele may be possible. This is why it is so important to know the genes involved in a

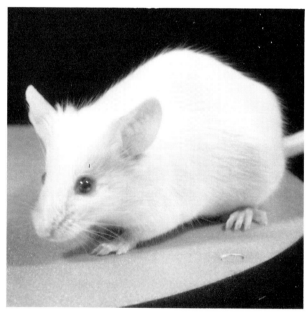

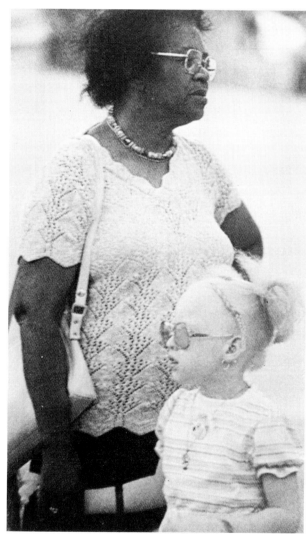

*These four photographs show two different phenotypes in rodents and in humans. Wild type (agouti) mice produce melanin. The same is true of Caucasian humans. Albinos do not produce any pigment. Albino individuals are recessive homozygotes in both species*

particular disease, their location and how the normal alleles work.

# Mendelian patterns in human pedigrees

All genes, except those carried on the sex chromosomes, are called **autosomal genes**.

## Autosomal dominant characters

They are inherited like *yellow* seed colour in Mendel's peas. For example, Huntingdon's disease, in which there is a progressive increase in uncontrolled movements, and dementia develops. Symptoms typically occur when people are in their 40s but the age of onset is very variable. Affected individuals usually die within 12–15 years from onset of the disease.

The characteristic features of an **autosomal dominant pedigree** are shown in Figure 3.
(i) Affected patients (**A–**) always have an affected parent (**A–**) so that the disease appears in every generation of the pedigree.
(ii) If an affected person marries an unaffected person, there is at least a 1 in 2 chance that each child will be affected (**Aa** × **aa** →

½**Aa** : ½**aa**, see Figure 2). Genetic diseases are quite rare so that most affected individuals had one normal parent. They are therefore heterozygotes.
(iii) Both sexes are equally affected.
(iv) Both sexes are equally likely to pass the disease on.

There are complications to this simple pattern. Genes often show variable expression so that a disease may be severe in one person and so mild in another that they do not realize that they have it. Variable expression is particularly confusing in human pedigree analysis because individuals in previous generations may be put in the wrong category.

## Autosomal recessive characters

These are inherited like Mendel's *green* peas. An example is cystic fibrosis. All mucous secretions are too viscous, leading to recurrent lung congestion and infection, and pancreatic defects lead to poor food absorption. The primary cause of the disease is the alteration of a cell membrane protein, that affects chloride ion transport. Affected individuals usually die in early adulthood.

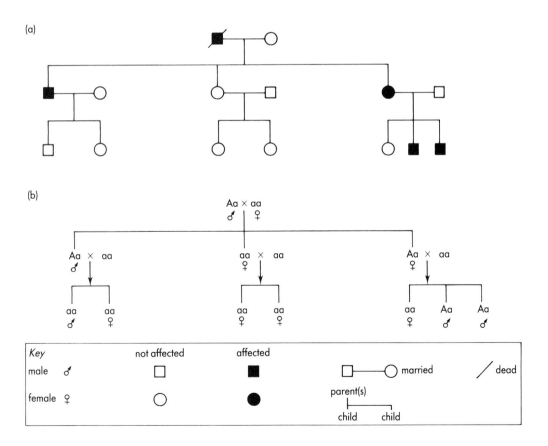

***Figure 3*** *(a) An autosomal dominant pedigree pattern, and (b) Mendelian interpretation of this pattern*

The characteristic features of an **autosomal recessive pedigree** are shown in Figure 4.

(i) Heterozygote individuals are unaffected, but they are **carriers**. When two carriers have children, the cross is (**Aa** × **Aa**). One or more of their children may be affected (**aa**).

(ii) If an affected person (**aa**) marries, all their children are unaffected (**aa** × **AA** → **Aa**) unless they marry a carrier. This means that the disease can skip generations.

(iii) There is an association of the disease with marriages between close relatives who are both likely to have inherited the same gene (**a**) from an immediate ancestor (**Aa** × **Aa** × → some **aa**).

(iv) Both sexes are equally affected.

# Genetic counselling

Now that the genetic basis of some diseases is understood, medical geneticists are able to offer genetic counselling to people who come from families in which a disease is known to be inherited. This means that parents can be told the likelihood of their having an affected child.

It is usually easier to give an estimate to a couple that has already had an affected child. In this case, if the genetics of the disease are well understood, the medical geneticist can predict the genotypes of the parents accurately. They can then be told, with some certainty, the likelihood that their next child will be affected. For example, if unaffected parents already have a child with cystic fibrosis, they must both be heterozygotes (see above). The probability of the next child having the disease is 1 in 4 because this is the proportion of recessive homozygous offspring when two heterozygotes mate. The fact that one child has already been born with the disease has no effect on the probability that the next one will have the disease; each child is an independent event.

An unaffected individual from a family with a history of a disease can consult a medical geneticist to find out the risk of having an affected child. This is much more difficult to estimate because the geneticist has to predict the genotype of the unaffected individual and also the genotype of their spouse. There are a number of problems.

(i) To estimate whether or not an individual is carrying a particular gene, there has to be accurate information from the family pedigree.

(ii) The frequency of the gene in the population as a whole must be known. The likely

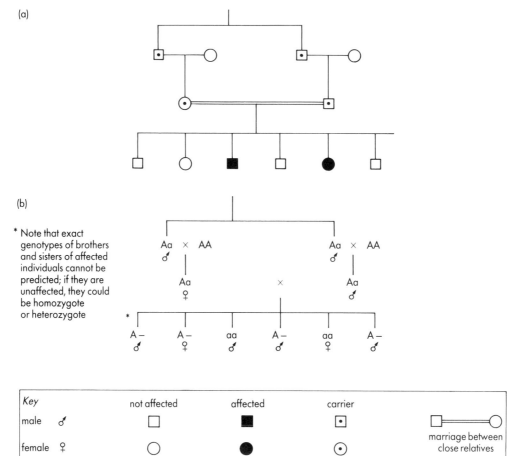

*Figure 4   (a) Autosomal recessive pedigree pattern, and (b) Mendelian interpretation of this pattern*

genotype of the spouse can then be estimated.

(iii) It is important to know to what extent the husband and wife are related to each other. If they have recent ancestors in common, they are more likely to have inherited the same gene than if they are distantly related.

Molecular genetics can help to solve counselling problems using DNA extracted from blood samples. For diseases like DMD and cystic fibrosis, this DNA can be screened for the presence of the mutant gene. If husband *and* wife agree to give blood samples, there is a good chance that their genotypes can be determined accurately. They can then decide whether they wish to conceive a child. This does not solve the problem completely because they can only be told the *probability* that they will have an affected child. However recent medical advances make it possible to test the genotype of the foetus at a very early stage of development. There are two techniques (Figure 5).

### Amniocentesis
A sample of the amniotic fluid surrounding the developing foetus is removed. This contains cells of the same genotype as the embryo. These cells can be cultured and tested.

### Chorionic villi sampling
Dividing cells are removed from the embryonic part of the very early placenta and cultured. This technique can be performed much earlier in development than amniocentesis and, as the cells are already dividing, they can be cultured more rapidly.

Using these techniques, it is possible to test for protein markers, DNA markers, or chromosomal abnormalities. These tests are not without risk but, if carried out early enough, the parents can be offered the possibility of an abortion. This opportunity may be very important for them, particularly if the disease is debilitating and incurable.

# 3.6 MULTIPLE ALLELES
## Animals
Many organisms have characters with more than two alternatives. The shell of the landsnail, *Cepaea nemoralis*, is either brown or pink or yellow. These colours are determined by three alleles, $C^B$ (brown), $C^P$ (pink) and $C^Y$ (yellow). An individual can only carry two alleles, but with multiple allelic systems there are several *combinations* of two alleles. For example, snails with brown shells can be $C^BC^B$ or $C^BC^P$ or $C^BC^Y$. Those with pink shells may be $C^PC^P$ or $C^PC^Y$. Snails with yellow shells are all $C^YC^Y$. Note there is a dominance hierarchy with pink shell colour recessive to brown, but dominant to yellow.

Several medically important human characters are determined by multiple allelic systems. e.g the ABO blood group, and the HLA tissue incompatibility system.

### The ABO blood group
Dominance hierarchies are common but not universal in multiple allelic systems. In humans, there are three alleles ($I^A$, $I^B$ and $i$) which determine three different forms of a particular glycoprotein (**antigen**) on the surface of red blood cells. These are the A, B or O antigens (Table 3). An understanding of the ABO blood group alleles

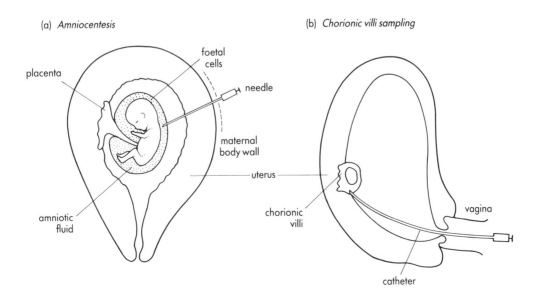

(a) *Amniocentesis*  (b) *Chorionic villi sampling*

**Figure 5**  *Taking cell samples from tissue which has the same genotype as the developing human embryo*

and other blood group genes is important in medicine because there may be severe problems in blood transfusion if donor and recipient genotypes are not matched. Table 3 shows that some genotypes produce antibodies to glycoprotein antigens present on the surface of red blood cells. They do not produce **antibodies** to antigens present on *their own* red blood cells. Thus $I^B i$ individuals produce anti-A antibodies in their blood serum and have B antigens on their own cell surfaces.

*Table 3  Genotypes and antigenic phenotypes of the ABO blood groups*

| GENOTYPE | GLYCOPROTEINS PRESENT ON RED BLOOD CELL SURFACE | ANTIGENIC PHENOTYPES (BLOOD GROUP) | ANTIBODIES PRESENT IN SERUM |
|---|---|---|---|
| $I^A I^A$ | type A | A | anti-B |
| $I^A I^B$ | types A and B | AB | none |
| $I^A i$ | types A and O | A | anti-B |
| $I^B I^B$ | type B | B | anti-A |
| $I^B i$ | types B and O | B | anti-A |
| i i | type O | O | anti-A and anti-B |

There is no dominance between the A and B antigens, the heterozygote $I^A I^B$ produces both antigens. The **i** gene product is non-antigenic so both $I^A I$ and $I^B i$ individuals produce a *single* antigen. Thus $I^A$ and $I^B$ are both dominant over **i**. Table 3 gives the antibodies present in the blood serum of the various ABO genotypes, and shows that an $I^A I^B$ individual can accept blood from any other genotype as their own blood contains A and B antigens and neither antibody. **ii** individuals can only accept blood from someone of the same genotype because they lack antigens and produce anti-A and anti-B antibodies.

The role of the ABO multiple allelic system in transfusion is well understood; its role in normal body function is less clear.

### The HLA tissue incompatibility system

There are three different genes, HLA–A, HLA–B and HLA–C; the proteins produced by these genes are present in the cell membrane of every cell in the body. There are at least 20 alleles for gene **A**, 40 alleles or gene **B** and 8 alleles for gene **C**. With so many alleles of each gene, an individual is likely to inherit different alleles from each parent. *Further*, unrelated individuals are likely to contain very different combinations of alleles.

The genes are involved in the normal immune response of the body. The immune system of a recipient will recognise a donor tissue as foreign, and therefore reject it, if the donor contains an allele of either the **A**, **B** or **C** genes which the

recipient does *not* carry. For example, a recipient which is heterozygous **A1A2 B5B8**, and homozygous **C3C3**, will reject tissue from an **A1A1 B5B7 C3C3** donor because this tissue carries **B7** which is absent from the recipient. Tissue from **A1A1 B5B8 C3C3**, or **A2A2 B5B5 C3C3** donors, among others, would be accepted because all the donor alleles are also present in this recipient.

## Plants

In flowering plants, male and female reproductive organs are usually present in the same flower. This allows self-fertilisation, and indeed this does occur in garden peas, wheat and several other species. However, in some species, there are inhibitory tissue interactions between pollen and the surface of the style. These mating incompatibility interactions are usually controlled by multiple allelic systems. If pollen and style contain the same alleles then the pollen tube is inhibited and fertilisation is prevented. This is shown in Figure 6 for the wild cherry *Prunus avium*.

| female parent | possible male parents | | | | | |
|---|---|---|---|---|---|---|
| | $S_1 S_2$ | | $S_2 S_3$ | | $S_3 S_4$ | |
| style | pollen $S_1$ or $S_2$ | | pollen $S_2$ or $S_3$ | | pollen $S_3$ or $S_4$ | |
| $S_1 S_2$ | 0 | 0 | 0 | + | + | + |
| $S_2 S_3$ | + | 0 | 0 | 0 | 0 | + |
| $S_3 S_4$ | + | + | + | 0 | 0 | 0 |

Pollen is a gametophyte and therefore contains only one allele in each nucleus. The style is part of the sporophyte and therefore contains two alleles per nucleus

*Key*

0 :  no fertilisation (pollen and stigma are incompatible)
+ :  pollen tube formation and fertilisation occur (pollen and stigma are compatible)

Note:  the greatest number of fertilisations is possible between plants with completely different alleles at the incompatibility locus; some species have 100 alleles at the locus

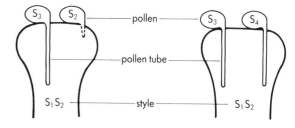

*Figure 6   The genetically determined interactions which control pollen tube growth in* **Prunus avium** *(wild cherry)*

These incompatibility mechanisms encourage outbreeding between genetically different, and often unrelated, individuals. This helps to maintain genetic variation in natural populations.

Plant reproductive incompatibility systems have also played an important part in the development of hybrid seed for horticulture and agriculture. Hybrid seed formed from genetically different parents often combine the best characteristics of both parents and make useful crop plants. To produce hybrid seed economically, it is an advantage to grow many plants of the two parent strains together on a large scale, knowing that self-fertilisation is impossible (see page 149).

(see page 149)

Mating systems can now be altered by DNA manipulation. Belgian molecular biologists have discovered genes which are only active in anthers. They have modified the DNA making up these genes and introduced it into oil seed rape plants which are normally self-fertile. These modified plants do not produce fertile pollen and are therefore self-infertile. However they make ideal female parents for the large scale production of hybrid seed when grown with other strains of oil seed rape which produce fertile pollen as usual. It should be possible to introduce the modified DNA into many other crop plants which are normally self-fertile. This is just one example of the advantages of molecular genetics.

# BIBLIOGRAPHY

Peters, J A (1959) *Biological Science Series, Classic Papers in Genetics* (contains English translation of Mendel's paper) Prentice Hall

Suzuki, D T, Griffiths, A J F, Miller, J H and Lewontin, R C (1989), *An Introduction to Genetic Analysis* 4th Edn W H Freeman and Co

Davies, K E and Read, A P (1988) *Molecular Basis of Inherited Disease* IRL Press, Oxford

Fisher, R and Yates, F (1967) *Statistical Tables* 6th Edn Oliver and Boyd.

# QUESTIONS

1 How would you determine the genotype of an individual showing a dominant characteristic, if that individual is (a) a higher animal, (b) a cross-pollinating plant, (c) a self-pollinating plant?

2 Mendel concluded that his first experiments supported his idea that an organism's characters were determined by pairs of internal factors but only one of each pair could be represented in a gamete.
  a) Give the modern names for (i) Mendel's factors; (ii) alternative forms of a factor; (iii) an organism containing two different forms of a factor.
  b) Explain how these factors occur in pairs in animals (diplont) and higher plants (haplodiplont). Explain how a fungus mycelium (haplont) would differ from the animal or plant.

3 A gardener received four samples of tomato seeds. He planted the samples of seeds separately and as they grew he noted if they had hairy or hairless stems. The results were as follows:

| SAMPLE | TOMATO PLANTS | |
| --- | --- | --- |
| | HAIRY | HAIRLESS |
| 1 | 152 | 0 |
| 2 | 0 | 110 |
| 3 | 24 | 76 |
| 4 | 98 | 89 |

Assign genetic symbols for this character and indicate the genotypes in the seed samples and their likely parents. Use a Chi-squared analysis to test whether the results for sample (4) conform to your genetic hypothesis.

4 Four babies were born to different parents at the same time in a maternity hospital. Unfortunately there was a power cut soon after the births and the babies identities were confused. The babies were found to have different ABO blood groups; these were A, B, AB, O. The blood groups of the parents were:
Mr and Mrs Smith      A × B
Mr and Mrs Jones      B × O
Mr and Mrs Carter      O × O
Mr and Mrs Miles      AB × A
Are these blood groups genotypes or phenotypes? Explain if it possible to assign any of the children to particular parents using this blood group information.

5 Give the most probable explanation of the inheritance pattern for the genetic disease shown as shaded symbols in the following pedigree. What are the likely genotypes of
(i) individuals (1) and (2) in generation I;
(ii) individuals (4) and (5) in generation II;
(iii) individual (16) in generation III?

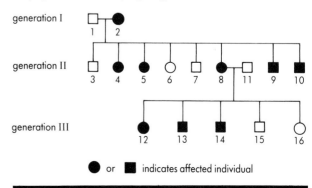

● or ■ indicates affected individual

# 4 INHERITANCE PATTERNS FOR MORE THAN ONE GENE

The experiments in chapter 3 show, that, given alternative forms of a character, controlled breeding will demonstrate that at least one gene determines a character. Thus Mendel concluded that alternative seed colours in peas are determined by alternative forms of a single gene.

Mendel went on to investigate the inheritance of the other pea characters and showed that they were each determined by a single gene. He also showed that these genes were quite distinct from each other. His methods and interpretation are summarised in this chapter. These methods have been applied to a variety of different organisms with some surprising results. In some cases, they show that a single character must be determined by the interaction of quite separate genes, all of which can have alternative forms.

## 4.1 DIVERSE CHARACTERS AND DISTINCT GENES

Mendel extended his breeding experiments to include two characters. He showed that the different characters were determined by separate genes, each of which is now called a **gene locus**. A locus is a position on a chromosome which is occupied by a particular gene (see chapter 6). Different alleles of a gene can substitute at its locus, for example **A** and **a** could be alleles at one locus; **B** and **b** could be alleles at a second locus determining a different character. The separate

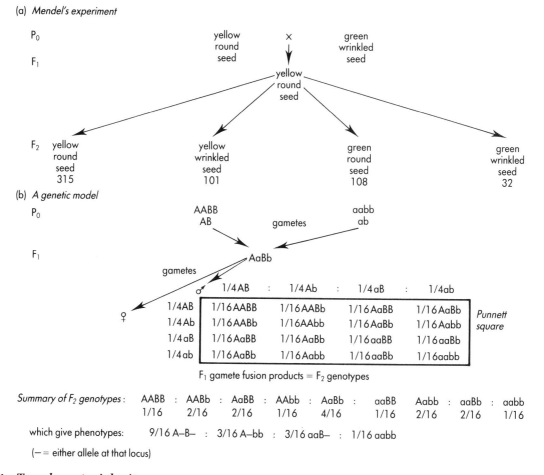

*Figure 1    Two character inheritance*

gene loci studied by Mendel were inherited independently of each other.

Figure 1a shows the results of Mendel's experiments involving two characters: seed colour and seed shape. If each character is considered on its own, the distribution of alternative seed colours and alternative seed shapes in the $F_2$ are as follows:

| **Seed colour** | | yellow | : | green | total |
|---|---|---|---|---|---|
| | | 315 + 101 | : | 108 + 32 | |
| | = | 416 | | 140 | 556 |

| **Seed shape** | | round | : | wrinkled | total |
|---|---|---|---|---|---|
| | | 315 + 108 | : | 101 + 32 | |
| | = | 423 | | 133 | 556 |

Neither the seed colour nor the seed shape result is significantly different from a 3:1 ratio in the $F_2$. Thus if the two characters are considered separately, each behaves as if it were determined by two alleles at a single gene locus.

Does this mean that there is one gene locus with two alleles which control a complex of many characters? If so, the parental ($P_0$) alternatives, yellow with round seeds and green with wrinkled seeds could not be split. They would be the only ones to reappear in the $F_2$ and they would be in a 3:1 ratio. However, yellow with wrinkled seed, and green with round seed combinations in the $F_2$ show that the parental ($P_0$) combinations *can* be split. This suggests that seed colour and seed shape are determined by *separate* gene loci.

The proportions of the four phenotypes in the $F_2$ suggest that seed colour and shape must be determined by two **independently inherited** gene loci. This is shown in Figure 1b. The gametes produced by an $F_1$ parent must be ½**A** and ½**a** to account for the inheritance of seed colour, and ½**B** and ½**b** to account for seed shape. If a gamete gets **A** or **a** and, quite independently, **B** or **b**, then there must be the four gamete types: ¼**AB**, ¼**Ab**, ¼**aB** and ¼**ab**. i.e. the **A/a** and **B/b** loci **recombine at random** (see the Multiplication Rule in the box on page 37).

The Punnett square in Figure 1b shows that if the four types of male and female gametes are equally common, then all possible fusions would be expected to give nine different genotypes. Because of dominance, these give four phenotypes in the ratio 9 yellow round : 3 yellow wrinkled : 3 green round : 1 green wrinkled. Table 1 compares observed and expected results.

With four comparisons there are three degrees of freedom and the probability of obtaining such a small $\chi^2$ value by chance is between 90 and 95 times in 100. Hence, the data obtained by Mendel do satisfy his genetic model.

The second fundamental of Mendelian genetics is that a double heterozygote forms four gamete types in equal frequency. It shows that different characters are determined by independent genes. The hypothesis can be confirmed by a test cross of the heterozygote to the double recessive homozygote. If **A/a** and **B/b** are independent, the heterozygote **AaBb** produces four gametes at equal frequency 1**AB** : 1**Ab** : 1**aB** : 1**ab** but, the homozygote aabb can produce only 1 gamete type **ab**. This means that the progeny phenotypes (1AB : 1Ab : 1aB : 1ab) directly reflect the constitution of the heterozygote's gametes. Counting the different progeny from a test cross scores the heterozygote parent's gametes.

Mendel used the double heterozygote for seed colour and shape as either the male or female parent in reciprocal test crosses to the recessive homozygote. He obtained the progeny shown in Table 2. Each heterozygote must have produced four types of gametes in equal numbers (1**AB** : 1**Ab** : 1**aB** : 1**ab**). There are no differences between the male and female heterozygotes, both sexes transmit seed colour and seed shape genes into their gametes as independent units. These test cross results obtained by Mendel confirm the independent assortment and random recombination of alleles at two loci.

There are probably about 50 000 – 100 000 gene loci making up a human. Are they all inherited quite independently? This idea is considered in chapter 5.

---

*Table 1*

| | F_2 SEED CHARACTERS | | | |
|---|---|---|---|---|
| | YELLOW ROUND | YELLOW WRINKLED | GREEN ROUND | GREEN WRINKLED |
| Observed number | 315 | 101 | 108 | 32 |
| Expected fraction | $\frac{9}{16}$ | $\frac{3}{16}$ | $\frac{3}{16}$ | $\frac{1}{16}$ |
| Expected number | 312.75 | 104.25 | 104.25 | 34.75 |
| Obs. no. − exp. no. | 2.25 | −3.25 | 3.75 | −2.75 |
| $\frac{(\text{Obs. no.} - \text{exp. no.})^2}{\text{Exp. no.}}$ | 0.016 | 0.10 | 0.14 | 0.218 |

$$\chi^2_{(3)} = 0.016 + 0.10 + 0.14 + 0.218 = 0.470$$

**Table 2** *Test cross offspring for two pairs of contrasting characters in the pea. A yellow round seed heterozygote (AaBb) was crossed to a double recessive green wrinkled seed parent (aabb)*

| | HETEROZYGOTE PARENT | OFFSPRING | | | |
|---|---|---|---|---|---|
| | | yellow round seed **AaBb** | yellow wrinkled seed **Aabb** | green round seed **aaBb** | green wrinkled seed **aabb*** |
| Cross 1 | Female (AaBb) | 31 | 26 | 27 | 26 |
| Cross 2 | Male (AaBb) | 24 | 22 | 25 | 26 |
| | Total | 55 | 48 | 52 | 52 |

*Offspring genes from heterozygote parent are in bold.

# 4.2 GENE INTERACTION

Breeding experiments with a number of different organisms have shown that it is possible to count several different gene loci which interact with each other to produce *one* character. In fact, most characters are affected by gene interaction.

## Complementary genes

White flowered sweet peas (*Lathyrus odoratus*) have appeared in horticultural collections several times. It must have been a surprise to William Bateson, a famous English geneticist, when he crossed two of these white flowered varieties to obtain only purple flowered plants among the progeny. When these were self-fertilised, they produced several plants with purple flowers but nearly as many with white flowers (Figure 2). Careful analysis of the numbers in the F₂ showed that there were 9/16 purple flowered plants: 7/16 white flowered ones. This is a modified 9 : 3 : 3 : 1 ratio, 9 purple : (3+3+1) white. Bateson pointed out that these results can be satisfactorily explained if two independently inherited gene loci each with two alleles (**A/a** and **B/b**) are involved in the cross. The effect of **A** is dominant over that of **a**, and the effect of **B** is dominant over that of **b**. The production of purple pigment is stimulated by the *combined* activities of genes **A** and **B**. If either **A** or **B** is absent from a plant, then the flowers are unable to produce purple pigment and are white. Thus genotypes **AAbb, Aabb, aaBB, aaBb** and **aabb** share a common white phenotype because none of them contain both the **A** *and* **B** alleles which are necessary to produce purple pigment.

## Epistasis

In dominant epistasis, the dominant allele at one locus *inhibits* the expression of alleles at a second locus. An example is the variation in band pattern on the shell of the landsnail *Cepaea nemoralis* (Figure 3a).

In a cross between snails with unbanded shells and snails with five banded shells (Figure 3b), all the F₁ are unbanded. But in the F₂ there are three phenotypes in the proportion 12 unbanded : 3 midbanded : 1 five banded. The modified 9:3:3:1 again suggests two independently segregating loci. In this case, one locus determines whether bands are present (**a**) or absent (**A**) and the latter is dominant. A second locus determines the number and position of bands, midband (**B**) or fiveband (**b**); alleles at this locus cannot be expressed if an **A** allele is present. So **aabb** are five banded, **aaB–** are mid banded and **A–––** are unbanded (– means that either alleles may be substituted at the appropriate locus, see Figure 1).

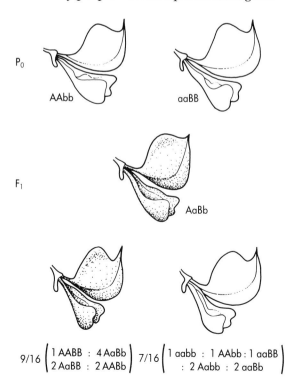

P₀   AAbb    aaBB

F₁   AaBb

$\frac{9}{16}\left(\begin{array}{l}\text{1 AABB : 4 AaBb}\\\text{2 AaBB : 2 AABb}\end{array}\right)$ $\frac{7}{16}\left(\begin{array}{l}\text{1 aabb : 1 AAbb : 1 aaBB}\\\text{: 2 Aabb : 2 aaBb}\end{array}\right)$

**Figure 2** *The inheritance of purple and white flower colour in the sweet pea*

(a) *The band patterns*

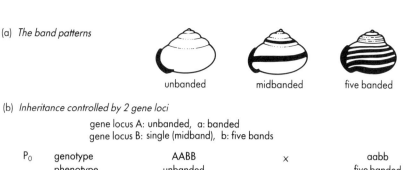

unbanded     midbanded     five banded

(b) *Inheritance controlled by 2 gene loci*

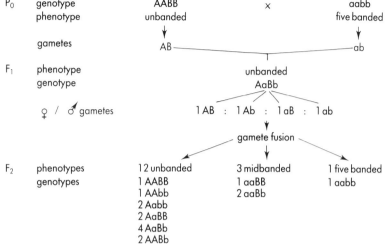

gene locus A: unbanded,  a: banded
gene locus B: single (midband),  b: five bands

$P_0$   genotype    AABB    ×    aabb
   phenotype   unbanded    five banded

gametes   AB ——————— ab

$F_1$   phenotype    unbanded
   genotype    AaBb

♀ / ♂ gametes    1 AB : 1 Ab : 1 aB : 1 ab

gamete fusion

$F_2$   phenotypes

| 12 unbanded | 3 midbanded | 1 five banded |
|---|---|---|
| 1 AABB | 1 aaBB | 1 aabb |
| 1 AAbb | 2 aaBb | |
| 2 Aabb | | |
| 2 AaBB | | |
| 4 AaBb | | |
| 2 AABb | | |

*Figure 3   The inheritance of shell band patterns in the snail* Cepaea nemoralis

## Interactions involving more than two gene loci

Most characters are produced by the activities of genes at many loci. However, breeding experiments will only show this if there is allelic variation at each of the loci involved. Coat colour in mammals is an example with more than one allele at several of the loci involved. House mice (*Mus musculus*) in natural populations have a greyish brown (agouti) coat with pigments unevenly distributed along the hair shaft. Mice with different coat colours have appeared since humans have kept them as pets. The genetic basis of coat colour has been established by.

  (i)  carrying out controlled breeding experiments,
 (ii)  studying the cellular and biochemical differences between the various colour forms.

Just three loci will be considered here. The agouti genes have been shown to control the distribution of melanin pigments along the hair shaft. Pigments are present as a mid-shaft band in the wild type (agouti) state, but they are uniformly distributed in other forms. Breeding experiments show that this is an allelic difference with agouti (**A**) dominant over uniform distribution (**a**). Other experiments showed that a second (**B/b**) locus determines the intensity of pigmentation, black or brown. A third (**C/c**) locus determines whether or not melanin pigment is manufactured in the hair cells. **A–B–C–** animals are agouti (wild type); **aaB–C–** mice have black coats; **aabbC–** mice are chocolate brown; **––cc** mice lack melanins. The **––cc** mice are albino with a white coat and pink

eyes (due to red blood pigments showing through).

The alleles at each locus have large effects. The **a** allele spreads pigment all along the hair so the **aa** genotype produces a uniform colour; the colour depends on genes present at other loci, e.g. the **B/b** locus. As the albino mutation, **c**, prevents melanin synthesis, it suppresses the effect of other coat colour genes, so **cc** genotypes are albino whatever **A/a** or **B/b** genes are present in the animal.

Hence the colour of an animal's coat is influenced by the activity of many different gene loci. A famous geneticist, Sewall Wright, worked on the genetics of guinea pig coat colours. In 1917, he suggested that some of the genes he discovered might affect the activity of enzymes and produce different pigments in his animals' coats. However, it was nearly 30 years before George Beadle and Edward Tatum gave the first convincing proof that a gene can act by controlling the activity of one enzyme (chapter 8).

## 4.3 QUANTITATIVE CHARACTERS

Differences in the colour of a flower are usually clear cut, e.g. purple and white flowers. This character shows a difference in *quality*. However, variation in characters such as height, weight or milk yield are not so distinct. These types of character are measured, weighed or counted, and differences between individuals are often small.

When many individuals are measured, they cover a range of measurements and the extremes can be very different, e.g. very tall and quite short (see photograph). These characters differ in *quantity* and they are continuously variable between extremes. A simple way to describe this variation is given in the box on page 51.

Both qualitative and quantitative characters are determined by Mendelian genes, and both may involve several different gene loci. However, allelic substitutions for qualitative characters have large effects and different gene loci usually have *different* effects. On the other hand, allelic substitutions at the various gene loci determining a *quantitative* character have a similar, usually small, and often *additive* effect. The genes at these loci are called **polygenes**. The additive effect of polygenes and the pattern of inheritance they produce means that it is seldom possible to count separate genes. In addition, variation can be caused by the environment. e.g. a starved youngster will not grow as tall as a well fed one, although both may have the same genetic potential. In the analysis of quantitative characters geneticists measure the variation in the character and estimate how much of this variation is likely to be genetic.

# 4.4 CONTINUOUS VARIATION

Suppose that the weight of an organism is determined by two independently inherited gene loci, each with two alleles which increase weight by 2.5 g (**l** and **m**) or 5 g (**L** and **M**). If there is no dominance or interaction between the two loci, a genotype **llmm** will have a genetic weight

contribution of $2.5 + 2.5 + 2.5 + 2.5 = 10$ g. The weight of an **LLMM** individual will be $5 + 5 + 5 + 5 = 20$ g. The genes are acting additively; their effect on weight on two groups of homozygous parents, their $F_1$ progeny and $F_2$ progeny are shown in Figure 4.

All **llmm** homozygotes have a genetic contribution to weight of 10 g, but if a number of such homozygotes were weighed, some would weigh more and others less than this. It is unlikely that they would all have eaten exactly the same amount of food. Environmental variation superimposes on the genetic effect and cause weight to vary.

In a controlled breeding experiment starting with homozygote parents, the weight distributions of parents, $F_1$ and $F_2$ offspring will follow the pattern shown in Figure 4. There are genetic differences between the two types of homozygous parent, but no genetic variation within either parent strain. All $F_1$ individuals are heterozygous for both genes so they must also be genetically uniform. Any variation within these three groups must be *environmental*. If the three genotypes are exposed to the same range of environments and respond to them in the same way, they should all show the same amount of weight variation.

Segregation of alleles at each locus, and random recombination between the two loci, produce a genetic variation in weight among the $F_2$ generation. This can be calculated as follows. With one locus segregating (**L/l**), there are three genotypes in the $F_2$ (1/4**LL** : 2/4**Ll** : 1/4**ll**). With two unlinked loci segregating, the $F_2$ generation has $3 \times 3 = 9$ genotypes:

(1/4 **LL** + 2/4 **Ll** + 1/4 **ll**) $\times$ (1/4 **MM** + 2/4 **Mm** + 1/4 **mm**) = (1/16 **LLMM** + 2/16 **LLMm** + 1/16 **LLmm** + 2/16 **LlMM** + . . . + 1/16 **llmm**). This is another way of calculating the results of a Punnett square (figure 1).

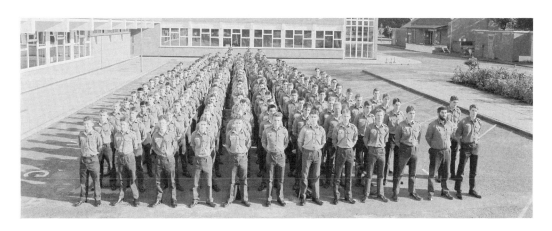

*The differences in height among a group of trainee naval engineers, HMS Sultan*

## Mean and Variance

There are 219 men in the photograph. If their heights had been given as a list or in a table it would have been difficult to see any pattern in the men's heights. The pattern is easy to see in the picture which groups people of the same height (measured to the nearest inch). It is a pictorial summary called a **histogram**. It shows that most people are near average height, but there is a spread. If more men had been measured and the tops of the columns in the histogram joined by a line, the histogram woud become a *bell shaped curve*. This is called a **normal distribution**. If we assume that the heights actually measured are normally distributed we can summarise all the data in the histogram by two figures:

   (i) the **mean**, which is a measure of the 'middle' height;

   (ii) the **variance**, which measures how much spread there is about the mean.

We can calculate the mean and variance of the sailor's heights using a calculator, but mean and variance are best understood if the data are set out as follows:

'n' is the number in each height class, 'x' is the height class (in metres for ease of calculation).

| n | x | nx | $n(x - \bar{x})$ | $n(x - \bar{x})^2$ |
|---|---|---|---|---|
| 15 | 1.676 | 25.140 | −1.575 | 0.165 |
| 20 | 1.702 | 34.040 | −1.580 | 0.125 |
| 26 | 1.727 | 44.902 | −1.404 | 0.076 |
| 35 | 1.753 | 61.355 | −0.980 | 0.027 |
| 24 | 1.778 | 42.672 | −0.072 | 0.000 |
| 36 | 1.803 | 64.908 | 0.792 | 0.017 |
| 28 | 1.829 | 51.212 | 1.344 | 0.065 |
| 18 | 1.854 | 33.372 | 1.314 | 0.096 |
| 10 | 1.880 | 18.800 | 0.990 | 0.098 |
| 0 | 1.905 | 0.000 | 0.000 | 0.000 |
| 4 | 1.930 | 7.720 | 0.596 | 0.089 |
| 1 | 1.956 | 1.956 | 0.175 | 0.031 |
| 2 | 1.981 | 3.962 | 0.400 | 0.080 |

| $\Sigma$n | $\Sigma$nx | $\Sigma n(x - \bar{x})$ | $\Sigma n(x - \bar{x})^2$ |
|---|---|---|---|
| 219 men | total height 390.039 m | 0.000 | 0.869 |

The mean is calculated by adding all 219 heights, and dividing the total by the number of men whose height is measured. In the table, nx represents the total height in each class and $\Sigma$nx is the total height of the 219 men, so the mean height $\bar{x}$ is:

$$\bar{x} = \frac{\Sigma nx}{\Sigma n} = \frac{390.039}{219} = 1.781\,m$$

Variance is expressed as difference of each measured height from the mean height. Some heights are less and others are greater than the mean. So, when all the height differences are added (the sum of n(x-$\bar{x}$)), the positive and negative differences cancel each other out. Thus $\Sigma$n (x-$\bar{x}$) = 0.00. To make all the differences positive, the values are squared. The sum of all the squared values is obtained by adding the values in the n(x-$\bar{x}$)$^2$ column; this is 0.869. The variance is estimated by dividing this by $\Sigma$n, the number of men measured (or more accurately $\Sigma$n − 1 as the data were used once to find $\bar{x}$ before this is used to find variance):

$$\text{variance} = \frac{\Sigma n(x - \bar{x})^2}{\Sigma n - 1} = \frac{0.869}{218} = 0.0040$$

The variance is the average squared deviation of all the heights about the mean height. The square root of the variance is called the **standard deviation** (s.d.). It is a linear measure of deviation and the mean ±2 s.d. encompasses 95% of all measurements in the sample.

For these sailors, the standard deviation = $\sqrt{\text{variance}}$ = $\sqrt{0.0040}$ = 0.06 m, so 95% of the men's heights lie between 1.78 − (2 × 0.06) = 1.66 m and 1.78 + (2 × 0.06) = 1.90 m.

Calculators use other versions of the formulae given here to calculate mean and standard deviation automatically. This means that you do not have to group your data as done here. You just feed each of your measurements into the machine, one after another and in any order, but remember to check all your calculations.

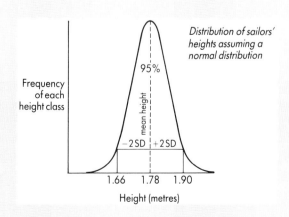

*Distribution of sailors' heights assuming a normal distribution*

95%

Frequency of each height class

mean height

−2 SD | +2 SD

1.66   1.78   1.90

Height (metres)

By applying the weights due to each allele, the five weight classes in the F₂ histogram shown in Figure 4 can be quickly worked out.

Figure 4 shows that several genotypes in the F₂ have the same genetic weight. However, just like the other two generations, some individuals of each genotype will weigh more or less than their genetic weight because they grew in different environments. If a genetic weight is shifted up or down by the environment, it becomes impossible to state the genotype of any individual in the F₂ generation from its measured weight. If it is not possible to estimate genotypes, it is not possible to count the number of different genes.

With more gene loci contributing to weight, there are more genetic classes in the F₂ and it will be even more difficult to distinguish between

them. Consider an example in which four gene loci each have a pair of alleles contributing 2.5 g or 5 g. If heterozygotes for all four loci are mated they will give $3 \times 3 \times 3 \times 3 = 81$ different genotypes. Given the allelic weight contribution, these genotypes fall into 9 weight classes varying from 20 g to 40 g but differing by only 2.5 gms (Figure 5a). It would be very difficult to predict the genotype of any F₂ individual from their weight, particularly with overlying environmental variation. Figure 5b shows the weight of 2000 new born humans. Various

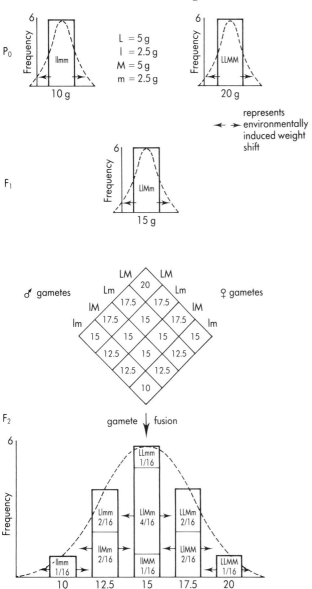

Figure 4   Genetic and environmental components of weight variation in an organism with two gene loci contributing to weight

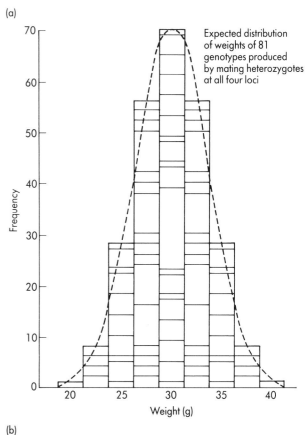

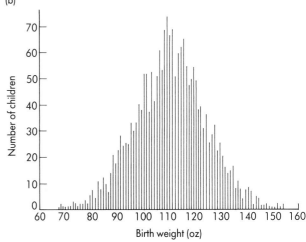

Figure 5(a)   Genetic effect on weight of independent segregation at four gene loci, and (b) distribution of weights among new born babies

methods of analysis suggest that human weight does have a large genetic component, but it is not possible to count the number of genes that are contributing to this continuously varying character.

# 4.5 HERITABILITY

It is not usually possible to count the number of genes underlying a quantitative character so geneticists often do a controlled breeding experiment and ask the general question, 'How much of the observed variation is genetic and how much is due to the environment?'. In practice, this approach needs quite sophisticated statistics, including the analysis of variance, but the basic idea is straightforward.

The weight models just described showed that all the variation among the two parent types, and the $F_1$ was due to the environment. The variation in the $F_2$ was partly due to genetic variation but environmental variation was added to it. So simply:

$$V_{F2} = V_G + V_E$$

where $V_{F2}$ represents the variation in the $F_2$ generation, and $V_G$ and $V_E$ represent the genetic and environmental components of this variation. If all generations in a controlled breeding experiment for a quantitative character are maintained in the same environments, then $V_E$ can be measured in $P_0$ and $F_1$ generations where all variation is environmental. $V_E$ is often measured as the *average* of the variation of the two parents ($P_0$) and the $F_1$. The *overall* variatiion of the $F_2$ generation can also be measured. $V_G$ is then:

$$V_G = V_{F2} - V_E$$

It is then possible to estimate how much of the $F_2$ variation is genetic. This proportion is called the **heritability** of a character:

$$\text{heritability} = \frac{V_G}{V_{F2}}$$

Note that the heritability can only be calculated if all the generations are exposed to the *same* environments because only then can the variation in the $P_0$ and $F_1$ give a measure of $V_E$ in the $F_2$.

If heritability of a character is *high*, much of the $F_2$ variation is due to *genetic* differences between individuals. If this were true of milk yield, for example, a cross between a cow with good milk yield and a bull whose mother had a good milk yield should produce daughters with a good yield. But if heritability is low, most of the variation is environmentally induced and there is less likely to be a positive correlation between parent and progeny performance.

In the model set out above it has been assumed that all the genetic variation is due to additive effects of the polygenes, each gene adding a small amount to the weight, height or whatever is measured. However, as for qualitative genes some polygenes may be dominant over their alleles, or epistatic over polygenes at other loci. These interactions will affect the genetic variation in the $F_2$, so $V_G$ (the estimate of genetic variability) is actually the *sum* of the *additive* effects of polygenes $V_A$ plus the *interaction* effects $V_I$:

$$V_G = V_A + V_I$$

Methods of analysis have been developed to separate the effects of dominance and epistatic interactions from the additive effects of polygenes. It is therefore possible to work out how much of the observed variability is due only to the additive effect of polygenes. This estimate is called the **narrow heritability**, or **$h^2$**:

$$h^2 = \frac{V_A}{V_{F2}}$$

This is an important estimate of genetic variation for the development of improved strains in agriculture and horticulture because it predicts most accurately how likely it is that a polygenic character is going to respond to selective breeding (chapter 11).

# 4.6 INTELLIGENCE

Intelligence in humans can be considered a quantitative character because individuals can be tested and given numerical IQ scores. However it is very difficult to obtain heritability estimates because it is impossible to do controlled breeding experiments. People bring their past (unmeasured) environment as well as their genetics to be tested. The problems can be illuminated by investigations involving maze learning in rats. Table 3 summarises the numbers of mistakes made by two strains of rats when run in the same maze. One strain was genetically 'bright' and the other was genetically 'dull'. If both strains were brought up in a normal laboratory environment and then tested, 'dull' rats made many more mistakes in the maze than 'bright' rats. However when rats from the two strains were brought up in a very restricted or a very stimulating environment the differences between them disappeared.

Hence, genetics can only be separated from the environmental contribution to behaviour if both strains of rats are brought up in the same range of environments. This also applies to human behaviour so estimates of genetic differences in intelligence between different families or ethnic groups should be treated with great caution.

*Table 3 Genotype-environment interactions in rat learning behaviour. 'Bright' and 'dull' rat strains, brought up in three different environments, were tested in a maze; data are number of mistakes by rats from different environments*

|  | RESTRICTED ENVIRONMENT | NORMAL ENVIRONMENT | STIMULATING ENVIRONMENT |
|---|---|---|---|
| Bright rats | 170 (many) | 120 (few) | 112 (few) |
| Dull rats | 170 (many) | 165 (many) | 120 (few) |

# BIBLIOGRAPHY

Suzuki, D T, Griffiths, A J F, Miller, J H and Lewontin, R C (1989) *An Introduction to Genetic Analysis* 4th Edn W H Freeman and Co.

# QUESTIONS

**1** A cross was carried out with *Drosophila melanogaster* which differed for two characters: long versus short wing, and grey versus ebony body colour. One parent had grey body and short wings, the other had ebony body and long wings. The $F_1$ flies were all grey bodied and long winged. They were mated among themselves to produce an $F_2$ generation as follows:

| Type of fly | Numbers of flies |
|---|---|
| grey body, long wings | 95 |
| ebony body, long wings | 36 |
| grey body, short wings | 24 |
| ebony body, short wings | 5 |

a) How many genes are segregating in this cross?
b) Do either of the characters show dominance?
c) Give the genotypes of all the flies in each generation.
d) What other parental genotypes could give these $F_2$ results.
e) Test your genetic hypothesis for this cross by means of a Chi-squared test.

**2** a) Define complementary gene activity.
b) A geneticist crossed a tall pea plant with purple flowers with a short, white flowered plant. A few $F_1$ plants were self-fertilised but only 14 $F_2$ seeds were produced. When these seeds were germinated, none produced a white flowered short plant. Explain why this might be.
c) What would be the most probable number of tall plants with white flowers in this sample of 14?

d) What would be the minimum number of plants in the $F_2$ generation to fulfil the predictions of Mendel's second hypothesis? Would it be possible for all four types of plant expected in the $F_2$ to appear in a sample of 14 $F_2$ plants?

**3** The effects of three mouse coat colour gene loci was explained on page 49. The three loci are agouti/non-agouti (A/a), black or brown melanin (B/b) and pigmented or albino (C/c). Upper case letters show the dominant allele at each locus. Describe the coat colours of the parents and their off spring in the following mouse crosses:
(i) AABBCc × aabbCc,
(ii) aaBBcc × aabbCC.

**4** There are a number of different forms of comb on the heads of poultry. Birds from a pure breeding 'pea comb' strain were mated to a pure breeding 'rose comb' strain. The $F_1$ of this cross all had a 'walnut comb'. When the $F_2$ were mated among themselves, all three comb types appeared among the $F_2$ birds but there was an additional type of bird carrying a 'single comb'. Numbers of birds among the $F_2$ phenotypes were as follows:

| walnut | rose | pea | single |
|---|---|---|---|
| 40 | 10 | 16 | 3 |

Test these results to see if they conform to a 9 : 3 : 3 : 1 ratio. Give the genotypes of the various birds in each generation. What does this experiment tell you about the minimum number of gene loci involved in forming poultry combs?

**5** Suppose a quantitative character in a particular species is found to have a very low heritability. Does this mean:
a) The character is not inherited?
b) The character is not influenced by the environment?
c) There is little genetic variation underlying this character?
d) This species lives in a relatively uniform environment?
Give your reasons for rejecting or accepting any of these conclusions.

# MEIOSIS

This chapter considers how chromosome behaviour in meiosis can explain the behaviour of genes in controlled breeding experiments.

Controlled breeding experiments, like those summarised in chapters 3 and 4 demonstrate that inheritable units (genes) exist. However, breeding experiments do not show where genes are found within an organism. Molecular genetic experiments like those reviewed in chapter 2 have shown that DNA is the genetic material and that this molecule is located in chromosomes. As discussed in chapter 1, nuclear division by meiosis is a major component of sexual reproduction in all eukaryote life histories. So can the behaviour of chromosomes during meiosis explain the behaviour of genes in sexual reproduction?

## Cell preparation for meiosis

In eukaryote cells, two identical copies of every DNA molecule are produced well before they are separated into different daughter cells. i.e. DNA replication always precedes, and is separate from, segregation of daughter DNA molecules which happens during nuclear division. DNA replication before meiosis often takes several hours, e.g. 14 hours in the mouse. DNA replication is usually followed by a 'rest' period before nuclear division. However the length of this period between replication and meiosis varies between species.

In many animals, including humans, the cells which are going to produce the reproductive cells are set aside very early in the embryo. These **germ line** cells multiply by mitosis and then undergo meiosis to produce gametes.

## 5.1 MEIOSIS

Meiosis consists of two nuclear divisions. The first division produces two daughter nuclei. In the second division, each daughter nucleus divides into two. There is no DNA replication between the first and second divisions which means that the four products of meiosis have half the quantity of

DNA that was in the original nucleus. Meiosis occurs in diploid cells which have two copies of every chromosome (except the sex chromosomes – see below). Each of the four nuclei produced contains one copy of those chromosomes, i.e. they are haploid.

Meiosis is a continuous process. There are steady changes in the organisation of the chromosomes which can be observed under the light microscope. Biologists have divided meiosis into various stages. The sequence of the two divisions is set out stage by stage as follows:

| 1st MEIOTIC DIVISION | | 2nd MEIOTIC DIVISION |
|---|---|---|
| Prophase 1 | ('beginning') | Prophase II |
| leptotene | ('thin thread') | |
| zygotene | ('paired thread') | |
| pachytene | ('thick thread') | |
| diplotene | ('double thread') | |
| diakenesis | ('moving through') | |
| Metaphase I | ('middle') | Metaphase II |
| Anaphase I | ('ending') | Anaphase II |
| Telophase I | ('end') | Telophase II |

Meiosis may last less than a day, but in many organisms it takes longer than this. In some female mammals, it runs over several years. Before a woman is born, many cells called **oocytes** start meosis in her immature ovary. The oocytes do not develop beyond prophase of the first division; they complete meioses one, or a few, at a time. The first meiosis is completed at puberty when she is in her 'teens. The last one is completed at menopause some 40 years later. In contrast, in the testes of the human male, many thousands of meioses are completed every few days from puberty to the end of the man's reproductive life.

The diagrams in Figure 1 show the behaviour of two of the smaller chromosomes and the X sex chromosome during meiosis in a male grasshopper. Note that the chromosomes steadily become shorter and fatter through each nuclear division. When the chromosomes are condensed in this way, they can be moved about within the cell more easily. the important features of meiosis are described below.

(a) Chromosomes appear as single strands – ends attached to nuclear membrane

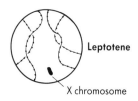

**Leptotene**

X chromosome

(b) Homologous chromosomes pair – role of 'synaptonemal complex'

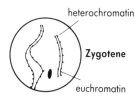

heterochromatin

**Zygotene**

euchromatin

(c) Chromosomes divide into chromatids; one or more chiasmata form

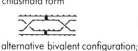

alternative bivalent configuration; two chiasmata and central centromeres

centromere

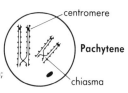

**Pachytene**

chiasma

(d) Centromeres of a bivalent repel each other; chiasmata hold bivalent together

**Diplotene**

(e) Chromosomes and bivalents condense

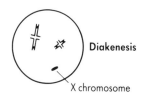

**Diakenesis**

X chromosome

(f) Bivalents lie on spindle equator with a centromere on either side; chiasmata hold bivalent together

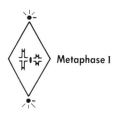

**Metaphase I**

(g) Sister chromatids repel each other; chiasmata fall apart and two chromosomes in a bivalent move to opposite poles

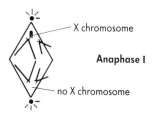

X chromosome

**Anaphase I**

no X chromosome

(h) Chromosomes reach spindle poles; nuclear membranes form round both groups which may decondense or pass straight into prophase II

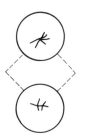

**Telophase I**

(i) Each daughter nucleus contains one member of each homologous pair of chromosomes; chromosomes decondense at this stage

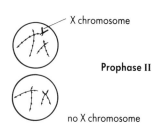

X chromosome

**Prophase II**

no X chromosome

(j) Chromosomes form upon the spindle equator quite independently of each other

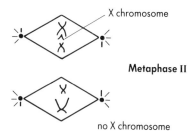

X chromosome

**Metaphase II**

no X chromosome

(k) Centromeres split and pull chromatids to opposite spindle poles

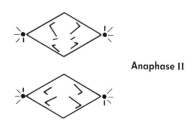

**Anaphase II**

(l) All four nuclei contain one haploid chromosome set, except that half these male gametes contain an X chromosome, the other half do not

**Telophase II**

*Figure 1   Progression of meiosis in the male grasshopper (**Chorthippus bruneus**)*

## Prophase I

The nuclear membrane remains intact through this part of meoisis.

**Leptotene (Figure 1a).** Each chromosome appears as a single thin thread. So although each chromosome must contain two copies of its DNA molecule, they are not yet visibly separate. Electron microscopy suggests that the ends of the chromosomes are attached to the inner nuclear membrane at this stage.

**Zygotene (Figure 1b).** Chromosomes pair off. Both members of a pair appear the same, they are **homologous**. We know that one chromosome of each pair comes from the individual's mother and the other from its father. The homologous chromosomes are the same length and each one has a **centromere** in the same position. Centromeres are very important in the movement of chromosomes later in meiosis.

**Pachytene (Figure 1c).** Each chromosome is split along its length into two sister **chromatids**, except at the centromere. So each pair of chromosomes (a **bivalent**) consists of two sets of sister chromatids. Two of these chromatids break at one or more sites along the length of the bivalent. The same two chromatids are not necessarily involved at all sites. The result of this break and exchange can be seen under the light microscope as a **chiasma** (cross-over) between two chromatids. Chiasmata are important for two reasons:

(i) They hold the chromosomes in a bivalent together. In doing so they ensure that each daughter nucleus eventually gets one chromosome from each bivalent and therefore one complete set of chromosomes.

(ii) They can produce new combinations of genes strung along the homologous chromosomes.

**Diplotene (Figure 1d).** The two centromeres of a bivalent move apart and separate the homologous chromosomes, except at chiasmata where sister chromatid attraction holds chromosomes together (Figure 2). The molecular mechanisms of these processes are not yet understood.

**Diakenesis (Figure 1e).** The bivalents are approaching their most condensed state. They move apart from each other. The nuclear membrane breaks down and a spindle is formed. This stage marks the transition from prophase to metaphase.

## Metaphase 1 (Figure 1f)

The spindle consists of **microtubules** made of the protein **tubulin**. Microtubules are also an essential component of a cell's cytoskeleton. In a spindle, two sets of tubules radiate out from opposite centres (**poles**) and overlap at the spindle **equator**. The centromeres of the bivalents attach to some spindle fibres and the bivalents are moved to the spindle equator. Every bivalent has two

(a) *Bivalent with terminal centromeres and a single chiasma*

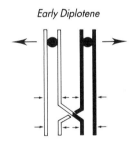

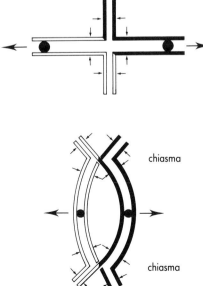

(b) *Bivalent with mid centromeres and two chiasmata*

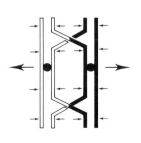

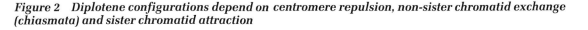

Key    centromere repulsion ➔    chromatid attraction →

*Figure 2    Diplotene configurations depend on centromere repulsion, non-sister chromatid exchange (chiasmata) and sister chromatid attraction*

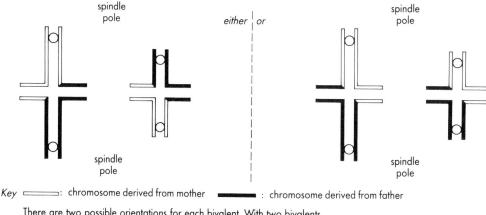

Key ⊏══⊐ : chromosome derived from mother   ▬▬▬▬ : chromosome derived from father

There are two possible orientations for each bivalent. With two bivalents
there are two possible combinations: like with non-like, and like with like,
(shown above). If bivalent orientation is random, the two combinations
should be equally frequent over a number of meioses

**Figure 3**   *Random orientation of two chromsome bivalents on the first meiotic metaphase spindle*

centomeres so that one lies above the spindle
equator and one below it. Centromeres orientate
on the spindle at random (figure 3). At this stage a
bivalent is still held together by one or more
chiasmata.

### Anaphase/Telophase 1 (Figure 1g and 1h)
The attraction between sister chromatids turns to
repulsion and the chiasmata therefore fall apart.
The two centromeres of each bivalent are moved
to opposite spindle poles by the microtubules.
This separates the homologous chromosomes and
halves the number of chromosomes in the two
daughter nuclei. Nuclear membranes reform
round the two groups of chromosomes in some
organisms, but not all.

In many organisms the chromosomes at each
pole move quickly into the second meiotic
division.

### Prophase II (Figure 1i)
Each nucleus is haploid, i.e. there is only one
copy of every chromosome. The chromosomes
consist of two chromatids which were formed in
the first meiotic division. The chromosomes
condense. The nuclear membranes, if formed,
break down and a spindle is produced for each
nucleus.

### Metaphase II (Figure 1j)
The centromere of each chromosome attaches to
microtubules and is moved to the spindle equator.
Note that in this second metaphase there is only
one copy of each chromosome so that its
centromere lies *on* the spindle equator. Also,
microtubules from both spindle poles attach to
opposite faces of every centromere.

### Anaphase II (Figure 1k)
Each centromere splits and the chromatids from
each chromosome are moved to opposite spindle
poles. Each chromatid has now become a
*chromosome.*

### Telophase II (Figure 1l)
Nuclear membranes form round the groups of
chromosomes and meiosis is complete.

# The products of meiosis
Nuclear division is followed by cell division so
that the nuclei are distributed to two cells at the
end of the first division and there are four cells at
the end of the second division. In many female
animals and in higher plants, only one of the
meiotic products acts as a gamete. In animals this
is a large cell called an **ovum**. Large amounts of
RNA and protein are required for development to
continue after the ovum is fertilised and before
the new individual can feed for itself. These
molecules are synthesised in the cytoplasm
during prophase I of meiosis and they are all
distributed to one meiotic product. The others are
often broken down or shed as small polar bodies,
one from the first meiotic division and another
from the second meiotic division. All four
products of meiosis in male organisms usually
survive. In several male animals the cells remain
connected to each other until meiosis and male
gamete development is completed.

# Sex chromosomes
One of the chromosomes in Figure 1 is unpaired.
A similar chromosome was discovered in a male
hemipteran insect in 1891. The discoverer was
not sure that it was a chromosome so he labelled it
'X'. In 1905 it was shown that a female
hemipteran has a pair of X chromosomes which
behave like all the other paired chromosomes in
meiosis. This means that all the female meiotic
products receive an X. In the male, the X
chromosome passes to one nucleus at meiosis I, so
only half the male gametes receive an X
chromosome (Figure 1g–1l). Fusion of an ovum

with a sperm carrying an X chromosome produces a female insect (which is XX). Fusion of an ovum with a sperm lacking an X produces a male insect (this is XO).

Other species have a chromosomal sex-determining mechanism but the details are different. In many species, including *Drosophila* and humans, the male has two sex chromosomes, one X and one Y. The female is XX. X and Y chromosomes are usually very different from each other. In contrast to these organisms, female butterflies and birds are XY whereas the males are XX.

The mechanisms by which sex is determined are not universal. Even in *Drosophila* and humans, which both have XY males and XX females, the switch mechanism is different. The first evidence for this came from the data set out in Table 1.

**Table 1  Sexual characteristics of Drosophila and humans with unusual sex chromosome complements**

| SEX CHROMOSOMES | DROSOPHILA | HUMAN |
|---|---|---|
| XO | male | female |
| XYY | male | male |
| XXY | female | male |
| normal complements | | |
| XX | female | female |
| XY | male | male |

In humans and mice, presence of one Y switches development to male. There must be at least one gene present on the Y chromosome that makes this switch from the female pattern. One such gene has been isolated from male mice and introduced into female embryos by DNA manipulation. The embryos develop as sterile male mice. In *Drosophila*, the sex of the fly seems to be determined by the ratio of X chromosomes to non-sex chromosomes (**autosomes**). 1X to 3 pairs of autosomes makes the individual a male, 2Xs to 3 pairs of autosomes makes it a female. Somehow this difference activates a cascade of genes switching them one way or the other. The molecular detail of this gene activation is currently under investigation.

An X or Y chromosomal switch for sex is not universal. For example, female honey bees (both queens and workers) are diploid, whereas males are haploid. A queen bee takes part in only one mating flight early in her adult life. Thereafter she lays eggs which she fertilises with sperm she has stored in a special part of her reproductive tract. Fertilised eggs develop as females, usually workers and occasionally as a new queen. At certain times the queen lays unfertilised haploid eggs which develop as males.

Many reptiles do not have an obvious chromosomal switch for sex either. Their sex-determining genes are temperature-sensitive. The females usually bury a clutch of eggs and the temperatures at which the embryos develop determine whether they are going to be male or female.

## Unusual meioses

Various animals and plants reproduce from *unfertilised* ova. This mode of reproduction is called **parthenogenesis**. The cytoplasmic development of the female gametes is normal as this is essential for normal development of the embryo. However, many organisms which reproduce by parthenogenesis cease meiosis in prophase I so that the ovum and the embryo which develops from it remain diploid. The individuals which are reproduced contain only their mother's chromosomes so they are identical to her and are female. Many generations of female aphids are produced parthenogenetically in the summer; but in autumn males and females are produced and undergo normal meiosis and sexual reproduction.

## Genetic importance of meiosis

There are three features of meiosis which are important in genetics.

(i) **Segregation of alleles**. Homologous chromosomes are bound together at the beginning of meiosis as bivalents. Bivalents are orientated at metaphase I so that two homologous chromosomes will segregate into different nuclei/cells at anaphase I. This halves the chromosome number and can segregate alleles.

(ii) **Independent assortment and random recombination**. Homologous chromosomes are bound to each other and are therefore dependent on each other until anaphase I. In contrast, different pairs of chromosomes are quite independent of each other throughout meiosis. This means that genetic information carried on different pairs of chromosomes is sorted independently and can be recombined at random.

(iii) **Linkage**. Different genes on the same chromosome tend to be inherited together. Genes at different positions on the same chromosome can only be recombined when a chiasma occurs between them.

## Segregation of alleles

Figure 4 illustrates the four critical steps in meiosis needed to explain segregation of alleles in a Mendelian breeding experiment. Two alleles in a heterozygote, Aa, are carried at identical

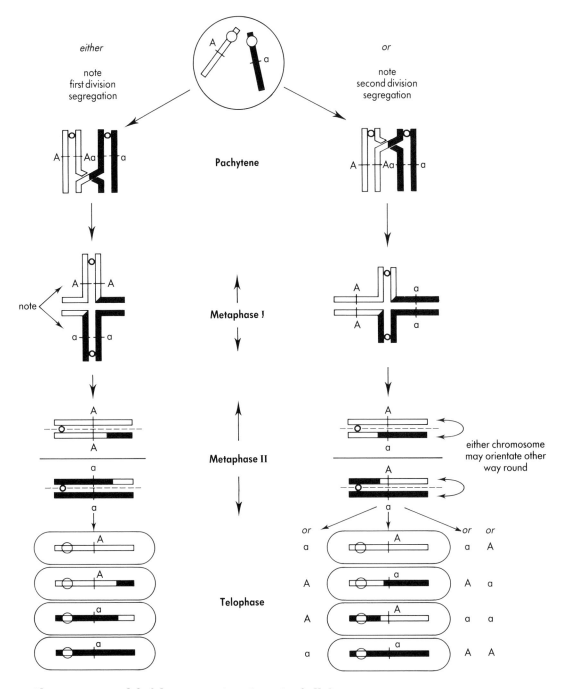

*either*

note
first division
segregation

*or*

note
second division
segregation

Pachytene

Metaphase I

note

Metaphase II

either chromosome
may orientate other
way round

Telophase

*Figure 4   Chromosome model of the segregation of a pair of alleles*

positions on two homologous chromosomes. Chromatid division separates two copies of each allele. At least one chiasma must occur to hold the bivalent together. Let's assume that these are small chromosomes and one chiasma is the norm. There are only two possible positions for the chiasma:

   (i)  Outside the locus-centromere distance (Figure 4 'either'). In this sort of meioses the *first* division segregates **A** from **a**.

   (ii)  Between the locus and the centromere (Figure 4 'or'). In this sort of meiosis, the *second* division segregates **A** and **a**.

Both types of meiosis produce equal numbers of nuclei containing **A** and **a** so that over all the meioses there must be 1**A**:1**a**. This is what Mendel said must happen in his breeding experiments (chapter 3, Figure 1).

## 5.2 SEX LINKAGE

A sex-linked character shows a different pattern of inheritance among males and females. Sex linkage was discovered in the fruit fly *Drosophila melanogaster* quite early in this century. Reciprocal crosses for red and white eyed fruit

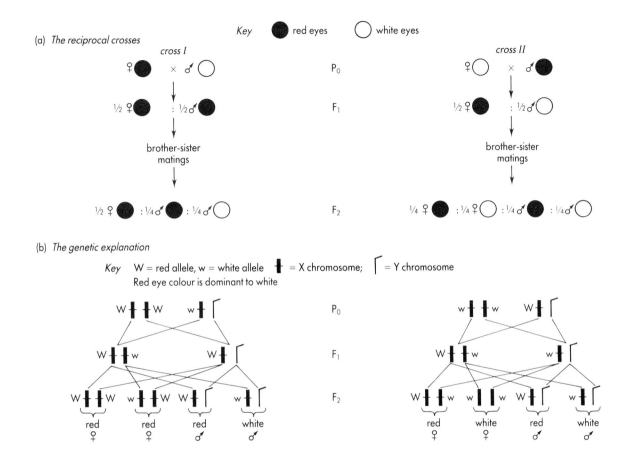

*Figure 5  Sex-linked inheritance of eye colour in* **Drosophila melanogaster**

flies are shown in Figure 5a: in one cross the $P_0$ male fly is red eyed, in the other cross the $P_0$ male is white eyed. Note:

  (i) Males and females are equally frequent in the $F_1$ and $F_2$ generations of both crosses.
  (ii) The patterns of inheritance of eye colour are different in the reciprocal crosses.

These results were first understood when it was discovered that the male and female have different chromosome complements. The diploid chromosome number is 8 in both sexes. But males have an X and a Y as well as three pairs of autosomes (non-sex chromosomes), whereas the female has three pairs of autosomes plus a pair of X chromosomes.

The inheritance of red and white eyes in *D. melanogaster* can be explained if the gene locus which determines this difference is present on the X chromosome but absent from the Y (Figure 5b). Such gene loci are said to be **sex-linked**. Note that the character has nothing to do with the actual sex of the fly, it is merely one of the genes carried on the X chromosome.

A male must receive its Y chromosome from its father and therefore always inherits any gene carried on the X chromosome from its mother. Males carry only one X chromosome so the genes on that chromosome are always expressed. This means that dominance cannot obscure the expression of sex-linked genes in males. in controlled breeding experiments, brothers and sisters may therefore have different phenotypes as in cross II in Figure 5. The $F_1$ females are heterozygotes expressing the red eye allele obtained from their father; their brothers have white eyes as this was the allele carried on both their mother's X chromosomes.

The patterns of inheritance of eye colours in crosses I and II are consistent with their genes being carried on the X chromosome. The correlation between the transmission of sex chromosomes and the patterns of inheritance of sex-linked genes was one of the first pieces of evidence that genes are indeed carried on chromosomes.

# 5.3 HUMAN PEDIGREE ANALYSIS

(a) *Sex-linked recessive pedigree pattern*

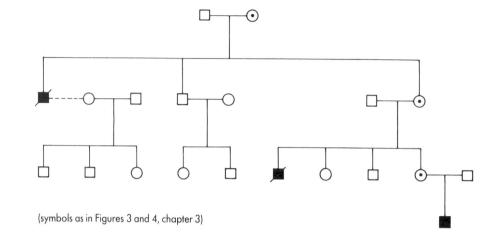

(symbols as in Figures 3 and 4, chapter 3)

(b) *Genetic explanation*

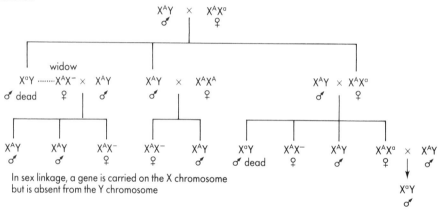

In sex linkage, a gene is carried on the X chromosome but is absent from the Y chromosome

**Figure 6** *A sex-linked recessive pedigree pattern and its genetic explanation*

There are several examples of human genetic diseases that are determined by **sex-linked recessive genes**, including Duchene muscular dystrophy (DMD) and haemophilia A. DMD boys are slow to walk and have difficulty in running. They show progressive muscular weakness, are in a wheelchair by age 10 and are usually dead by 20. In haemophilia A, the blood will not clot because of low Factor VIII (a blood clotting protein) activity. The disease can be crippling as the result of bleeding into joints and internal haemorrhaging, but the severity of the disease is variable. The specific features of sex-linked recessive pedigrees are (Figure 6):

(i)  The disease affects mainly males.
(ii) Affected males (**a**) have unaffected parents (♀ **Aa**, ♂ **A**) but may have affected maternal uncles (**a**).
(iii) The disease is transmitted by carrier women (**Aa**) who usually do not show any symptoms of the disease. Half their sons are likely to be affected (½**A**:½**a**) and half their daughters are likely to be carriers (½**Aa**:½**AA**).
(iv) Affected girls (**aa**) can be born if an affected male (**a**) survives long enough to marry a carrier woman (**Aa**) and have children.

Until recently haemophiliac men had a short life expectancy and boys with DMD still do. This means that there has been a very small chance of an affected male, with either disease, having children. However in recent years donated blood from non-haemophiliacs has been processed to provide Factor VIII. Haemophiliacs can inject this into their bloodstream and live relatively normal lives. This advance in medicine has decreased the selective disadvantage of carrying this gene (see chapter 10). It is therefore likely to increase in frequency in the human population, giving an increased likelihood that haemophiliac women will be born.

# 5.4 INDEPENDENT ASSORTMENT

Mendel showed that two gene loci can segregate independently and therefore recombine at random. This causes a double heterozygote **AaBb** to form gametes in a proportion 1 **AB** : 1 **Ab** : 1 **aB** : 1 **ab**. A chromosome model for a double heterozygote **AaBb** is shown in Figure 7. The alleles **A** and **a** are carried on one chromosome pair, and **B** and **b** are carried on a second pair. This will account for Mendel's results.

In this model, cross-overs occur outside the locus-centromere distance. Note that the chromosome pairs orientate quite independently at metaphase so there are two possible types of meiosis. In the first, **AA** and **BB** orientate together so **aa** and **bb** must go in the opposite direction. In the second, **AA** and **bb** co-orientate so that **aa** and **BB** must go together. Figure 7 shows that each meiosis can produce only two types of nuclei with either **AB** and **ab**, or **aB** and **Ab**. Over many meioses, the two alternatives are equally likely so that all four haploid combinations **AB** : **Ab** : **aB** : **ab** should be equally common.

The two chromosome model shown in Figure 7 satisfactorily accounts for the independent assortment and random recombination of alleles at two loci. This model can be extended to include a chiasma between either locus and its centromere. When all possible combinations of chiasma positions are considered the model continues to produce all four combinations of alleles (**AB:Ab:aB:ab**) in equal proportions. Independent assortment and random recombination are thus guaranteed if loci are carried on different pairs of chromosomes.

# 5.5 LINKAGE

Thomas Henry Morgan discovered linkage in 1911. He was investigating patterns of inheritance in *D. melanogaster* and discovered that some characters did not recombine at random. Many hundreds of different gene loci have been discovered in *D. melanogaster*, but there are only four different chromosomes in this species. It is therefore not possible for each locus to be carried on a different chromosome. Similar arguments apply to other species. Linkage is most easily

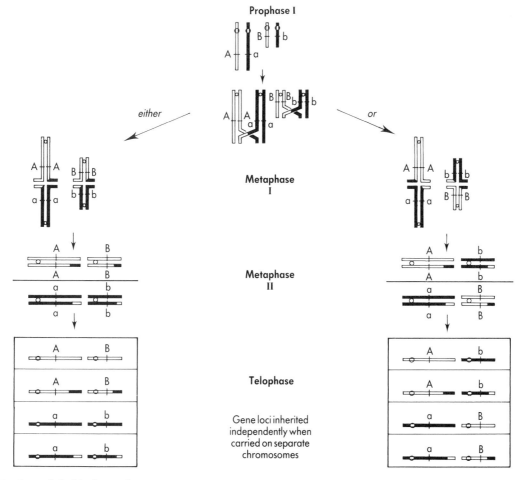

*Figure 7    A model of independent assortment*

understand in terms of chromosome behaviour at meiosis.

What happens during inheritance if different genes are carried on the same chromosome? Figure 8a shows the chromosome constitution of a double heterozygote **AaDd** which received one chromosome carrying **AD** from its mother and a second carrying **ad** from its father.

The combinations of alleles at different loci that a heterozygote receives from its parents are called the **parental combinations**. In this case they are **AD** and **ad**; in other individuals they could be **Ad** and **aD**.

Suppose that the heterozygote with **AD** and **ad** on homologous chromosomes undergoes meioses prior to reproduction. A single exchange can occur outside the two loci or between them. The effects of these two exchange positions are shown in Figure 8b and 8c. In the first case (8b) the parental combinations are transmitted to the gametes unchanged. In the second case (8c) half the gametes contain parental combinations of alleles and the other half contain two new recombinant combinations.

(a) *Parental combinations of alleles*

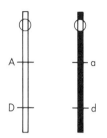

(b) *Exchange outside loci*

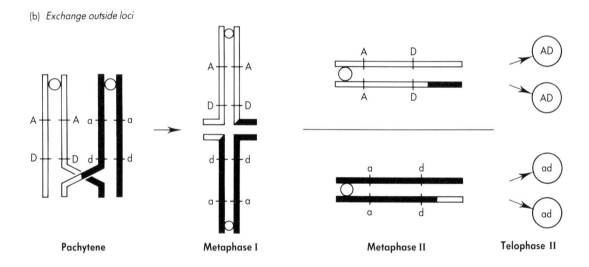

(c) *Exchange between loci*

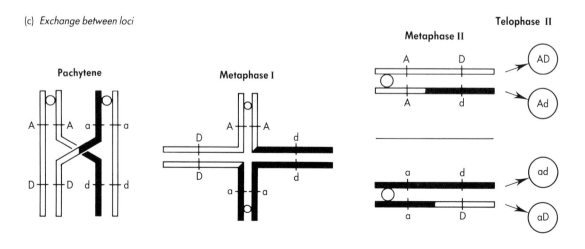

**Figure 8**   *The effect of the position of an exchange on the types of gamete produced by a double heterozygote A/a D/d when the two loci are linked on the same chromosome*

If all meioses were the first type, only parental combinations would be transmitted to the gametes and there would be no recombinants. This is **complete linkage**. If all meioses were of the second type, then 50 per cent of the gametes would be parental (**AD** and **ad**) and 50% would be recombinant (**Ad** and **aD**), giving four gamete types at equal frequency.

It is likely that some meioses will have a cross-over between the two loci, but others will have a cross-over outside them. In this case there will be some recombinant gametes but less than 50%. This is **partial linkage**. A model is provided in Figure 9. If 20% of meioses have a cross-over between the two loci, then the frequency of recombinant gametes is 10%.

recombination frequency

$$= \frac{\text{Number of recombinant gametes}}{\text{total number of gametes}} \times 100$$

Note that this recombination frequency is half the frequency of meioses with an exchange between the two loci (20/100 = 0.2 or 20%)

because only half the products of such meioses are recombinant.

If a cross-over can occur at random anywhere along a chromosome, and A/a and D/d have fixed positions on the chromosome, then any heterozygote for these genes should produce similar frequencies of recombinant gametes. They will not always be exactly 10% of the total because of the effects of chance, but they should always be close to 10%. If two other loci (J/j and K/k) are closer together on the chromosome, then exchange should occur less often between them than they do between A/a and D/d. Similarly if other loci (M/m and N/n) are further apart then exchanges should occur between them more often. Each of these pairs of loci should have a particular and repeatable recombination frequency.

The frequency of recombinant gametes can be estimated from controlled breeding experiments. In chapter 2 it was shown that the phenotypes of the progeny from a test cross directly reflect the gametes of the heterozygote parent.

Total number of meioses = 100
Number of meiosis with an exchange between A/a —— D/d = 20
Total number of gametes = 400

Number of gametes produced

| | AD | Ad | aD | ad | Totals |
|---|---|---|---|---|---|
| 80 meioses no exchange between loci (80 × 4 gametes) | 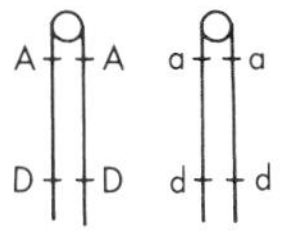 160 | | | 160 | 320 |
| 20 meioses with an exchange between loci (20 × 4 gametes) | 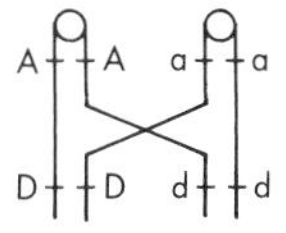 20 | 20 | 20 | 20 | 80 |
| | 180 | 20 | 20 | 180 | 400 |

Parental combinations are produced by both types of meiosis and must be most frequent among the gametes

Frequency of recombinant gametes (Ad and aD)

$$= \frac{\text{number of recombinant gametes}}{\text{total number of gametes}} = \frac{20 + 20}{400} = 0.1 \text{ or } 10\%$$

***Figure 9    The effect of chiasmata on linked genes, and calculation of recombination frequency (heterozygotes are AaDd and parental combinations are AD and ad)***

*Test cross*
Red eyed and long winged heterozygous females mated to males showing recessive white eye and miniature wing characters

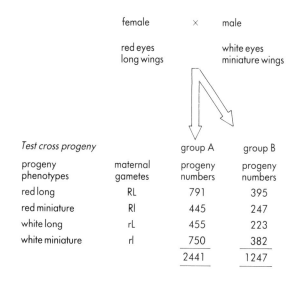

| Test cross progeny | | group A | group B |
|---|---|---|---|
| progeny phenotypes | maternal gametes | progeny numbers | progeny numbers |
| red long | RL | 791 | 395 |
| red miniature | Rl | 445 | 247 |
| white long | rL | 455 | 223 |
| white miniature | rl | 750 | 382 |
| | | 2441 | 1247 |

$$\text{Recombination frequency} = \frac{\text{number of recombinants}}{\text{total number of progeny}} \times 100$$

$$\text{For group A} = \frac{445 + 455}{2441} \times 100 = 36.9\%$$

$$\text{For group B} = \frac{247 + 223}{1247} \times 100 = 37.7\%$$

**Figure 10    Test cross results for Drosophila melanogaster. Group A data from Morgan (1911), Group B data from Sturtevant (1913)**

Figure 10 gives the data for two test crosses carried out two years apart. Female *Drosophila melanogaster* heterozygous at the miniature wing and white eye loci were mated to males carrying only the recessive alleles at these loci. Red eyes with long wings and white eyes with miniature wings are the most frequent progeny classes and must have been the parental combinations in the heterozygote female. The recombination frequency estimate for Morgan's data is 36.9 per cent, and for Sturtevant's data it is 37.7%. It is clearly repeatable as the linkage model predicts. This model is T H Morgan's great contribution to genetics.

Until very recently it was impossible to locate the physical position of any gene on the chromosomes of any organism. With the advent of DNA technology it has been possible to locate the positions of some genes in a few organisms like *Drosophila*, humans and some viruses. However, it is still generally true that we cannot see genes on the chromosome so we do not know how far apart they are. This means that it is not possible to predict the recombination frequency for linked

genes. It is only by carrying out the appropriate test cross that the recombination frequency can be measured.

# BIBLIOGRAPHY

Peters, J A (1959) *Classic Papers in Genetics* Biological Science Series (contains Morgan's paper on sex linkage) Prentice Hall.

Lewis, K R and John, B (1972) *The Matter of Mendelian Heredity* Longman.

# QUESTIONS

1 Suppose that the cells of a simple animal contain four chromosomes with a total of $10^7$ nucleotide pairs before DNA replication. How many chromosomes and how many nucleotide pairs of DNA will there be in the cells of this animal when they are:
   a)   in meiotic metaphase 1,
   b)   in meiotic metaphase II,
   c)   post meiotic gametes?

2 Consider two meioses in a heterozygote for three gene loci (Aa, Bb, Cc) arranged on one pair of homologous chromosomes as follows, with the centromeres at one end of the chromosomes, to the left of A and a.

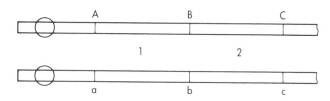

Explain by means of diagrams (showing pachytene and metaphases I and II), which genes will segregate at meiosis I and which ones will segregate at meiosis II with:
   a)   a meiosis with a single chiasma in region 1,
   b)   a meiosis with a single chiasma in region 2.

3 Define the terms *complete linkage* and *partial linkage*. How do these types of linkage differ from sex linkage?

4 In the following human pedigree circles indicate females and squares indicate males.

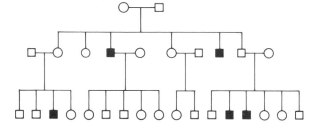

Filled in circles and squares indicate red-green colourblind individuals; open circles and squares indicate normal vision. Give the genotypes of as many individuals in the pedigree as possible and give the name of this pattern of inheritance.

5 Female flies were collected from a pure breeding stock of *Drosophila melanogaster* with bodies which were yellow and covered with small twisted bristles. They were mated to males from a pure breeding stock which had grey bodies covered with long straight bristles. In the $F_1$, all the sons were like their mother (yellow and twisted) and all the daughters were like their father (grey and straight). The $F_1$ brothers and sisters were mated and number of their offspring scored for body colour and bristle type as follows:

| | Number of males | Number of females | Totals |
|---|---|---|---|
| grey body straight bristles | 33 | 37 | 70 |
| grey body twisted bristles | 18 | 12 | 30 |
| yellow body straight bristles | 14 | 18 | 32 |
| yellow body twisted bristles | 37 | 31 | 68 |

a) Give the genotypes of the parents and the $F_1$ males and females.
b) Is there any evidence from these data that the two characters are linked? If they are linked give the recombination frequency.
c) Can you decide if either gene is carried on a particular chromosome?

# GENETIC MAPS

This chapter is concerned with the methods that have allowed geneticists to work out the positions of different genes on an organism's chromosome(s). All the methods involve two steps:
  (i) identification of each gene,
  (ii) tracing the arrangement of these genes on maps of the chromosome(s).
There are now two general methods by which genes can be placed in position on a map:
  (i) Genetic methods involving mating organisms which contain different alleles of the genes to be mapped. These methods produce **genetic maps**.
  (ii) Physical methods involving isolation of the DNA from a species. The positions of genes on that DNA are worked out and **physical maps** are produced.
Genetic maps have been prepared for a variety of organisms including several viruses, some bacteria and a number of eukaryotes (fungi, plants and animals). The genetic maps for some bacterial viruses, the bacterium *E. coli* and the fruit fly *Drosophila melanogaster* show the positions of a large number of those organisms' genes. However, the only complete genetic maps are a few viral ones.

Methods for DNA sequencing were introduced in chapter 2. These methods, still in their infancy, are most important for producing physical maps. Once a complete nucleotide sequence is known, it is fairly straightforward to locate the appropriate genes. At the moment there are only complete physical maps for some viruses.

## 6.1 EUKARYOTE GENETIC MAPS

Eukaryote genetic maps are **linkage maps**. They are based on recombination frequencies obtained from controlled breeding experiments. These experiments were introduced in chapters 4 and 5. Some different genes, e.g. the genes for seed colour and seed shape in the garden pea *Pisum sativum*, are inherited independently. This means that in a test cross of a double heterozygote (**AaBb**)

to a double recessive (**aabb**), all four types of offspring are equally frequent and the recombination frequency is 50% (chapter 5).

Other genes are inherited as if they are linked together, e.g. genes for eye colour and wing length in *Drosophila melanogaster* (chapter 5). For these two genes, repeated test crosses produced an average recombination frequency of 37%. The original (parental) combinations of alleles in the heterozygote parent (e.g. **CD** and **cd**) are more often inherited by the offspring of the cross than new (recombinant) combinations (e.g. **Cd** and **cD**). The parallels with the behaviour of chromosomes in meiosis suggests that two independently inherited genes are carried on different chromosomes, whereas two linked genes are carried on the same chromosome. New combinations of linked genes can only be produced if a chiasma (cross-over) happens between them.

Once genetic information accumulates for one species and different alleles are discovered at several gene loci, it becomes possible to carry out test crosses for various pairs of these genes (e.g. **L/l** with **M/m**, **L/l** with **N/n**, **M/m** with **N/n**, etc.) If such test crosses show a group of recombination frequencies which are less than 50%, then all the gene loci in this group must be linked to each other. These genes form a single **linkage group** on a chromosome. So what is the order of these genes along the chromosome? This can be worked out using the recombination frequencies between them. This is **linkage mapping**.

## Linkage mapping

Linkage mapping is based on the following ideas.
  (i) A chiasma can form at many different sites along a pair of homologous chromosomes although each site is occupied by a chiasma quite rarely.
  (ii) If (i) is true, a chiasma is most likely to occupy one of the many sites between two distant gene loci. It is least likely to occupy one of the few sites between two loci that are close together.
  (iii) Following from (ii), several meioses are likely to have a chiasma between two

distant loci whereas only a few will have a chiasma between two adjacent loci. The proportion of meioses with a chiasma between two loci therefore measures the distance apart of those loci. Unfortunately, scoring chromosome preparations is no use. There is no way to position any gene on a chromosome stained for light microscopy, so it is not possible to relate a chiasma to two particular loci.

(iv) However, if every chiasma forms recombinants according to the chromosome model (chapter 5), the frequency of recombinant progeny in a test cross is an estimate of the chiasmata frequency and a measure of the distance between the two gene loci.

On this basis, a recombination frequency for two linked genes is converted directly into **map units (m.u.)** e.g. 1% recombination frequency is 1 map unit.

The procedure for mapping the positions of several genes in a linkage group is as follows. Consider three loci in *D. melanogaster*:

eye colour – red (**W**) or white (**w**)
wing length – long (**M**) or miniature (**m**)
eye shape – bar (**B**) or round (**b**)

Three separate test crosses gave the following recombination frequencies = map units:

eye colour – eye shape = 50 m.u.
eye colour – wing length = 35 m.u.
eye shape – wing length = 15 m.u.

Chiasmata must have formed more often between eye colour genes **W/w** and eye shape genes **B/b** than between eye colour genes **W/w** and wing length genes **M/m** or between eye shape genes **B/b** and wing length genes **W/w**. Comparison of the

three map distances gives the order of the loci:

| < | 50 m.u. | | > |
|---|---|---|---|
| B/b | M/m | | W/w |
| < | 15 m.u. | >< | 35 m.u. | > |

i.e. the distance beteen W/w and B/b is the *sum* of the other two distances.

Maps showing the order of several loci and the distances between them can be built up from a series of paired crosses:

| Gene order | N/n | X/x | Z/z | Y/y | P/p | G/g | F/f |
|---|---|---|---|---|---|---|---|
| map distance (m.u.) | < 12 >< | 5 >< | 10 >< | 7 >< | 2 >< | 8 > | |

However, mapping is not quite as simple as this because chiasmata do not always give rise to recombinants. If two chiasmata occur simultaneously, they sometimes cancel each other out (Figure 1). Several chiasmata are most likely to form between distant gene loci. This means that a recombination frequency for a pair of genes that are far apart on a chromosome will tend to underestimate the distance between them. Various techniques have been worked out to overcome this sort of problem but they are beyond the scope of this book.

Quite detailed linkage maps have been prepared for several eukaryotes. In every case the number of linkage groups has been found to equal the number of different chromosomes. In *Drosophila melanogaster* there are four different chromosomes (chapter 2) and four linkage groups. Some of the genes on the linkage map of the X chromosome are shown in figure 2.

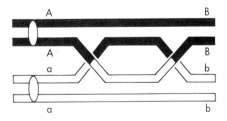

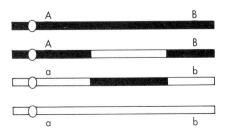

Recombinants for A/a and B/b genes are not produced, so these two chiasmata cannot be detected in a test cross for these loci

*Figure 1    An effect of two simultaneous chiasmata*

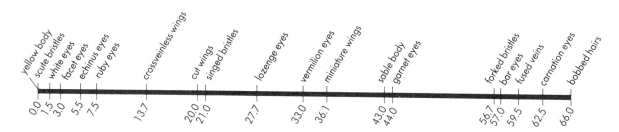

map of X chromosome

*Figure 2    A linkage map of some genes on the X chromosome of* Drosophila melanogaster *(from E W Sinnott, L C Dunn and T Dobzhansky* Principles of Genetics *5th edn. McGraw Hill)*

# 6.2 GENE MAPPING IN BACTERIA

Bacteria and viruses are relatively simple organisms. Their genetics has been concentrated on so that they may be completely understood and the principles applied to other more complex organisms.

### Variation in bacteria

Bacteria can be cultured in the laboratory. Many of them are able to synthesise all their component molecules from a simple **minimal medium** containing a sugar and various inorganic salts. *Escherichia coli*, a bacterium from the human gut, has been cultured and studied in laboratories all over the world for about 70 years. More is known about its genetics than probably any other organism. Many cultures have been treated with mutagens and a large number of mutants have been isolated. A **mutation** is an altered form of a gene, and a **mutant** is an organism which shows the mutation (chapter 7).

A most useful type of mutation is one that alters a gene so that the bacterium cannot synthesise one essential organic molecule from simple precursors in a minimal medium. e.g. a mutant strain unable to synthesise the amino acid arginine since it has the gene *arg⁻*. The original strain has an *arg⁺* gene and can synthesise arginine. Many other mutants are known, each one unable to synthesise a different organic molecule. This type of mutant dies if cultured on minimal medium but it can be kept alive by culturing on a minimal medium supplemented with the appropriate organic molecule. e.g. an Arg⁻ mutant will only grow on a minimal medium supplemented with arginine (Figure 3).

Mutants like Arg⁻ are called **auxotrophic mutants** because they cannot synthesise all the

organic molecules they need to survive. They are one type of **conditional lethal mutation** i.e. they will survive one set of conditions (supplemented medium) but not another (minimal medium). Conditional lethal mutants are very useful in biochemical and molecular genetics. Other conditional lethal mutants may grow at one temperature but not at another (page 76). This sort of mutation occurs in viruses, prokaryotes and eukaryote cells.

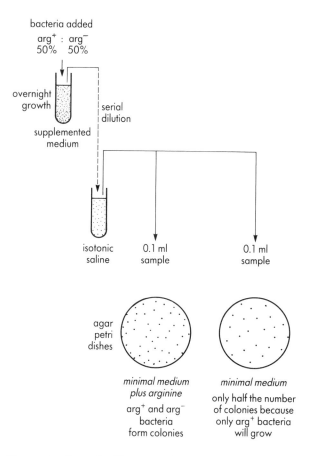

*Figure 3    Growth of bacterial colonies from mixed culture on minimal medium or on supplemented minimal medium*

## Methods for growing and counting bacteria

Bacteria can be grown in a liquid in a flask, or on an agar surface in a petri dish (an agar plate). Both liquid and agar may be made up as a minimal medium or a supplemented minimal medium. Bacteria divide into two about every 20 minutes (chapter 9), so after a few hours a liquid culture may contain 1000 million bacteria per ml. In genetics, the phenotype (characters) of individual organisms must be known if mutants are to be separated from the rest. Often the various types have to be counted to determine mutation or recombination rates. Individual bacteria can be separated out of $10^9$ per ml and counted in the following way.

**Serial dilution.** A liquid culture can be serially diluted as follows: a 1 ml sample is added to 9 mls isotonic saline and shaken well. This is a 1 in 10 dilution. 1 ml taken from this mixture and added to a further 9 ml of saline is a further 1 in 10 dilution, but the original sample has now been diluted 1 in 100. Six transfers of this kind produces a millionfold ($10^{-6}$) dilution; so if the original concentration of bacteria was 1000 million ($10^9$) per ml, a $10^{-6}$ dilution means there will now be 1000 ($10^3$) per ml. This is a small enough number to think of counting, but each of these bacteria is about 0.005 mm

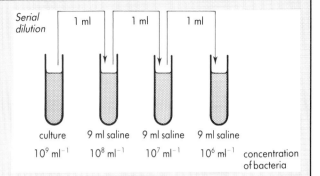

Serial dilution

| | 1 ml | 1 ml | 1 ml |

culture — 9 ml saline — 9 ml saline — 9 ml saline

$10^9$ ml$^{-1}$ — $10^8$ ml$^{-1}$ — $10^7$ ml$^{-1}$ — $10^6$ ml$^{-1}$ — concentration of bacteria

long. This is far too small to see with the naked eye.

**Growing bacteria on agar.** Bacteria can be made visible and counted by spreading them on an agar plate. If a ⅟₁₀ ml sample of the $10^{-6}$ dilution in the previous series is spread on the surface of an agar plate, the few bacteria in the sample (about 100) are spread out. If they can grow on the agar medium, each bacterium will reproduce asexually and form a small colony over a few hours. These colonies can easily be counted, each one representing one bacterium from the original culture. By growing samples on agars supplemented in different ways, it is possible to find out how many different phenotypes there were in the original culture and to estimate the numbers of each of them.

## Bacterial recombination

There was no means of mapping bacterial chromosomes until Joshua Ledeberg discovered that different mutant strains of *E. coli* could produce recombinant offspring. He used two auxotrophic mutants: one strain was not able to synthesise the vitamin biotin or the amino acid methionine, but could synthesise the amino acids threonine and leucine ($bio^- met^- thr^+ leu^+$); the other strain was the reverse of this ($bio^+ met^+ thr^- leu^-$). Neither of these two parent types would survive on minimal medium but $bio^+ met^+ thr^+ leu^+$ bacteria produced by recombination would survive on this medium. This is a **selective technique** because not all types of bacteria grow. It allows geneticists to test many millions of bacteria on a single petri dish. Ledeberg discovered that *E. coli* exchanged chromosomal genes very rarely; only about 1 in a million bacteria were recombinant. Unfortunately, these were too few recombinants to map genes accurately.

Further work showed that recombinants arose when a bacterium of one strain the **F$^+$** strain, joined (**conjugated**) with another bacterium of an F$^-$ strain (see photo). About one in a million F$^+$

bacteria **donated** its chromosomal genes to an F$^-$ individual during **conjugation**. After the conjugants had separated, the F$^-$ alone formed recombinants. The rare bacteria which donated their chromosomes were isolated from an F$^+$ strain by chance. These donors were called **Hfr** because, when mixed with an F$^-$, they all donated their chromosomes to F$^-$ cells and produced a **h**igh **f**requency of **r**ecombinants for their chromosomal genes.

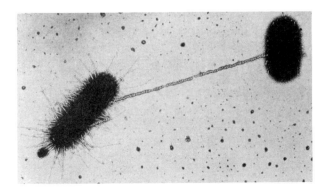

*This electron micrograph shows a pair of conjugating* Escherichia coli *bacteria*

## Chromosomes and plasmids in bacteria

It is now known that an Hfr bacterium is formed when a particular plasmid called the **F plasmid (fertility factor)** inserts into the bacterial chromosome. Remember from chapter 2 that bacterial chromosomes and most plasmids are circular. Figure 4 shows how a circular plasmid can integrate into a circular chromosome. F plasmids contain various short sequences which are also present at various **recognition sites** on the bacterial chromosome. An F plasmid can therefore integrate into one of a number of different recognition sites. F plasmids usually exist free of the bacterial chromosome. Bacteria with free F plasmids are $F^+$. In about 1 in a million $F^+$, the plasmid intergrates into the chromosome and the bacterium becomes an Hfr. In this state the bacterium can donate chromosomal genes to a recipient. Note that an $F^-$ recipient lacks a sex factor plasmid altogether.

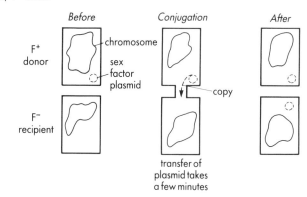

(a) $F^+$ donor

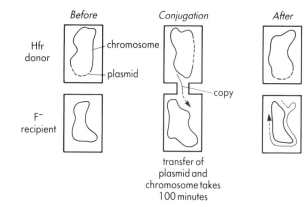

(b) Hfr donor

**Figure 5    Bacterial conjugation with (a) $F^+$, and (b) Hfr donors**

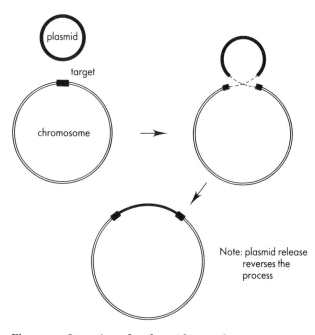

**Figure 4    Insertion of a plasmid into a bacterial chromosome**

An F plasmid carries the genes needed to make two copies of itself. It also carries the genes needed to make a conjugation tube. $F^+$ bacteria often conjugate with $F^-$, but they only transfer a copy of the *plasmid* to the $F^-$ bacterium (Figure 5). In Hfr bacteria, a plasmid is integrated with the bacterial chromosome. In this case the plasmid replication system copies the **chromosome** as well; one copy of the plasmid-chromosome is retained in the donor bacterium while the other one is transferred to the $F^-$ through a conjugation tube (Figure 5b). Which chromosomal gene is first through the conjugation tube depends at which site the F plasmid is integrated, and which end of the chromosomes is transferred first.

## Bacterial mapping

Once Hfr bacteria were isolated, François Jacob and Elie Wollman designed an experiment to map the chromosome in the Hfr bacterial strain. This is called the **interrupted mating experiment** and it measures the time taken (in minutes) for the donor bacterium to pass its genes through the conjugation tube into the recipient bacterium. The distances between genes on the *E. coli* map are therefore measured in minutes.

Jacob and Wollman were the first to suggest that if a donor chromosome had to pass into the recipient bacterium to form recombinants, it might pass in gradually, one end first. They argued that donor genes would therefore enter the recipient in linear order (Figure 6). They could test this by allowing a number of Hfr bacteria to conjugate with $F^-$ ones, separating some pairs at different times. If the bacteria were separated a short time after conjugation began, only the genes at the front end of the donor chromosome could pass into the recipient before the conjugation tube broke. In bacteria left to conjugate longer, genes further down the donor chromosome could pass into the recipient. To perform this experiment they used a recipient $F^-$ strain with

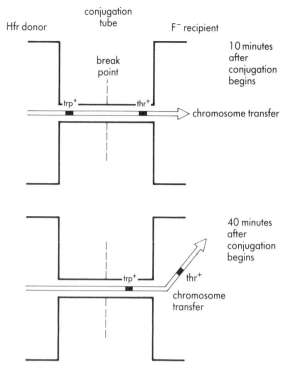

If conjugation tube is broken early in transfer, only genes at front end of donor chromosome are passed to recipient; if tube is broken later, genes further down are also passed to recipient

**Figure 6**  *Linear transfer of chromosome from donor to recipient bacterium*

several different auxotrophic genes (e.g. *thr⁻* and *trp⁻*) and a donor Hfr strain with the non-mutant alleles of these genes.

In the experiment, the first donor allele to enter F⁻ individuals was thr⁺. This happened 8 minutes after conjugation began. On the other hand, trp⁺ did not enter F⁻ individuals until 33 minutes after conjugation began. This suggests that thr⁺ was much nearer to the front end of the Hfr chromosome. Figure 7a gives the first linear map showing the order of these genes, and some others, on the Hfr H chromosome. The distance between them is also given, measured in minutes.

## The circular *E. coli* map

The circularity of the *E. coli* map was worked out when various other Hfr strains were isolated. These would also grow on minimal medium and therefore contained non-mutant genes. However, when they were tested against the original F⁻ strain it was found that each strain transferred the same genes in slightly different orders and all of them were different to the original Hfr H strain. Consider four different Hfr strains with the same five donor genes *gly⁺*, *met⁺*, *thr⁺*, *trp⁺* and *lac⁺*: these are concerned with the synthesis of the amino acids glycine, methionine, threonine and tryptophan and the breakdown of the disaccharide lactose for use as an energy source.

| HFR STRAIN | ORDER OF TRANSFER OF DONOR GENES TO THE F⁻ | |
|---|---|---|
| | **First** | **Last** |
| Hfr H | *thr⁺ lac⁺ trp⁺ gly⁺ met⁺* | |
| Hfr 2 | *lac⁺ thr⁺ met⁺ gly⁺ trp⁺* | |
| Hfr 4 | *met⁺ gly⁺ trp⁺ lac⁺ thr⁺* | |
| Hfr AB311 | *trp⁺ lac⁺ thr⁺ met⁺ gly⁺* | |

The results show three main features:
(i) different Hfr strains pass different genes to the F⁻ first,
(ii) apart from the first and the last genes, the same genes are always transferred next to each other by the different strains,
(iii) some donors transfer the genes in the reverse order of the other strains, e.g. Hfr H and Hfr 4.

The results indicate that the donor cell contains a single circular chromosome. During conjugation, different Hfr strains copy the circle from different origins depending on where the plasmid is inserted. A linear chromosome is transferred to the recipient. In some Hfr strains a gene is transferred early, but in other strains it is late. This depends on the orientation of the plasmid at the target site (Figure 7b). This experiment gave the first evidence that the bacterial chromosome is circular, and later electron microscopy confirmed this (chapter 2).

(a)

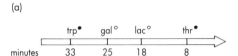

° genes needed to break down sugars, galactose or lactose
• genes needed to make amino acids, tryptophan or threonine

(b)

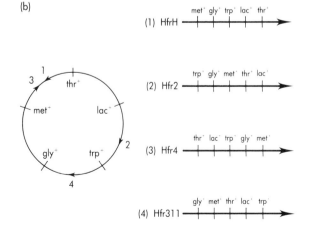

← = sites of integration and orientation of F plasmid into the chromosome. When an F plasmid is integrated the bacterium is Hfr. Position and orientation of F plasmid determines which genes pass through the conjugation tube first

**Figure 7**  *(a) First linear map of* Escherichia coli *chromosome, and (b) explanation of linear transfer of genes from a circular chromosome*

In the bacterial chromosome, genes that work together to carry out a particular function are often grouped together (figure 8) e.g. the five genes trp A, B, C, D, and E (which make the amino acid tryptophan from simpler precursors) and three genes lac Z, Y and A (which are involved in lactose breakdown). This is quite different from the eukaryotes where genes that are involved in the same function are often located on *different* chromosomes.

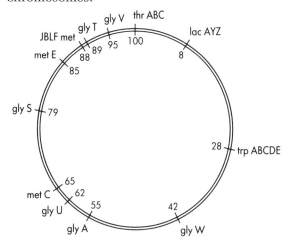

Some genes concerned with the same function are closely linked e.g. lac AYZ are three genes involved in lactose metabolism. Genes concerned with another function may be more widely spread e.g. gly genes involved in the synthesis of glycine

***Figure 8    Some gene positions on the circular* E. coli *chromosome. Map units are minutes***

## Transduction

Interrupted mating cannot resolve the order of genes within two minutes map distance. Fortunately there are other techniques which can be used to map closely linked bacterial genes. One of these is **transduction** in which bacterial genes are transferred between bacteria by viral infection. A combination of conjugation and transduction has been used to produce the *E. coli* linkage map.

Transduction was discovered in the 1950s by Joshua Ledeberg. He found that two nutritional mutant strains of the bacterium *Salmonella typhimurium* would produce recombinants when they were grown in the same liquid medium, but on either side of a bacteria-proof filter. The bacteria could not make physical contact across this filter. Further work has shown that bacterial genes were carried from one bacterium to the other by a virus. Since then, some viruses which infect *E. coli* have been found to be transducing. There are two sorts of transduction, carried out by viruses with different life histories (chapter 1).

(i) **General transduction**. Viruses with a virulent life history (chapter 1) carry out this type of transduction, and any bacterial gene can be transferred. The virus injects its DNA into a bacterial cell and then breaks down the bacterial chromosome into short lengths, each carrying one or a few genes (Figure 9). P1 is an example of a virus infecting *E. coli* in this way. Later in infection, viral progeny are put together inside the host bacterium by enclosing newly synthesised copies of viral DNA inside new viral protein. Occasionally, a fragment of the host DNA is included inside a viral protein coat instead of a copy of the viral DNA. When the bacterium bursts and the viruses are released, most are infective viruses carrying viral DNA but a very few are **transducing viruses** containing bacterial DNA. This DNA may contain a few bacterial genes, e.g. $a^+b^-$, which were next to each other on the bacterial chromosome.

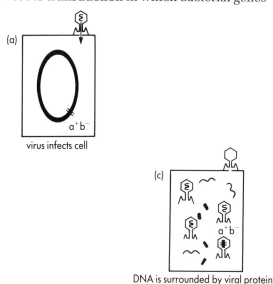

virus infects cell

DNA is surrounded by viral protein → progeny virus

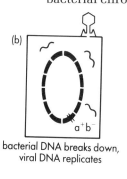

bacterial DNA breaks down, viral DNA replicates

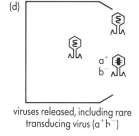

viruses released, including rare transducing virus ($a^+b^-$)

***Figure 9    The formation of a transducing virus***

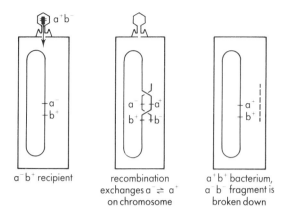

a⁻ b⁺ recipient | recombination exchanges a⁻ ⇌ a⁺ on chromosome | a⁺ b⁺ bacterium, a⁻ b⁻ fragment is broken down

**Figure 10** *Modification of a recipient bacterium by a transducing virus*

The viral progeny can be used to infect a second bacterial strain (the **recipient**) which has different alleles ($a^-b^+$) from the first host or **donor** $a^+b^-$. Most viruses inject viral DNA into the recipient bacteria and kill them. However, when a transducing virus carrying an $a^+b^-$ fragment of donor chromosome injects this DNA into a recipient bacterium, there is the possibility of recombination between the donor fragment and the recipient chromosome (Figure 10). The resulting $a^+b^+$ recombinant bacteria can be selected on a minimal medium and can be used to

order closely linked genes on the bacterial chromosome.

    (ii) **Restricted transduction.** Here, the transducing virus will transmit only a few very specific bacterial genes between donor and recipient. Viruses performing restricted transduction are temperate (chapter 1): they can **integrate** their DNA into the bacterial chromosome. There are several different temperate viruses and each one has a specific site of integration on its host's chromosome. An example is the lambda (λ) virus. This infects *E. coli* and inserts next to the bacterial gene for metabolizing galactose (gal, Figure 11). When the viral chromosome is integrated, the viral genes are switched off and the virus is inherited as part of the bacterial chromosome when the host divides to form daughter cells.

Occasionally a virus is activated: it excises from the bacterial chromosome and produces many viral progeny which are released as the bacterium bursts. As it excises, the λ virus may occasionally bring some of the adjacent bacterial genes with it and leave some viral chromosome behind. This is the λ transducing virus (Figure 11) and it will transmit *gal* genes between donor and recipient bacteria.

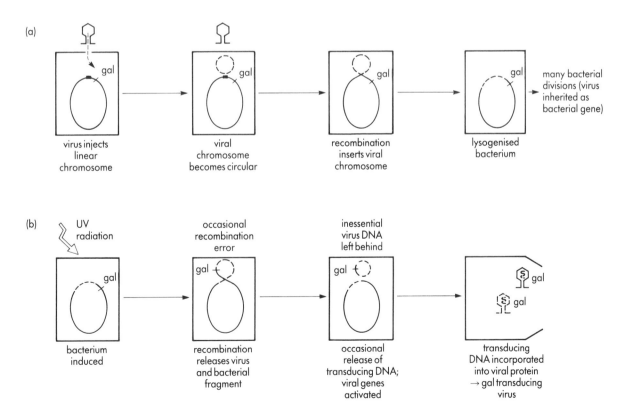

(a)

virus injects linear chromosome → viral chromosome becomes circular → recombination inserts viral chromosome → lysogenised bacterium → many bacterial divisions (virus inherited as bacterial gene)

(b)

UV radiation

occasional recombination error

inessential virus DNA left behind

bacterium induced → recombination releases virus and bacterial fragment → occasional release of transducing DNA; viral genes activated → transducing DNA incorporated into viral protein → gal transducing virus

**Figure 11** *(a) Integration and release of λ virus, and (b) occasional error on release forms a rare transducing virus*

# Transformation

Some bacteria will not conjugate, and transducing viruses may not have been isolated. Some of these bacteria will take up *naked* DNA from their environment. This is **transformation**. It has already been considered in chapter 2 because it provided the first evidence that DNA is the genetic material. Geneticists have used transformation to help map the chromosomes of several bacteria including the soil bacterium *Bacillus subtilis*. Note that *E. coli* will not normally take up free DNA. It can be made to do so by treating a culture with high $Ca^{2+}$ concentrations and low temperatures, and this is important for genetic engineering (chapter 11).

# 6.3 VIRAL CHROMOSOME MAPPING

Viruses considered so far have been of the complex form, e.g T2 and λ (chapter 1). But the ΦX174 virus that infects *E. coli* is small and regularly shaped, (see photo and Figure 12). There are three sorts of protein in its coat; they make up a **capsomere** and there are 12 capsomeres in the coat. The ΦX174 virus was the first organism to have a compete *genetic* map and a complete DNA sequence (or *physical* map) of its chromosome. The comparison of the two maps is informative.

## Viral gene mutation

Viruses rely on their host for all their materials so there are no viral auxotrophic mutations. Viruses are also much too small to see. However, a

number of conditional lethal mutants have been isolated in ΦX174 (and other viruses). For example a temperature-sensitive mutation is an alteration in the base sequence of a gene which makes the protein coded by that gene more sensitive to temperature than normal. The temperature-sensitive protein operates normally at 37°C (the **permissive temperature**) and the virus reproduces. At a higher **restrictive temperature** (40°C) the protein does not function and the virus does not reproduce. The methods for growing viruses and detecting a mutant are shown in the box.

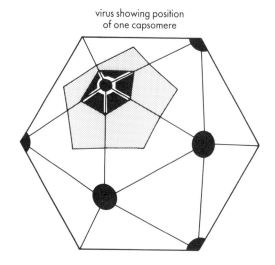

virus showing position of one capsomere

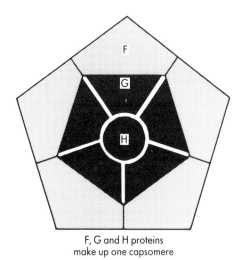

F, G and H proteins make up one capsomere

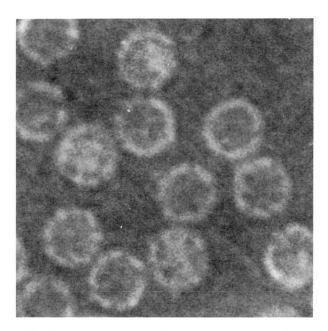

*This electron micrograph shows the structure of the ΦX174 virus. This structure is drawn out in Figure 12*

*Figure 12    The structure of virus ΦX174 (see photograph). (From D Friefelder* Molecular Biology *2nd edn. 1983 Jones and Bartlett Publishers)*

## Methods for culturing and counting viruses

Viruses infect a host cell when their protein coat attaches to the cell surface and the viral nucleic acid is transmitted to the host. The viral genes are transcribed into mRNAs which are translated into viral proteins on the host ribosomes. The raw materials and energy needed for this synthesis of viral progeny are produced by the host cell; the viral parent just provides the appropriate genetic instructions. This means that, before a virus can be cultured, it must be possible to culture its *host* cell. For this reason, bacterial viruses were the first to be studied in detail.

Large numbers of a bacterial virus can be produced by adding about $3 \times 10^8$ viruses $ml^{-1}$ to a colony of $10^8$ bacteria $ml^{-1}$ in a liquid medium at 37°C. Viruses of *E. coli* take about half an hour to reproduce about 100 progeny inside each infected bacterium. The bacterial cells then burst. $10^8$ bacteria $ml^{-1}$ make the liquid cloudy; viruses are too small to do this even at $10^{10}$ $ml^{-1}$, so the liquid clears as the bacteria burst and progeny viruses are released.

The actual number of viruses present can be counted by taking a sample from the cleared culture and serially diluting it (see box on page 71). This diluted sample containing relatively few viruses is then spread over the surface of a solid agar medium. This medium contains a large number of bacterial cells. As the bacteria grow, they make the agar opaque except in small regions where a virus particle has infected a cell. These regions remain clear because viruses kill infected host cells. The clear regions in the opaque lawn of bacteria are called **viral plaques**, each one representing a single virus in the original diluted sample. Temperature-sensitive mutants will produce plaques if the petri dish is incubated at one temperature but not at another.

## Complementation

A temperature-sensitive mutation can occur in any viral gene. However, whichever gene the mutation occurs in, the effect is just the same. The mutant virus has a normal life cycle at the permisive temperature but will not reproduce at the restrictive temperature. Two temperature-sensitive mutants found on different occasions could be mutant in the same gene. In this case they would be represented as $a^-$ mutants of an $a^+$ gene which codes for protein A. On the other hand, they could be mutants $a^-$ and $b^-$ in different genes, $a^+$ and $b^+$, coding for proteins A and B. These two possibilities can be distinguished by a **complementation test** as follows.

The two mutant genes are brought together into common cytoplasm so that the gene products can interact. In viruses this is achieved by infecting a culture of host bacteria with *two* viral mutants. Each bacterium has more than one site where

viruses can attach so this mixed infection allows *both* viruses to inject their DNA into the same host cell. If the viruses are mutant in the same gene there will now be two different temperature-sensitive versions of that gene inside the host (**case I** below). However, if the viruses are mutant in different genes, there will be one normal copy of each gene (**case II**).

Consider what will happen to the viral life histories if the infected bacteria are moved to the restrictive temperature: if the viruses are mutant in the same gene (case I) all A proteins (in this example) will be temperature-sensitive and neither virus can complete their life cycle. If the two viruses are mutant in different genes (case II) the normal alleles will complement each other. Both viruses can use normal A and B proteins present in the cytoplasm to complete their life cycle inside the bacterial host and burst it to release offspring.

The complementation test is therefore carried

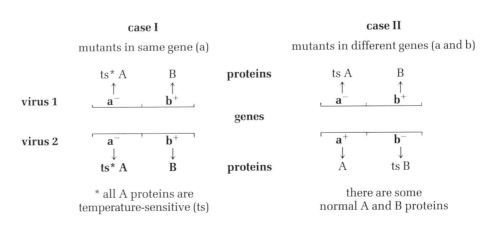

| | case I | | case II |
| --- | --- | --- | --- |
| | mutants in same gene (a) | | mutants in different genes (a and b) |

* all A proteins are temperature-sensitive (ts)

there are some normal A and B proteins

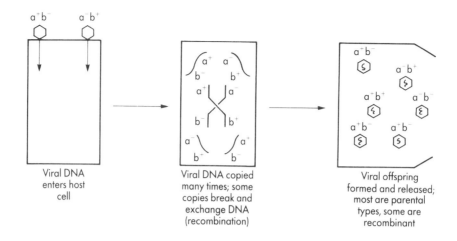

**Figure 13** *Mixed infection of host cell by two mutant viruses. The viral DNA is shown linear for simplicity; the ΦX174 chromosome is circular in reality*

out by infecting a host bacterium with two mutant viruses under restrictive conditions and waiting to see if the bacteria burst. If they do not burst, the viruses are mutant in the same gene. If they do, the viruses are mutant in different genes.

Complementation tests can be used to decide if two conditional lethal mutations are in the same gene, or different genes, in any kind of organism. All that is needed is some means of bringing the two mutations into common cytoplasm. Complementations tests have been carried out for bacterial genes, fungal genes and mammalian genes using cells in culture.

Notice that a complementation test does not show the *position* of the mutant sites on the chromosome. They may be close to each other or far apart. Position is determined by chromosome mapping, and viral maps are produced by linkage analysis or DNA sequencing.

## Viral linkage maps

As for eukaryotes, viral mutants are mapped by mating them and scoring their offspring for recombinants. This analysis is carried out as follows: two temperature-sensitive mutants (e.g. **a⁺b⁻** and **a⁻b⁺**, Figure 13) are mated by adding them both to host bacteria in liquid culture at the permissive temperature. There are no restrictions on growth of either virus at this temperature. if the mutations are at different sites, recombination can occur between them (Figure 13). Once the bacteria have burst, a sample of progeny viruses can be spread on a lawn of bacteria at the restrictive temperature. If recombination has occured then some viral progeny (**a⁺b⁺**) will be able to grow under these restrictive conditions. If another sample is spread on a bacterial lawn at the permissive temperature, then all progeny types will grow. The *proportion* of recombinant viruses can be estimated. Techniques similar to these

were used to count Φ174 genes and produce a linkage map. The map is circular and contains nine different genes. The actual role of these genes in the life history of the virus is now quite well established; the linkage map is shown in Figure 14a.

(a) *The linkage map*

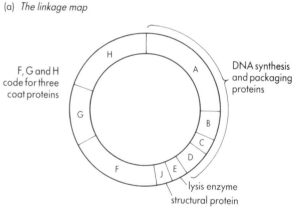

(b) *DNA sequence map*

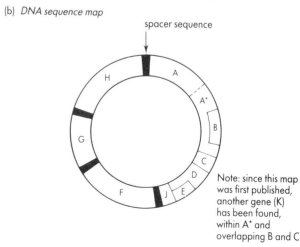

**Figure 14** *A comparison of the gene positions of ΦX174 as found by (a) linkage analysis, and (b) sequence analysis*

# Genetic and physical maps

Frederick Sanger chose ΦX174 to produce the first nucleotide sequence of a whole genome. This virus is relatively easy to grow in large quantities (and therefore get enough DNA to work with) and the chromosome was known to be quite small (the double stranded form was eventually found to consist of 5375 nucleotide pairs). It was thought that all the viral genes had been discovered and the amino acid sequence of most of the proteins produced by these genes was known. Sanger and his colleagues could therefore use the codon dictionary (see chapter 7) to locate the nucleotide sequence of each gene when the complete nucleotide sequence had been worked out.

The position of the genes on the physical map is shown in Figure 14b. It is in broad agreement with the linkage map, but there are some surprises. For example, the end of some genes overlap the beginning of their neighbouring genes; in two cases, one gene completely encloses another. Overlapping genes occur in several other viruses and some eukaryotes. Viruses probably use overlapping genes because this reduces the length of the DNA that needs to be packed inside the small viral particle. This example makes an important general point: a linkage map is only a *guide* to the organisation of a chromosome; to understand it fully, we need an accurate physical map.

## BIBLIOGRAPHY

Brown, T A (1989) *Genetics, a Molecular Approach* Van Nostrand Reinhold
Suzuki, D T, Griffiths, A J F, Miller, J H and Lewontin, R C (1989) *An Introduction to Genetic Analysis* 4th Edn W H Freeman and Co.

## QUESTIONS

1 What is the difference between a genetic map and a physical map?

2 *Drosophila* has four gene loci, a, b, c and d, each with a pair of alleles. A series of test crosses produced the following recombination frequencies between different pairs of loci:

| Gene loci | recombination frequency |
|-----------|------------------------|
| a – b | 35% |
| a – d | 20% |
| c – d | 10% |
| c – b | 25% |

a) What are the map distances between the gene loci?
b) Use these map distances to produce a map of the loci.
c) What other test cross results would confirm your map?

3 Briefly explain the three different ways that chromosomal DNA can be transferred from a donor bacterium to a recipient.

4 A series of interrupted mating experiments, using five different Hfr strains of *E. coli* with the same F⁻ and a total of ten different donor genes, produces the following linear gene orders of transfer:

| Hfr strain | order of transfer first | | last |
|-----------|-------|---|------|
| 1 | a  l  g | e | |
| 2 | c  m  b | i | |
| 3 | j  i  b | m | |
| 4 | a  o  c | m | |
| 5 | l  g  e | j | |

Draw a circular map to show the position of these genes and the insertion sites of the F plasmid in the different Hfr strains.

5 Three temperature-sensitive mutants were isolated in a bacterial virus. They were given the serial numbers A1, A2 and A3. Different bacterial cultures were infected with these mutants in pairs. After infection, the bacterial cultures were shifted to the restrictive temperature conditions. Mutants A1 and A3 would not complement under these conditions, but these mutants were both complemented by the A2 mutant. Explain how many viral genes are represented by these three mutations.

# 7

# MUTATION AND GENETIC VARIATION

**Mutation** is a change in the genetic material. A mutation is recognised because it alters some character of a cell or organism. The altered cell or organism is called a **mutant**. Mutant individuals arise spontaneously in populations in nature or in the laboratory, but spontaneous mutants are very infrequent and are therefore difficult to study. Mutations can be induced by a variety of experimental treatments allowing us to study the DNA changes involved. X-rays, ionising radiations, ultraviolet light, chemicals and insertion of DNA sequences into chromosomes have all been shown to cause mutations in a large number of different organisms.

Mutation is one of the most important topics in genetics. Without mutants, it would be impossible to trace patterns of inheritance and therefore to count genes and locate them on chromosomes. Mutations are fundamental to discoveries of how genes control the structure and function of cells, and the organisms that contain them. Mutation is the origin of all genetic variation in natural populations. Without it, evolution would not have occurred. Recent improvements of crop plants have depended on spontaneous and induced mutations. Geneticists can now alter the DNA of a gene exactly as they wish and there is no doubt this will be widely used in applied genetics in the future.

## Spontaneous mutations

**Spontaneous mutations** in single genes mostly occur at very low rates (Table 1). It is easiest to measure mutation rates in haploid organisms because they contain only one copy of most genes. If a particular gene mutates then the organism shows this alteration at once. In diploid organisms with two copies of every gene, mutation alters one copy of a gene but the other copy may cover the effect of the mutation (see explanation of dominance, chapter 3). Simple prokaryote organisms can also be grown in very large numbers which increases the likelihood of detecting rare mutants. However, spontaneous mutation rates have been measured in some genes in higher organisms. A human example involves a gene which contributes to blood clotting. This is a sex-linked gene so there is only a single copy in males (see chapter 4). Mutation of this gene alters its protein product (protein factor VIII) so that it cannot take part in the normal blood clotting reaction, resulting in the genetic disease haemophilia A. In every human generation, some three gametes in 100 000 carry a haemophilia A gene, newly-formed by mutation from its normal alternative. Note that the mutation rates for different genes shown in table 1 are all low *but* they are not all the same.

## Types of mutation

Mutations can be classified in many different ways but they are usefully separated into two groups depending on the number of DNA base

**Table 1**  *Mutation rates for some genes. The rates for all organisms except humans were measured by experiment, but not all in the same way*

| ORGANISM | PARTICULAR GENE | MUTATION RATE | |
|---|---|---|---|
| *Escherichia coli* | streptomycin resistance<br>histidine independence | $4 \times 10^{-4}$<br>$1 \times 10^{-9}$ | } mutant cells<br>} per cell division |
| *Zea mays*<br>(maize) | purple seed | $1 \times 10^{-5}$ | frequency<br>per<br>gamete<br>*per*<br>generation |
| *Drosophila melanogaster* | white eye | $3 \times 10^{-5}$ | |
| *Homo sapiens*<br>(humans) | Duchenne muscular dystrophy<br>Haemophilia A | $4 - 10 \times 10^{-5}$<br>$2 - 4 \times 10^{-5}$ | |

pairs that are involved in the mutation:

   (i) **Micromutations**. These are changes that alter one or a few nucleotide pairs in a DNA molecule. In almost all cases, this sort of change affects a single gene.

   (ii) **Macromutations**. These are mutations in which a large number of nucleotide pairs and several genes are affected.

In the past, **point mutations** have been distinguished from **chromosome mutations**. Point mutations referred to changes in a single gene, (e.g. for factor VIII), whereas chromosomal mutations involved many genes. However, DNA analysis has shown that point mutation and chromosomal mutation are both caused by the same sorts of changes in DNA. They differ only in a matter of scale, i.e. in the number of base pairs involved. Therefore, classification into (i) and (ii) is more useful.

# Agents causing mutations

The rate at which a gene or chromosome mutates is increased by exposing organisms to **mutagens**, the agents which cause mutation. Mutagens fall into four broad groups:–

   (i) ionising radiation (e.g. gamma rays and X-rays),
   (ii) chemicals,
   (iii) ultraviolet light (UV),
   (iv) short DNA sequences which insert into chromosomal DNA.

Most of these treatments damage DNA or alter its nucleotide sequence and therefore alter the genetic information. However, some mutagens which cause changes in chromosome *number* interfere with the normal processes of nuclear division. One chemical, colchicine, interacts with the protein tubulin and disrupts the spindle in nuclear division. This prevents chromosome segregation and it is important in the experimental manipulation of chromosome numbers (Chapter 11).

Biologists believe that mutations occur spontaneously in nature when an organism is exposed to a mutagen which happens to occur in its environment. We know now that cancers are due to mutations in somatic cells; exposure to the mutagenic chemicals in cigarette smoke is a contributory cause to many lung cancers. Exposure of various organisms to mutagens in the laboratory (particularly UV and certain chemicals) has increased our understanding of the molecular basis of mutation and has shown the existence of **repair enzymes** which correct many alterations to the DNA. Indeed, it seems that mutations are mostly rare because the majority of them are corrected by the various repair enzymes.

## Ionising radiations

Different *ionising radiations* are shown in Table

2. They are all energetic and will dislodge electrons of an atom if they hit it. X-rays and gamma rays are short wavelength members of the electromagnetic spectrum (which also includes light and radio waves). Particulate radiations are produced by fission of atomic nuclei. Neutrons, β particles (electrons) and α particles (helium nuclei) are all radiated by decaying nuclei. Some radiations have less energy than others e.g. α particles cannot penetrate a piece of paper, but gamma rays require a considerable thickness of concrete or lead to stop them.

**Table 2   Ionising radiations**

| Electromagnetic radiations | X-rays<br>gamma (γ) rays |
|---|---|
| Particulate radiations | neutrons<br>alpha (α) particles<br>beta (β) particles |

The mutagenic effect of ionising radiations can be summarised as follows:

   (i) All ionising radiations are mutagenic (as well as having other physiological effects).
   (ii) All ionising radiations cause chromosome breakage, often resulting in macromutations. They also cause micromutations.
   (iii) Low energy radiations tend to cause macromutations; high energy radiations tend to cause micromutations.
   (iv) Larger doses of radiation are more mutagenic than smaller doses, but the effects of several small doses are cumulative.
   (v) The consequences of irradiation are modified by a number of biological factors which are not fully understood. These include species differences, age effects and differences between tissues and cells.

The mutagenic effects of ionising radiations are of particular concern to workers in nuclear power and related industries, and so stringent safety procedures and continuous monitoring of exposure are essential.

# Chemical mutagens

Many different chemicals are mutagenic, e.g. nitrous acid removes an 'amino' ($-NH_2$) group from various bases in a DNA molecule and replaces it with a 'keto' ($=O$) group. One effect of nitrous acid is to convert cytosine to uracil. Cytosine forms three hydrogen bonds with guanine (Chapter 2). Uracil is the wrong shape to do this but it will form two hydrogen bonds with adenine. If the C→U base change is not repaired before DNA replication, the uracil acts as a template for the incorporation of *adenine* in the new strand (Figure 1). In this way, a C≡G nucleotide pair becomes U=A. After a further round of DNA replication, this becomes a T=A nucleotide pair. In this way one nucleotide pair in the sequence along the DNA molecule has altered.

This is the type of mutation predicted by Watson and Crick (chapter 2) and it is called a **nucleotide pair substitution** (Figure 2). It changes one genetic **codon** (a triplet of nucleotide pairs coding for one amino acid) and it may alter the amino acid sequence in the protein coded by the gene (chapter 7). An example in humans is a mutant gene causing haemophilia A. DNA sequence analysis showed that the gene differs from usual by having one C≡G pair replaced by a T=A pair. This nucleotide substitution happened to convert an amino acid codon into a 'stop codon' (chapter 8). This is a **nonsense mutation**.

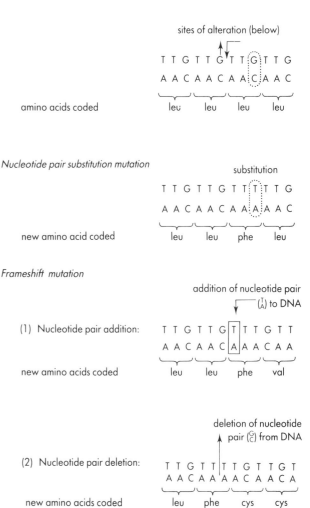

*Figure 2   The molecular basis of some mutations. A change in base pair sequence may cause a change in the amino acid sequence in the protein*

The result is a factor VIII blood clotting protein that is 124 amino acids shorter than normal and non-functional. The cause of this example of spontaneous mutation is unknown. Other nucleotide pair substitutions merely change a codon so that one amino acid is replaced by a different one in the protein coded by the gene; these are **mis-sense mutations**. They are often less damaging than nonsense mutations.

Other chemicals add a single base pair into a DNA molecule or remove a base pair from it (Figure 2). These are called **frame shift mutations**. Both these single base pair changes affect several adjacent codons. Addition of a nucleotide pair alters one codon and all the others downstream from it until the end of the gene. The same is true if a nucleotide pair is deleted (Figure 2); frame shift mutations have been shown to occur in human globin genes which code for haemoglobin proteins.

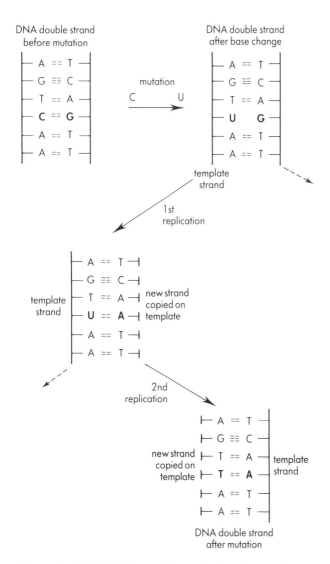

*Figure 1   Effect of change from cytosine to uracil on DNA sequence*

# Insertion of transposable DNA

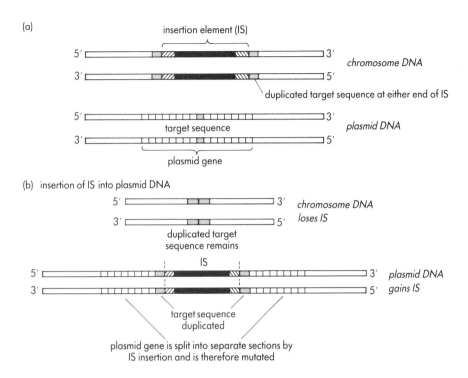

*Figure 3    The structure of an insertion sequence (IS) and the alteration to host DNA when an IS transposes into it*

During the 1960s, geneticists discovered some unusual mutants in bacteria. They were almost all irreversible and, if a plasmid (chapter 2) was introduced into a bacterium carrying one of these mutations in a chromosomal gene, then irreversible mutations soon appeared in any gene carried on the plasmid. It was as if the mutation was able to 'jump' (**transpose**) from the chromosomal DNA to the newly introduced plasmid DNA.

Further study showed that the mutated plasmid DNA had increased in length by about 1000 nucleotide pairs (np). It was then discovered that this 1000 bp DNA was inserted into the plasmid gene which had mutated. Different forms of these **insertion sequences** (IS) have been discovered. Nearly all of them consist of just one gene with a few flanking nucleotide pairs on either side of it (Figure 3a). The gene codes for an enzyme which allows the sequence to insert itself into other DNA molecules. An IS inserts into a short target sequence of nucleotide pairs in another DNA molecule (Figure 3b). When this happens, the host gene mutates because its coding sequence is interupted by the inserted nucleotide pairs.

Since these early discoveries, longer transposable elements have been discovered in bacteria, maize (*Zea mays*), *Drosophila melanogaster*, and humans. They have all been grouped together with ISs as **transposons**. Some transposons seem to have lost the ability to move about the genome on their own and human genomes contain several like this.

The pea 'wrinkled' allele used by Mendel, has also just been shown to contain a transposon. This is 824 base pairs long and it is absent from the round seed allele. In wrinkled peas, it has mutated the gene which codes for a starch branching enzyme (SBE). Wrinkled pea plants produce only the straight chain form of starch (*amylose*) and lack of SBE means that no branched chain starch (*amylopectin*) is formed. Plants which contain the round seed allele have an active SBE and produce both amylose and amylopectin. The type of starch laid down in the endosperm affects the shape and sweetness of the seed.

## Chromosome structure

This chapter has so far concentrated mainly on single nucleotide pair changes and on micromutations. But many micromutations and macromutations are caused by a structural change involving *several* nucleotide pairs. What distinguishes micromutations from macromutations is the number of nucleotide pairs involved. There are various types of structural change. They are summarised overleaf and are

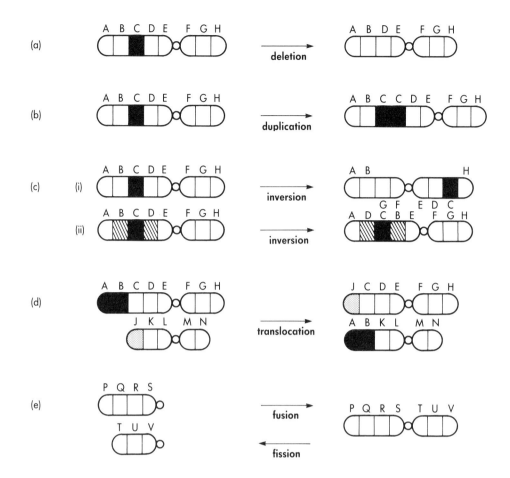

(a) → deletion

(b) → duplication

(c) (i) → inversion

(ii) → inversion

(d) → translocation

(e) → fusion ← fission

**Figure 4** *Changes in chromosome structure.*
*(Chromosomes are shown segmented to emphasise changes)*

shown in diagrammatic form in Figure 4 (the chromosome diagrams are divided into segments and lettered to make the changes easy to follow).

(i) **Deletion** (4a). Part of the DNA sequence is removed so that one or more genes are inactivated or lost.

(ii) **Duplication** (4b). A segment DNA is duplicted so that extra copies of a DNA sequence are added to a chromosome.

(iii) **Inversion** (4c). A segment of DNA is somehow cut out and replaced in reverse order.

(iv) **Translocation** (4d). A piece of DNA is moved from one chromosome to another.

(v) **Fusion/Fission** (4e). Two different chromosomes fuse at their centromeres, or a single chromosome becomes two by transverse division at the centromere.

These changes were first observed by inspection of stained chromosomes under the light microscope. i.e. They were macromutations. Now that it is possible to recognise changes in the base sequence of DNA, we know that the same types of structural alterations occur in many micromutations.

## (i) Deletions

**Deletion** (Figure 4a) means a loss of genetic material. A deletion may be quite short so only part of a gene is lost. If it is longer, several linked genes may be removed. Deletions are usually damaging and often lethal to the organism because one or more genes are inactivated or lost. The sex-linked dystrophin gene in humans (chapter 3) is very long and is spread over 2.3 million base pairs of DNA on the X chromosome. 70% of patients with Duchenne muscular dystrophy have a deletion of several thousand base pairs in the dystrophin gene and do not produce dystrophin protein. This protein is essential for muscle maintenance. Deletions such as this are usually recessive and are not expressed in the diploid heterozygote.

Deletions involving several genes can be observed under the light microscope in some organisms. The polytene chromosomes of *Drosophila melanogaster* were introduced in chapter 2. These large banded chromosomes show such deletions particularly clearly. Homologous polytene chromosomes lie close together along their whole length, except where one of them has a segment deleted. The non-deleted chromosome *loops out* in this position because it cannot pair with its partner (Figure 5).

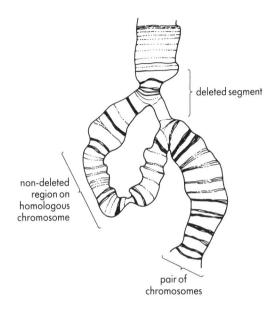

**Figure 5** *Polytene chromosomes of* **Drosophila** *to show deletion on one homologue*

### (ii) Duplications

**Duplications** (Figure 4b) are very important in evolution. In general simple organisms contain less DNA than more complex ones. In bacteria there is enough DNA for about 4000 different genes; in animals there are likely to be between 10–100 000 genes. There is good evidence that complex organisms evolved from simple ones and so we have to account for the increase in the number of genes.

A new gene can be formed if one gene is duplicated. The original copy retains its original function so the organism survives. The base sequence of the additional copy is free to change without damaging the organism. It therefore has the potential to become a new gene. Studies of various proteins and the genes that code for them suggests that this has often happened.

The different haemoglobin proteins and their genes are a good example. A human individual contains different haemoglobins at different stages of development. These proteins are adapted to carry oxygen under different physiological conditions. In the first few weeks after conception, the individual contains embryonic haemoglobin. In later embryos, this is replaced by foetal haemoglobin. At birth, foetal haemoglobin is replaced by adult haemoglobins. 98% of adult haemoglobin is haemoglobin A; about 2 per cent is haemoglobin A2. All these proteins consist of four polypeptide chains. The general structure of haemoglobins is two $\alpha$ polypeptides and two $\beta$ polypeptides (Figure 6a). Table 3 shows that every human haemoglobin contains two $\alpha$ polypeptides, and the proteins differ in their $\beta$ type polypeptides. The amino acid sequence of all these polypeptides has been worked out. $\beta$, $\delta$, $\gamma$ and $\epsilon$ polypeptides all contain 146 amino acids and their amino acid sequences are very much alike. e.g. $\beta$ and $\delta$ chains are identical at 136 of their 146 amino acids. $\alpha$ chains are 141 amino acids long, but even they have 64 amino acids in the same position as the $\beta$ chain. These similarities suggest divergence from a common origin for these polypeptides.

(a)  *Haemoglobin protein*

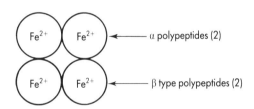

(b)  *Linkage map of genes*

**Figure 6    (a) The generalised structure of haemoglobins and (b) the linkage arrangement of genes which produce** $\beta$ **type polypeptides**

**Table 3    Comparison of the polypeptide chains present in human haemoglobins at different stages of development**

| | PROTEIN COMPOSITION | |
| HAEMOGLOBIN | $\alpha$ POLYPEPTIDES | $\beta$ POLYPEPTIDES |
| --- | --- | --- |
| Embryonic | 2 $\alpha$ | 2 $\epsilon$ |
| Foetal | 2 $\alpha$ | 2 $\gamma$ |
| Adult A2 | 2 $\alpha$ | 2 $\delta$ |
| Adult A | 2 $\alpha$ | 2 $\beta$ |

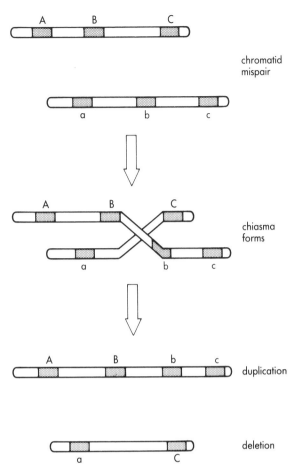

DNA sequencing techniques have shown that the β type polypeptides are coded by different genes which are arranged next to each other on human chromosome 11. (Figure 6b). There are two copies of the α globin gene next to each other on chromosome 16. The similarities of the polypeptides and the location of the genes make it very likely that the different human globin genes evolved by duplication from a common ancestral gene.

There is a lot of evidence which suggests that genes are duplicated by asymmetrical crossing over between chromosomes. Normally in meiosis a pair of homologous chromosomes lie exactly side by side (chapter 5). Occasionally they slip, so crossing over brings two copies of a gene onto one chromosome and removes the gene from the other chromosome (Figure 7). This means that asymmetrical crossing over forms duplications and deletions simultaneously.

## (iii) Inversions

**Inversions** play an important part in the evolution of many species. Some inversions include the centromere (Figure 4c), others do not. Inversions help to keep favourable groups of linked genes together to form one 'supergene'. Suppose that alleles cdef of four linked genes work well together, and so do CDEF. Other combinations may be less successful. If cdef is inverted compared to CDEF on the other (homologous) chromosome (Figure 8) then these two combinations are the ones that are most often passed on to the next generation. The reasons for this are as follows.

*Figure 7    The effect of chiasmata formation between chromatids of homologous chromosomes which are not exactly paired*

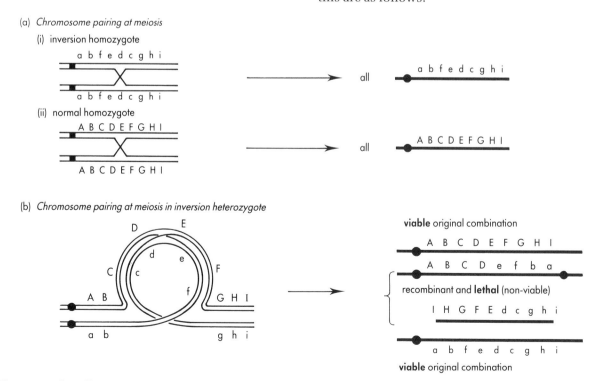

(a) *Chromosome pairing at meiosis*

  (i) inversion homozygote

  (ii) normal homozygote

(b) *Chromosome pairing at meiosis in inversion heterozygote*

*Figure 8    The effect of inversion on the production of recombinant chromosomes*

Individuals with two CDEF chromosomes, or two fedc ones (Figure 8a) can only produce one or other combination. In both sorts of individual meiosis is normal. The homologous chromsomes can lie side by side along their whole length. Cross-overs have no genetic effect in either individual because the genes are the same on both chromosomes. There is nothing for crossing over to reshuffle in either case. In individuals with a CDEF chromosome and an fedc one, meiosis is unusual. The only way chromosomes can pair is to form a loop as shown in Figure 8b. A cross-over within this loop produces non-viable recombinant chromosomes. Both are missing some genes: one has two centromeres the other has none, so they tend to be lost during meiosis. Two cross-overs may occur within the loop, but in a short length of chromosome they are rare. They do produce viable recombinants, but an individual containing normal and inverted chromosomes usually passes on the original combinations of genes.

In many organisms, including several species of *Drosophila*, there are multiple and overlapping inversions on the same chromosome. These very much reduce recombination in this region of the chromosome. Particular combinations of alleles at different loci are therefore inherited together as a single, tightly linked 'supergene'.

### (iv) Translocations

**Translocation** is the transfer of a piece of DNA from one chromosome to another non-homologous one (Figure 4d). This involves breaks in both chromosomes. The fragment from one chromosome is somehow rejoined onto the broken end of the other. In reciprocal translocation, the chromosomes exchange fragments.

Translocation can have a variety of effects. Meiosis in individuals with one translocated chromosome and one ordinary one (translocation heterozygotes) tends to produce many non-viable products. Individuals with translocated chromosomes have therefore been introduced into populations of some pest insects. For example, the tsetse fly is a serious medical and agricultural pest in tropical Africa; it spreads the parasite which causes 'sleeping sickness' in humans and their cattle. Translocations were induced in flies in the laboratory. The flies were introduced into the wild to mate with native flies and generate translocation heterozygotes in an attempt to control the population size of the flies.

Translocation can also alter the expression of a gene. e.g. A cancer of human white blood cells, which is common in Africa, has a small piece of chromosome 8 moved to a new position on chromosome 14. This translocation may be caused by viral infection. The position of the break-and-exchange is very specific and has been shown to alter the activity of at least one gene on chromosome 8, close to the join. This causes certain white blood cells to divide uncontrollably: a **cancer**.

### (v) Chromosome fusion/fission

Chromosome **fusion** (Figure 4e) occurs when two chromosomes unite at their centromeres. The fused centromeres become one so two different chromosomes with terminal centromeres become a single chromosome with a centromere in the middle. **Fission** is the reverse process. Successful fusions/fissions do not change the amount or the type of genetic material but merely rearrange it. An example of such rearrangements can be observed among various *Drosophila* species which have nearly identical genomes but these are distributed among a different number of chromosomes (Figure 9).

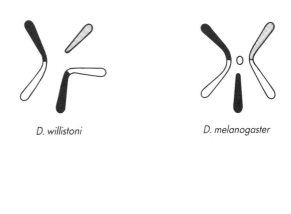

*D. willistoni*        *D. melanogaster*

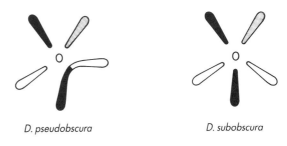

*D. pseudobscura*        *D. subobscura*

*Figure 9    The haploid chromosomes of four species of* Drosophila. *These chromosomes are related to each other by fission and fusion*

# Chromosome number

Some macromutations involve changes in the *number* of chromosomes that are present in the cells of an organism. In general, the cells of most organisms contain either a single set of chromosomes, or a double set. They are respectively haploid (n) or diploid (2n). Mutation can involve part of a chromosome set. This is called **aneuploidy**. When whole sets of chromosomes are involved in the mutation, it is called **euploidy**. The most important examples of euploidy involve *gains* in whole chromosome sets, so that the resultant organisms are *polyploid*.

## Aneuploidy

The most common aneuploids have either one chromosome less than the diploid set (2n − 1), or one chromosome in addition to a diploid set (2n + 1). This section will concentrate on human examples because of their medical interest.

In humans, the normal chromosome complement is 23 pairs (2n = 46). About 1 in 5000 female births are girls with only one X sex chromosome. They have 45 chromosomes in each of their nuclei (2n − 1) and their sex chromosome constitution is XO. These individuals are short and wide necked. They are sterile, but otherwise lead normal lives. About 1 in 1000 human males are born with an additional X chromosome. Their sex chromosome constitution is XXY and they have 47 chromosomes in each of their nuclei (2n + 1). These develop as lanky men who are often mentally retarded and sterile.

The X chromosome is one of the middle sized chromosomes and it is somewhat unusual for aneuploid individuals carrying a chromosome of this size to survive. Figure 10a shows that about 15% of human conceptions miscarry and are naturally aborted. Many of these foetuses have been shown to carry an extra autosome. Some

individuals with an extra autosome are born. The most frequent carry an extra chromosome 21 which is one of the smallest human chromosomes (chapter 3). These individuals show **Down's syndrome**. They are mentally retarded and about 1 in 3 die before they are 10. Babies with an extra chromosome 13 or 18 are severely handicapped and rarely survive more than a year.

Aneuploids arise when homologous chromosomes fail to separate at anaphase I of meiosis, or chromatids do not separate at anaphase II. If either happens, a daughter nucleus may receive an additional chromosome or miss one. The probability of having a child with an additional chromosome 21 increases with the age of the mother (Figure 10b). All meioses are initiated in a girl before she reaches puberty and they are completed individually during each menstrual cycle. The time an oocyte spends in prophase I of meiosis may affect the accuracy of the subsequent chromosome separations.

The reasons why most aneuploid imbalances in humans are lethal are not yet clear. The relatively small effect of loss or addition of a sex chromosome may be related to the condensation of all X chromosomes, except one, in every nucleus. In normal XX females, one of the X chromosomes is treated differently from all the other chromosomes and is condensed throughout most of the life of the cell. In stained nuclei, this chromosome can be seen as a **Barr body** (named after the person who first saw it). Normal XY

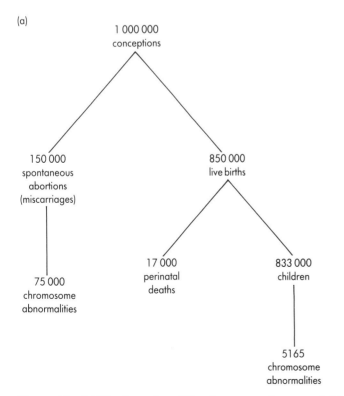

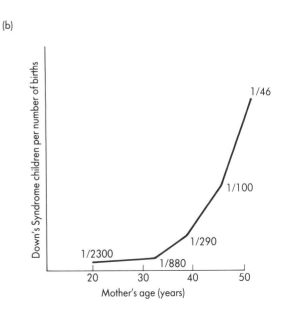

*Figure 10    (a) The fate of a million human embryos, and (b) maternal age and the birth of Down's Syndrome children*

males have only one X chromosome in each nucleus and do not have a Barr body.

Genetic analysis of females who are heterozygous (**Aa**) for sex-linked genes shows that for many such genes, one cell has only one active allele. Different cells have different alleles active (either **A** or **a**), so a female is a genetic 'mosaic' for most of her sex-linked genes. The implication is that XX females have mainly one X chromosome active in each nucleus, the same as every male nucleus. It is thought that chromosome condensation has a role in gene inactivation, so the Barr body is the inactivated X. XXY males have one Barr body in their nuclei and therefore one active X, XO individuals have no Barr body and so they too have one active X. The genetic imbalance in these individuals is probably partly counteracted in this way.

## Polyploidy

Increase in whole sets of chromosomes has occurred many times in the evolution of new species of flowering plant. It is less widespread among animal species. As well as being of great genetic interest, polyploidy is of considerable importance to human survival because many essential crop plants are polyploid (Table 4).

*Table 4   Some common polyploid crop plants. Ploidy is shown as multiples of the haploid (n) set of chromosomes*

| NAME | PLOIDY | NAME | PLOIDY |
|---|---|---|---|
| Bread wheat | 6n | sugar cane | 8n |
| Macaroni wheat | 4n | apple | 2n − 3n |
| Cultivated oats | 6n | European plum | 6n |
| Potato | 4n | strawberry | 8n |
| Peanut | 4n | banana | 3n |
| Alfafa | 4n | white clover | 4n |

In general terms, the leaves of polyploid plants are broader, thicker and greener than the diploid ones from which they are derived. Flowers are often much bigger, and many common flowering plants are polyploid. In some plants, nuclear volume and cell volume increase as the number of chromosomes increases. In many polyploids, fruit size is also increased (compare the wild and domesticated apples in the photograph). However, fertility may be markedly reduced and many domesticated plants have to be propagated asexually (from cuttings, or by plant tissue culture techniques).

Artificial methods of polyploid production have become important techniques for the plant breeder (see chapter 11). These methods have been developed from investigations into how polyploid plants arise spontaneously. There are two different ways.

(i) *Autopolyploidy*. Polyploids are formed within a species. The chromosome number in reproductive cells can double if meiosis is initiated but a spindle fails to form. If a diploid reproductive cell formed in this way fuses with a normal haploid cell, the resulting individual is triploid (3n) and contains three sets of homologous chromosomes. A triploid plant almost never produces viable reproductive cells. With more than two copies of each chromosome, bivalents (pairs of chromosomes) cannot form as normal at meiosis I and therefore chromosomes will not distribute evenly at anaphase. Meiotic products may therefore contain three copies of one chromosome, but none of several others. However, sterility may be a desirable characteristic in some crop plants, e.g. bananas (triploid and seedless), and recent strains of seedless cucumbers which are less bitter than their diploid relatives.

(ii) *Allopolyploidy*. These polyploids are formed after hybridisation *between* species. Suppose one species has a haploid genome, represented as R, distributed over nine chromosomes, diploid plants (RR) then have 2n = 18. Also suppose that the species grows in the same geographical region as a second species. The latter has a haploid genome, S, also distributed over nine chromosomes. Diploid plants of this species (SS) also have 2n = 18. Reproductive cells from the two species may sometimes fuse. This results in an RS individual with 18 chromosomes. If the R set of chromosomes is not homologous with the S set they cannot pair in meiosis.

*The larger apple is a domesticated polyploid cooking apple variety. The smaller variety is a diploid hedgerow apple*

However, if meiosis is incomplete, RS reproductive cells with *18* chromosomes may be produced. Fusion of two such cells would give an RRSS individual (2n = 36) with 18 pairs of homologous chromosomes (n = 9R + 9S = 18), but it is tetraploid (RR + SS = 36) compared with the two original diploid species. This pattern of events was achieved experimentally in an attempt to combine the root characteristics of the radish with the leaf characteristics of the cabbage. Unfortunately, the new plant had the root of the cabbage combined with the leaf of the radish!

However, allopolyploidy played a crucial part in the development of human culture from hunter-gatherer to settled farming communities in Eurasia. Wheat is a staple crop and wheat grains have been found in archaeological sites in the Near East dated from 10 000 years ago. It seems likely that wheat evolved in this region of the world. Modern bread wheat, *Triticum aestivum*, has 21 pairs of chromosomes (2n = 42). It appears that this is a hexaploid (6n) which arose spontaneously by combining chromosomes from three different species. The probable evolution of bread wheat is summarised in Figure 11 and this pattern is borne out by crosses between wild wheats collected from the Near East.

# Testing chemicals for mutagenic activity

In industrial societies, humans are continually coming into close contact with a range of chemicals that are important in manufacturing processes, agriculture, food production and other activities which help to maintain our standard of living. There has been increasing concern about the damage these chemicals may cause to human health and in many countries there is now a legal requirement for tests to determine the mutagenic activity of drugs, cosmetics, food preservatives, pesticides and compounds used in industry. Several of these compounds have been shown to be mutagenic (Table 5). Mutagenicity tests have often involved live mammals such as rats, guinea pigs and dogs, bred for the purpose. However there is an increasing awareness of unnecessary animal suffering, and so other test systems have been devised. One of the most widely used is the **Ames test**, invented by Bruce Ames in the 1970s. This test uses a strain of the bacterium *Salmonella typhimurium*: normal (wild type) *Salmonella* can make all the organic molecules it needs to survive and grow from a simple (minimal) medium. This contains glucose and inorganic salts. The glucose provides energy and the carbon skeleton needed by the bacterium to synthesise all its organic molecules. The inorganic salts provide the nitrogen, phosphorus, sulphur etc. for these organic molecules. The strain of *Salmonella* used in the Ames test is altered from the wild type. It cannot make the amino acid histidine from a minimal medium (although it can make other molecules as normal) so histidine must be added to the medium for this altered strain to grow.

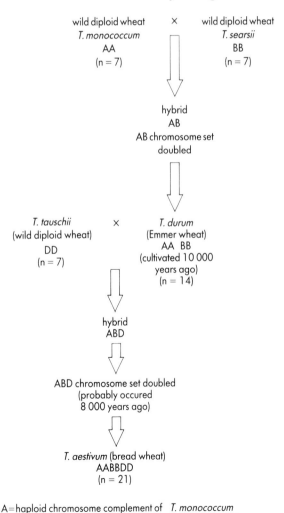

A = haploid chromosome complement of *T. monococcum* (7 chromosomes)
B = haploid chromosome complement of *T. searsii* (7 different chromosomes)
D = haploid chromosome complement of *T. tauschii* (7 other chromosomes)

**Figure 11** **Evolution of wheat (Triticum)**

**Table 5** *Some chemicals, used by man, which have been found to be mutagenic*

| USE FOR CHEMICAL | CHEMICAL |
|---|---|
| Synthetic food colour (kipper) | Brown FK |
| Food fumigant (grain) | Ethylene dibromide |
| Pesticide (fly papers) | Vapona (dichlorvos) |
| Hair dye additive | Mahogany silk |
| Industrial compound (PVC 'plastic' manufacture) | Vinyl chloride |

In the Ames test, a potential mutagen is added to a culture of the histidine-requiring *Salmonella*. The bacteria are then spread on a minimal agar medium in a petri dish. Only those bacteria which mutate to histidine independence will grow on this medium. These individuals will form colonies and can therefore be counted by eye. Comparison with control plates spread with bacteria untreated with the potential mutagen will show if the treatment has increased the number of mutations above background level.

The test uses a bacterium modified to prevent any DNA repair, therefore increasing sensitivity to the potential mutagen. The bacterium has also been genetically engineered so it is very unlikely to survive outside the laboratory environment. Oxidase enzymes from mammalian liver are also included in the test medium. They can oxidise some harmless chemicals and convert them into potent mutagens as they may do in the human body.

Bacteria and humans may differ in their sensitivity to mutagens but, for the moment, the quick and reliable Ames test offers the best solution for the widespread testing of mutagenic effects.

# BIBLIOGRAPHY

Brown, T A (1989) *Genetics, a Molecular Approach* Van Nostrand Reinhold
Suzuki, D T, Griffiths, A J F, Miller, J H and Lewontin, R C (1989) *An Introduction to Genetic Analysis* 4th Edn W H Freeman
Stebbins, G L (1971) *Chromosome Evolution in Higher Plants* Edward Arnold.

# QUESTIONS

1 Suggest two reasons why a gene appears to spontaneously mutate only rarely.

2 Explain why a mis-sense mutation is less likely to result in a mutant phenotype than a nonsense mutation. How damaging is a frameshift mutation likely to be?

3 Explain why transposition is always likely to produce mutants in prokaryotes, but is not always mutagenic in higher eukaryotes (page 103).

4 Give two reasons why micro-organisms such as bacteria are frequently used to study mutation.

5 A bacterial species has been investigated for spontaneous mutations. Two separate studies showed that 1 in 1000 bacteria carry gene X', the others carried gene X. Two other bacteria in 1000 carried gene m, the rest carried the alternative M. How many bacteria would you have to look at to find an individual carrying both gene X' *and* gene m?

6 Explain why it is incorrect to say the inversion heterozygotes do not produce recombinants for the gene loci within the inversion.

7 The plant genus *Brassica* contains a number of species of important vegetables and fodder plants, e.g. cabbage, swede and rape. Artificial hybridisation between the turnip species (*Brassica rape*, 2n = 20) and the black mustard species (*Brassica nigra*, 2n = 16) has produced the brown mustard (*Brassica juncea*, 2n = 36).
   a) How might these hybrids have been produced experimentally?
   b) What chromosomal change is likely to have occurred during the formation of the brown mustard hybrid?
   c) What is the term used to describe such a hybrid?
   d) Explain how the brown mustard hybrids are able to produce fertile seed.
   e) A black mustard plant has been produced with 32 chromosomes. What is the ploidy of this plant, what are its likely origins and why is it almost totally sterile?

# 8 GENE ACTION

Recent exciting advances in genetics are beginning to show how the information in genes is made into living organisms. There are two parts to the problem:

(i) How do genes form the materials which make up living organisms, e.g. keratin (the protein in animals skin cells), cellulose (for plant cell walls), or ATP (an energy carrier in animal and plant cells)?

(ii) How is gene activity regulated so there is just the right amount of material and in the right places, e.g. the correct amount of keratin is synthesised by skin cells and not at all by nerve cells?

The way genes act is well understood. The way some genes are controlled is also understood, but the picture is not complete. Our discoveries have depended on advances in equipment and technical innovation in biochemistry and molecular biology, as well as the ingenuity of scientists. This chapter deals with gene activity and shows how DNA determines the structure of proteins.

## 8.1 GENES AND ENZYMES

In 1941, George Beadle and Edward Tatum showed that many genes act by controlling cell metabolism in a very precise way. They summarised their work as the **one gene, one enzyme hypothesis** i.e each step in a biochemical pathway is catalysed by a different enzyme and the activity of each enzyme is controlled by a different gene:

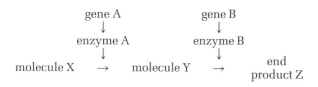

All biochemical reactions are catalysed by enzymes. If the activity of every enzyme is controlled by a gene, this explains how various genes act step by step to operate all the metabolic pathways needed to keep an organism alive.

Beadle and Tatum supported their idea with evidence from experiments using induced auxotrophic mutants (chapter 6). They used the bread mould, *Neurospora crassa*, that will normally grow on a minimal medium (glucose plus inorganic salts). Each auxotrophic mutant used required one organic supplement to the minimal medium, e.g. Paba$^-$ required para-amino benzoic acid for growth. When Beadle and Tatum crossed an auxotrophic mutant (Paba$^-$) with a non-mutant strain (Paba$^+$), they obtained equal numbers of mutant and non-mutant offspring. This suggests that the mutant and non-mutant states are determined by alternative forms of a single gene (figure 1a). Since it was known that synthesis of molecules inside an organism was catalysed by enzymes, Beadle and Tatum suggested that a mutation in one gene altered a single enzyme and made it non-functional. In an auxotrophic mutant therefore, one step in the synthesis of an essential organic molecule is blocked (Figure 1b). Beadle and Tatum received a Nobel Prize in 1958 for their work.

The hypothesis above has been confirmed by numerous other experiments. Mutations which make enzymes non-functional have been shown to account for many human inherited diseases. Figure 2 shows some of the steps in the metabolism of phenylalanine, an amino acid which humans obtain from their diet. They cannot synthesise it. Some individuals inherit a mutant gene and have an altered enzyme (phenylalanine hydroxylase) which cannot catalyse the normal conversion of phenylalanine to tyrosine. Excessive amounts of phenylalanine and other toxic byproducts build up in the cells, resulting in death. Fortunately, as diet is the source of this amino acid, the effects of the altered enzyme can be overcome by feeding an artificial diet which is very low in phenylalanine, but contains some tyrosine. If this is done soon enough in childhood, affected people can live normal lives.

Other mutant genes affect other enzymes in this pathway. One prevents the formation of melanin and produces albinos (Figure 2).

(a) *Results of cross*

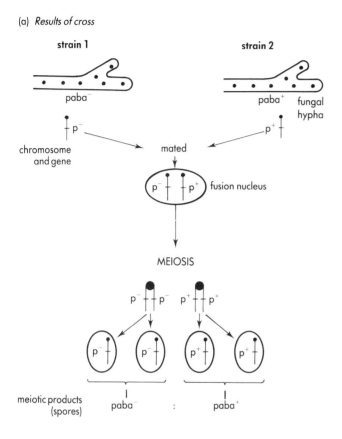

(b) *Interpretation of results (1 gene – 1 enzyme hypothesis)*

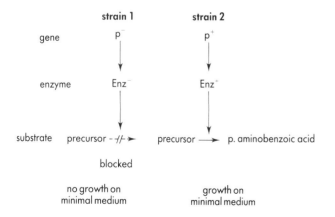

Figure 1    (a) Results of a cross between two fungal strains; one grows on minimal medium, the other needs a p-aminobenzoic acid supplement, and (b) interpretation of results using the one gene one enzyme hypothesis

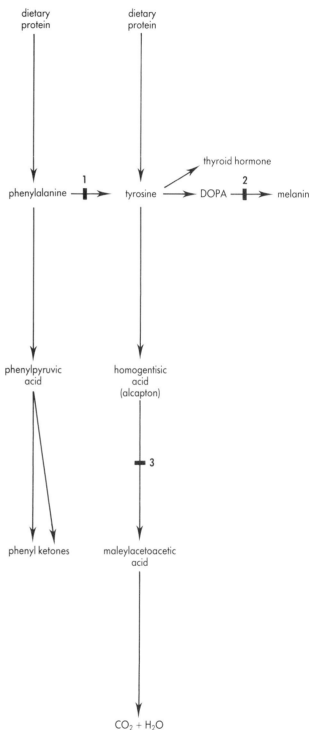

1 Step blocked in phenyl ketonuria
2 Step blocked in albinism
3 Step blocked in alkaptonuria (urine turns black in air – no severe symptoms; first discovered human genetic disease)

Figure 2    Phenylalanine metabolism in humans

# 8.2 PROTEINS

It has been known for some time that enzymes are proteins. All proteins, whether they are enzymes such as phenylalanine hydroxylase, or structural proteins like keratin, are made up from 20 different **amino acids**. These amino acids have the same basic structure:

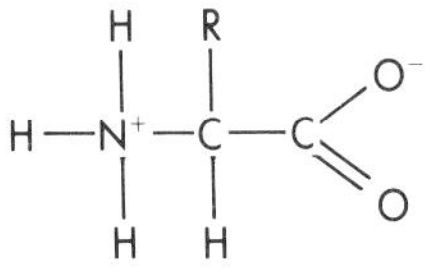

Proteins are chains of amino acids formed by a condensation reaction between the $COO^-$ of one amino acid and the $N^+H_3$ of the next. The link between the two amino acids is called a **peptide bond**:

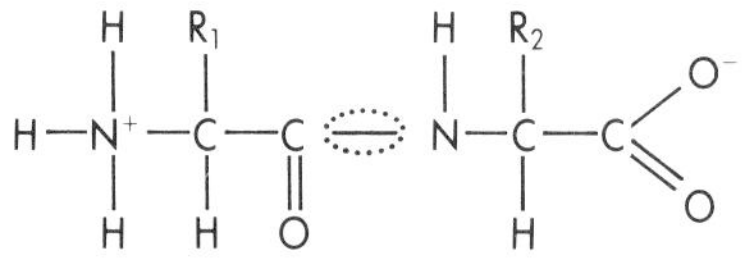

Amino acids differ in the side chains substituted at R ($R_1$, $R_2$ etc.) and this gives them different properties (Table 1). The side chains of a few amino acids are shown in Figure 3. When Frederick Sanger invented a method to work out the exact sequence of amino acids in a protein (see box ), it was soon found that each protein has a unique sequence of amino acids. A chain of amino acids forms the **primary structure** of the protein (Figure 4a). Depending on which amino acids are present and their order along the chain, the protein takes on various **secondary structures**.

There are two main elements to secondary structure:

(i)  In many proteins, much of the primary amino acid chain is wound into a spiral, the $\alpha$ **helix** (Figure 4a).

(ii)  Other parts of a sequence may be folded back and forward to form a **'pleated sheet'** (Figure 4b).

$\alpha$ helices can kink, especially where the amino acid **proline** is present in the primary sequence. This means that the helix can bend back on itself and form a globular **tertiary structure** (Figure 4c). Other proteins have a more elongated tertiary structure.

The amino acid **cysteine** also has an effect on protein structure (Figure 3). Two cysteine moleules can form an S–S double bond by oxidation of the two sulphydril, −SH groups. This bond may hold different protein chains together

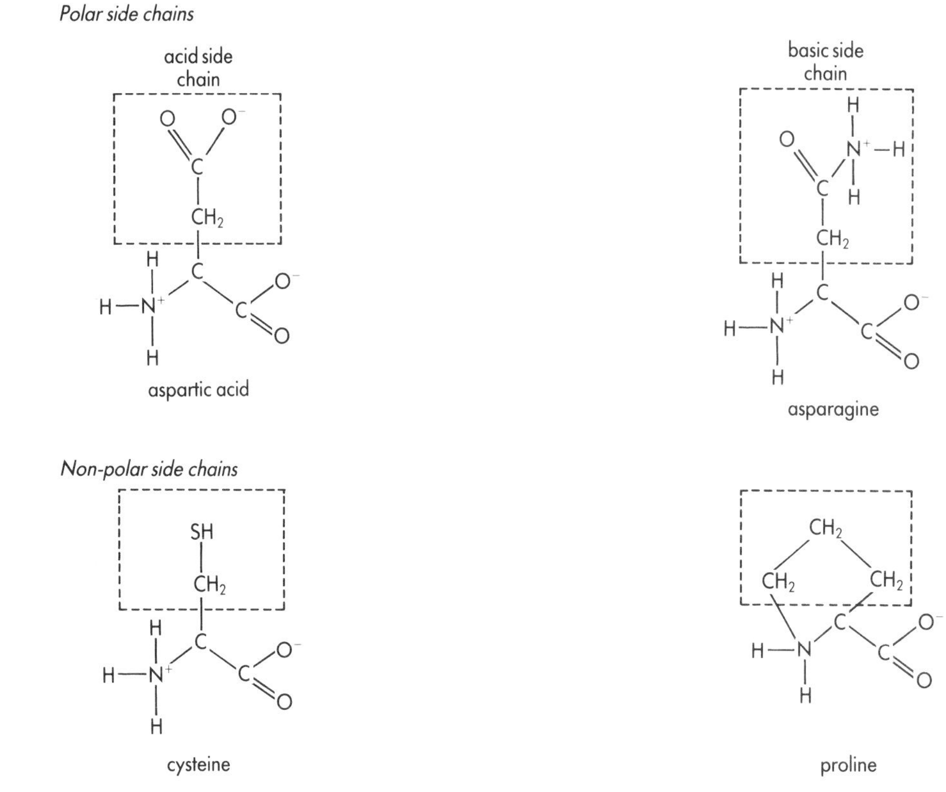

*Polar side chains*

acid side chain

aspartic acid

basic side chain

asparagine

*Non-polar side chains*

cysteine

proline

*Figure 3    The side chains of two small polar amino acids and two small non-polar amino acids*

(a) *α helix*

(b) *Pleated sheet*

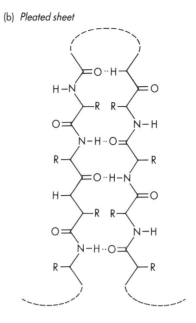

(c) *Tertiary structure of a globular protein*

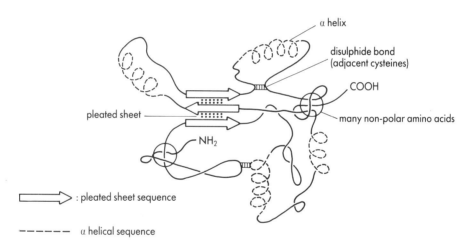

α helix

disulphide bond
(adjacent cysteines)

COOH

many non-polar amino acids

pleated sheet

NH₂

⬜➡ : pleated sheet sequence

------ α helical sequence

**Figure 4    Secondary and tertiary structures of proteins. (c) is redrawn from D Friefelder Molecular Biology 2nd edn. 1983 Jones and Bartlett Publishers**

to form a single functional protein, e.g. antibodies (Figure 5) which circulate in human blood to defend the body against infection. Figure 5 shows that antibodies are made of two different proteins, the shorter light chain and the longer heavy chain. If a protein is made up of separate chains of amino acids, these chains are called **polypeptides.**

Different amino acid sequences give proteins different secondary and tertiary structures, and hence different shapes. The shape of a protein determines its function. Folding can bring together amino acids that are in quite different positions in the primary chain, and certain amino acids brought close in this way are often very important in the activity of the protein.

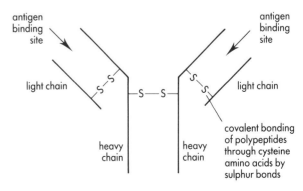

antigen binding site

light chain

heavy chain

antigen binding site

light chain

covalent bonding of polypeptides through cysteine amino acids by sulphur bonds

heavy chain

Note:  there are 4 polypeptides per antibody, 2 heavy and 2 light

**Figure 5    Line diagram of the structure of an immunoglobulin G antibody**

## Table 1 Amino acids commonly found in proteins

| TYPE | AMINO ACID AND ABBREVIATION | | | |
|---|---|---|---|---|
| Small polar | glycine* | gly | serine+ | ser |
| | aspartate* | asp | asparagine+ | asp |
| Large polar | glutamate* | glu | glutamine+ | gln |
| | lysine* | lys | arginine+ | arg |
| Intermediate polarity | tyrosine | tyr | histidine | his |
| | tryptophan | trp | | |
| Small non-polar | alanine | ala | threonine | thr |
| | proline* | pro | cysteine | cys |
| Large non-polar | valine | val | isoleucine | ile |
| | leucine | leu | methionine | met |
| | phenylalanine | phe | | |

NOTE Amino acids marked * have acid side chains.
Those marked + have basic side chains.

### Method for working out the amino acid sequence of a protein

It is not technically possible to remove amino acids one by one from the end of a complete protein chain. However, if proteins are cut into very short fragments, amino acids can be removed from them one by one and scored. The problem is to know where each fragment fits into the complete chain. Sanger's method to overcome this problem is as follows:

(i) A quantity of each protein chain is purified. If a protein consists of several different polypeptides, they have to be separated first.

(ii) The solution, containing many copies of a purified polypeptide is divided into different samples.

(iii) One sample of the polypeptide is cut into fragments by one set of enzymes and chemicals, e.g. the enzyme trypsin cuts a peptide bond at the amino acids lysine or arginine. The small fragments produced by this digestion are separated and their amino acid sequences are worked out. The position of the fragments in the protein is not known.

(iv) A second sample of the polypeptide is cut in different places by a different set of enzymes and chemicals e.g. the enzyme chymotrypsin cuts at phenylalanine and tyrosine. This digestion gives another group of unordered fragments and their amino acid sequences can be worked out.

(v) As the same protein was cut in different places by the two digestions, the two sets of fragments must overlap, i.e. a fragment in one set will have an amino acid sequence which is split between next door fragments in the other set (see below). Comparison of the amino acid sequences in the two sets of fragments will give the proper order for the fragments and the complete amino acid sequence of the protein, e.g.:

trypsin fragments (two):

leu−tyr−cys−glu−arg ↓ gly−phe−lys

chymotrypsin fragments (three):

leu−tyr ↓ cys−glu−arg−gly−phe ↓ lys

Therefore amino acid sequence in protein is:

leu−tyr−cys−glu−arg−gly−phe−lys

( ↓ : sites where endopeptidases cut protein chain.)

# 8.3 GENES AND PROTEINS

Studies of sickle cell anaemia demonstrate that a gene determines the function of a protein by coding its amino acid sequence. The disease is the result of an unusual human haemoglobin. Some children in East Africa have the disease and it is inherited as if it were due to a mutation in a single gene. Children with the disease have haemoglobin S (HbS) which has a lower affinity for oxygen than the normal haemoglobin A (HbA) found in unaffected children. HbA is made up of two different protein chains, the α and β **globins** (chapter 7). They have now been completely sequenced. Early work showed that the β globin in HbS is different from the one in HbA by *one* amino acid: the sixth amino acid of the 146 in the β chain is valine instead of glutamic acid.

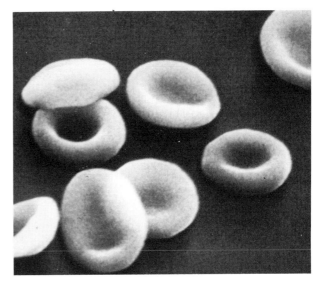

*This electron micrograph shows normal human red blood cells. They contain haemoglobin A*

| amino acid position | 1 | 2 | 3 | 4 | 5 | 6 | 7 | 8 | — | — | — | 146 |
|---|---|---|---|---|---|---|---|---|---|---|---|---|
| HbA β globin | val | – his | – leu | – thr | – pro | – **glu** | – glu | – lys | – | – | – | |
| HbS β globin | val | – his | – leu | – thr | – pro | – **val** | – glu | – lys | – | – | – | |

This difference is sufficient to radically alter the properties of the haemoglobin and it has widespread physiological effects, including a change of shape of the red blood cell (as shown in the photographs).

## Messenger RNA

If genes determine the structure and function of proteins, and DNA is the genetic material (chapter 1), then DNA must somehow determine the amino acid sequence of proteins. However, many different experiments have shown that chromosomal DNA is confined to the nucleus whereas proteins are only synthesised in the cytoplasm. So how is information passed from the DNA in the nucleus to the sites of protein synthesis in the cytoplasm?

Frances Crick suggested that there must be a 'messenger' molecule to carry the code for a protein from the DNA in the nucleus to the sites of protein synthesis in the cytoplasm. This is a single stranded ribose nucleic acid (RNA) called **messenger RNA (mRNA)**

## Evidence that mRNA exists

An experimental technique called **nucleic acid hybridisation** is an important method of finding a particular gene or nucleic acid sequence among many different sequences.

We can use nucleic acid hybridisation to prove the existence of mRNA: it depends on mRNA's ability to bind to the DNA from which it was copied but not to any other DNA. When a virulent virus infects a bacterium, the bacterial genes become inactivated. Any new RNA that is synthesised in the infected cell is likely to be viral

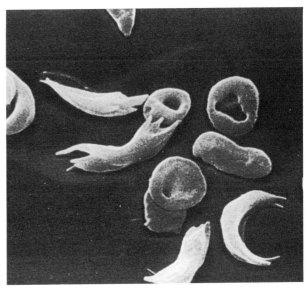

*This electron micrograph shows sickle-shaped red blood cells. Sickle cells contain haemoglobin S*

mRNA. This can be radiolabelled by adding a labelled RNA precursor (e.g. $^{3}$H uridine 5′ triphosphate) to the culture medium. If the mRNA was copied from the viral DNA, it will be complementary to one of the strands of that DNA. If extracted from the infected cells, the labelled viral RNA should base pair *in vitro* to the viral DNA strand from which it was copied. It should not bind to any other DNA because the base sequences will be different. In order to form DNA-RNA hybrid molecules, DNA must be extracted

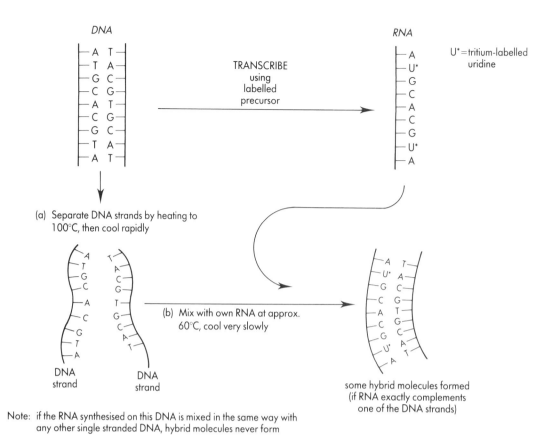

DNA

RNA

U* = tritium-labelled uridine

TRANSCRIBE
using
labelled
precursor

(a) Separate DNA strands by heating to 100°C, then cool rapidly

(b) Mix with own RNA at approx. 60°C, cool very slowly

DNA strand

DNA strand

some hybrid molecules formed (if RNA exactly complements one of the DNA strands)

Note: if the RNA synthesised on this DNA is mixed in the same way with any other single stranded DNA, hybrid molecules never form

*Figure 6    DNA/RNA hybridisation*

from mature viruses and the two strands of the DNA molecule must be separated. This can be done by heating a solution of the DNA molecules – heat energy separates the hydrogen bonds holding the strands together. If the mixture is then cooled rapidly the strands remain apart (Figure 6a). The labelled RNA is then added to this single stranded DNA. The mixture is warmed and then allowed to cool very slowly. This allows strands with a complementary base sequence to base pair to form double stranded molecules (Figure 6b). Double stranded molecules have different physical properties from single stranded ones; they can be separated from each other in a number of ways. The DNA-RNA hybrid molecules can be picked out from the other double stranded molecules because they are radiolabelled.

This early experiment using nucleic acid hybridisation showed that newly synthesised RNA from viral infected bacteria would bind to the viral DNA but not to bacterial DNA. The RNA must have been synthesised using one strand of the viral DNA as a template, i.e. it was **viral mRNA**.

## Transcription

Synthesis of an RNA molecule using one strand of a DNA molecule as a template is called **transcription** (Figure 7). A prokaryote RNA

polymerase enzyme that catalyses RNA synthesis on *E. coli* DNA was discovered in 1958. It is a very large molecule made up of four types of polypeptide. One of these, the sigma (σ) polypeptide, causes the enzyme to bind to a DNA molecule at a short sequence of nucleotide pairs which precedes every *E. coli* gene (Figure 7). This sequence is a '*bind here to start RNA synthesis*' signal and is called a **promoter**.

When RNA polymerase binds to DNA, it separates a few base pairs to form a **transcription bubble** (Figure 7b). The enzyme initiates a new RNA molecule in this bubble, using one of the DNA chains as a template. The RNA grows in the 5' to 3' direction (chapter 2). The polymerase progresses along the DNA and opens up a few base pairs as it goes; they close again behind it. In this way, the transcription bubble moves along the DNA and the RNA molecule increases in length (Figure 7c). Shortly after the end of every *E. coli* gene, there is a '*stop transcription*' signal called a **terminator sequence**. This is a binding site for other proteins which halt the polymerase.

**E. coli** RNA polymerase will transcribe mRNAs from all the bacterial genes. Each bacterial mRNA that is synthesised is broken down within a matter of seconds. This has very important implications for the regulation of bacterial gene activity (chapter 10). Bacterial RNA polymerase also transcribes two other types of RNA from the

(a) *RNA polymerase binds to promoter*

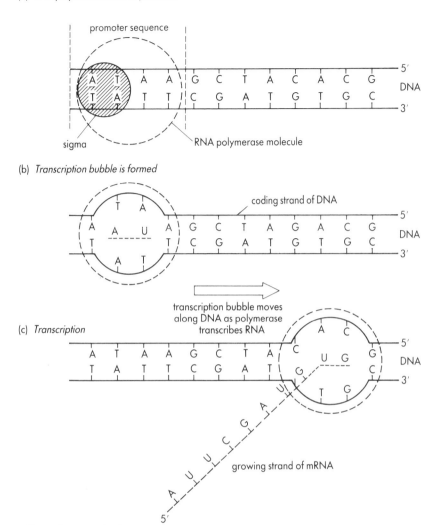

(b) *Transcription bubble is formed*

(c) *Transcription*

**Figure 7    An outline of transcription**

bacterial DNA. These are ribosomal RNA (rRNA) and transfer RNA (tRNA). Ribosomal RNA is combined with protein and lasts longer than mRNA. As discussed below, rRNA and tRNA are essential components in the cytoplasmic system for translating mRNAs into proteins.

It took longer to isolate RNA polymerases from eukaryotes. They are larger and more complex than the bacterial enzyme. There are three different RNA polymerases in a eukaryote nucleus, one for mRNA, one for rRNA and another for small RNAs including tRNA. Some eukaryote mRNAs are very stable, e.g. human globin mRNA survives in the enucleate red blood cell for several days.

## The triplet genetic code

In 1953, James Watson and Frances Crick worked out the structure of DNA (chapter 1) and pointed out that the sequence of nucleotide pairs along the DNA could be a code for amino acid sequences in proteins.

As there are 20 different amino acids in proteins, but only four different nucleotide pairs in DNA (chapter 2), 1 nucleotide pair cannot code for 1 amino acid. There are 16 different sequences of two nucleotide pairs, but this is still not enough to code for 20 different amino acids. However, there are 64 possible sequences of three nucleotide pairs, more than enough to code for 20 amino acids (Figure 8). Each triplet is called a **codon**.

Crick and his colleagues carried out an experiment which strongly supported the idea that each codon is a **triplet of nucleotide pairs**. They induced frame shift mutations in one gene in a virus. These mutations are due to the addition (+) or deletion (−) of a single nucleotide pair in the DNA (chapter 7). They created viruses with either 1, 2, or 3 frame shift mutations of the same sign (Figure 9) in a small part of a gene coding for a viral protein. If the protein was non-functional, the virus would not reproduce. One frame shift, or two frame shifts close together, in the gene prevented the viruses from reproducing. However,

There are 20 amino acids but only 4 nucleotide pairs

Let nucleotide pair A = T be represented as A
Let nucleotide pair T = A be represented as T
Let nucleotide pair C ≡ G be represented as C
Let nucleotide pair G ≡ C be represented as G

There are:

(a) *4 different nucleotide pairs*: A, T, C, G, so if single pairs are read, there are not enough for 20 amino acids

(b) *Nucleotides read in 'doublets'*

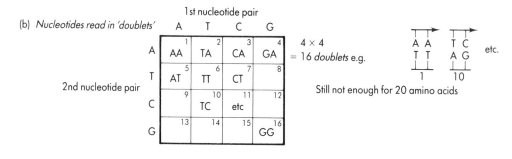

(b) *Nucleotides read in 'triplets'*

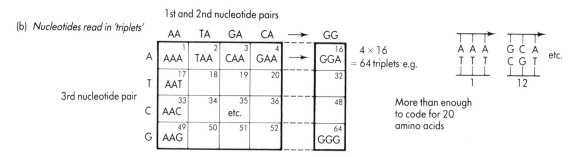

**Figure 8   *Evidence that each amino acid must be coded by a minimum of three base pairs***

with *three* frame shifts, the virus did reproduce, i.e. the protein must have been functional. These results are interpreted in Figure 9. One or two frame shifts of the same sign alter the whole downstream nucleotide sequence and produce an inactive protein. Three frameshifts add a complete triplet, and so most of the nucleotide sequence in the gene returns to normal and can produce an active protein.

This explanation only holds if the code for each protein is read from a fixed starting point and the code is non-overlapping. This means that no nucleotide in a mRNA can be part of two adjacent codons, i.e. the system which is synthesising a protein must read three nucleotides, then move along to the next three in the sequence and so on until the protein is completed.

## *In Vitro* protein synthesis

We can now break open *E. coli* cells (and other cells such as immature rabbit red blood cells or wheat germ cells) to produce a cell extract that will incorporate radiolabelled amino acids into protein in a test tube. These cell extracts can be used to dissect protein synthesis to find the molecules and organelles involved and how they

function. Table 2 summarises the components which are needed for protein synthesis.

The ability to synthesise proteins in vitro has made two major contributions to the study of gene action:

(i) By manipulating the system, it has been possible to discover which triplets of bases in mRNA code for the 20 different amino acids in protein. This is called the **codon dictionary**.

(ii) It has shown how the coding sequence carried in the mRNA molecule is made into an amino acid sequence in a protein. This is called **translation**.

**Table 2   *Cell components needed for* in vitro *protein synthesis***

a) *20 different amino acids,*
b) *20 amino acid activating enzymes,*
c) *about 60 different tRNAs,*
d) *a pool of ribosomes,*
e) *mRNA molecules coding for a protein,*
f) *several essential proteins present in the cell supernatant,*
g) *ATP and GTP.*

Nucleotide pairs are represented as follows:   A= T → A; T = A → T; G ≡ C → G; C ≡ G → C

Amino acids are given their three letter abbreviation (Table 1)

| | coding sequence | | | | amino acid sequence | |
|---|---|---|---|---|---|---|
| **normal code** | start ↓ A A A | T T T | C A C | G C G | start → lys ... phe ... his ... ala | original sequence |
| one nucleotide pair added | A A A | (G) T T | T C A | C G C   G | → lys ... val ... ser ... arg | altered sequence |
| two nucleotide pairs added | A A A | (G)(C) T | T T C | A C G   C G | → lys ... ala ... phe ... thr | altered sequence |
| three nucleotide pairs added | A A A | (A)(G)(C) | T T T | C A C   G C G → | lys ...[ser]... phe ... his ... ala | original sequence plus one amino acid |

**Figure 9** *The effect of frame shift mutations on the triplet genetic code with a fixed start point. All the mutations shown are caused by nucleotide pair additions. If all were nucleotide pair deletions, the effect would be similar*

# The codon dictionary

Marshall Nirenberg and others made long synthetic mRNA molecules of known base composition, added these to cell extracts, and analysed the newly synthesised protein to find out which amino acids it contained. One of the first mRNAs to be synthesised was polyuracil:

$$5'UUUUUUUUU--3'$$

This gave proteins consisting entirely of the amino acid phenylalanine:

$$NH_3{}^+phe-phe-phe---COO^-$$

This suggested that the mRNA codon for phenylalanine is:

$$5'UUU\ 3'$$

In a living organism, this would have been copied from a template on one strand of a DNA molecule which had the sequence:

$$3'...AAA...5'$$

This would have been transcribed by RNA polymerase.

Nirenberg devised a remarkable experiment to show which of the 64 possible mRNA triplets coded for which amino acids. He worked out a way to synthesise very short mRNAs consisting of three nucleotides. He was able to use this method to synthesise all 64 triplets. He discovered that a mRNA of this sort would bind with its amino acid to a ribosome, so $5'UUU3'$ would bind phenylalanine to the ribosome, i.e. the very short mRNA began the process of protein synthesis but that was all.

To find out which triplet coded for a particular amino acid, Nirenburg designed the following experiment. 20 tubes of the protein-synthesising extract were set up, each one with all 20 amino acids *but* with a different amino acid radiolabelled in each tube (Figure 10). The same

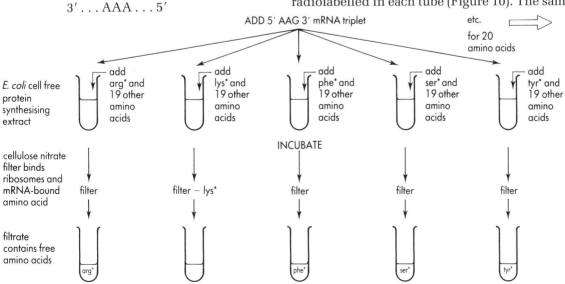

* indicates labelled amino acid and its location at the end of the experiment

**Figure 10**   *Experiment to show that the triplet AAG codes for the amino acid lysine*

**Table 3 The codon dictionary of the mRNA genetic code**

| | | SECOND BASE | | | | | | | | | |
|---|---|---|---|---|---|---|---|---|---|---|---|
| | | U | | C | | A | | G | | | THIRD BASE |
| | U | UUU<br>UUC<br>UUA<br>UUG } phe | | UCU<br>UCC<br>UCC<br>UCA } ser | | UAU } tyr<br>UAC<br>UAA stop<br>UAG stop | | UGU } cys<br>UGC<br>UGA stop<br>UGG trp | | U<br>C<br>A<br>G | |
| | C | CUU<br>CUC<br>CUA<br>CUG } leu | | CCU<br>CCC<br>CCA<br>CCG } pro | | CAU } his<br>CAC<br>CAA } gln<br>CAG | | CGU<br>CGC<br>CGA } arg<br>CGG | | U<br>C<br>A<br>G | |
| FIRST BASE | A | AUU } ileu<br>AUC<br>AUA } met<br>AUG | | ACU<br>ACC } thr<br>ACA<br>ACG | | AAU } asn<br>AAC<br>AAA } lys<br>AAG | | AGU } ser<br>AGC<br>AGA } arg<br>AGG | | U<br>C<br>A<br>G | THIRD BASE |
| | G | GUU<br>GUC } val<br>GUA<br>GUG | | GCU<br>GCC } ala<br>GCA<br>GCG | | GAU } asp<br>GAC<br>GAA } glu<br>GAG | | GGU<br>GGC } gly<br>GGA<br>GGG | | U<br>C<br>A<br>G | |

U = uracil (in RNA replaces thymine (T) found in DNA)
C = cytosine
A = adenine
G = guanine
The explanation of the three letter amino acid symbols is given in table 1. Stop codons stop translation and release the completed protein from the ribosome

mRNA triplet was added to all 20 tubes. After incubation, each mixture was passed over a separate filter. The ribosome-mRNA-amino acid complexes were too big to pass through the filters but all unbound amino acids were small enough to pass through. All the filters were tested for radioactivity to discover which amino acid had been bound to the ribosome by that triplet. As an example, when 5'AAG3' was added to all 20 tubes, the only filter which became labelled was from the tube containing labelled lysine. None of the labelled amino acids in the other tubes was retained by this triplet. Therefore one mRNA codon for lysine is AAG. Nirenberg shared a Nobel prize with two other workers for this contribution to the solution of the codon dictionary.

The complete list of mRNA triplets and the amino acids they code for is given in Table 3. Note that most amino acids are coded by more than one triplet. Amino acids like serine and arginine which are common in many proteins are coded by six codons, whereas amino acids like methionine and tryptophan are coded by only one. The different triplets coding for the same amino acid are **synonyms**. Many synonomous triplets differ in their third base, e.g. alanine has four codons: they all begin with GC but there are four possibilities for the third nucleotide. A code with several different triplets coding for the same amino acid is said to be **degenerate**.

There are two sorts of triplets that act as 'punctation codons'. The three codons UAA, UAG and UGA in Table 3 did not retain any amino acid in Nirenberg's filter test. They are all **stop codons**, and one or more of them are found towards the end of a mRNA molecule. They tell the protein synthesising system that the end of the message has been reached and the protein is complete. Translation stops and the protein is released from the ribosome. The first AUG of a protein-coding sequence on the mRNA is a **start codon** and all proteins start with methionine as their first amino acid (although it may be chopped off later).

## Universality of the genetic code

For many years the genetic code was thought to be the same in all organisms. The codon dictionary shown in Table 3 appeared to have the same meaning for the protein synthesising machinery of every type of organism that was tested; e.g. an *E. coli* cell, or a toad oocyte, would recognise a rabbit globin mRNA injected into them and both would make rabbit globin.

However, exceptions are beginning to accumulate. All codes remain triplet but the meaning of some codons is altered. This is true of nuclear genes in some ciliate protozoa, and mitochondrial and chloroplast genes in various eukaryotes.

In chapter 2, it was explained that cells contain extrachromosomal DNA. In eukaryotes most of

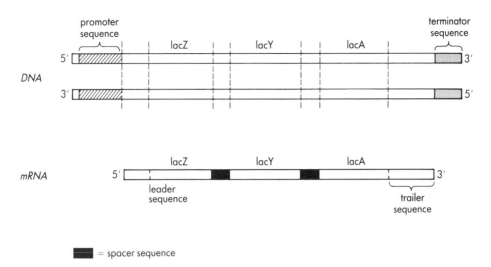

**Figure 11**  E. coli *lactose-catabolising genes are linked. They are all transcribed in a single mRNA, a common feature of prokaryote transcription*

this DNA is located in various organelles, particularly mitochondria and chloroplasts. Both of these organelles have their own internal protein-synthesising systems. E.g. mitochondrial DNA codes for some mitochondrial proteins and its own tRNAs and rRNA. Most mitochondrial proteins are coded by nuclear genes and synthesised in the cytoplasm; they then enter the mitochondrion. However, a few mitochondrial proteins are synthesised on mitochondrial ribosomes inside the organelle. These are coded by mitochondrial DNA. The mitochondrial genetic code is sometimes different from the

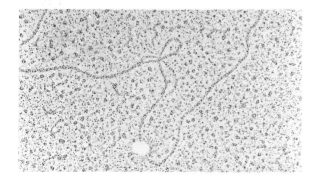

*This electron micrograph shows hybridisation of* β *globin mRNA with a copy of the* β *globin gene*

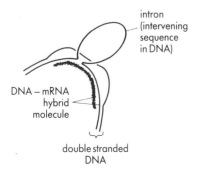

**Figure 12**  *Hybridisation of* β *globin mRNA with a copy of the* β *globin gene*

nuclear one. Thus, in yeast, the mitochondrial triplets CU– (where – stands for any one of the four bases) code for threonine not leucine. Yeast nuclear genes use these triplets to code for leucine as usual.

## Gene sequence and mRNA sequence

Gene manipulation techniques have made it possible to isolate particular messenger RNAs and the genes from which they are transcribed (chapter 11). This has shown that the structure of prokaryote and eukaryote genes is usually different. Prokaryote and eukaryote mRNAs are also differently organised.

In prokaryotes, transcription *alone* generates a functional mRNA molecule; the base sequence in one strand of the DNA is identical to the RNA copied from it. Mapping bacterial genes has shown that several genes involved in the same biochemical pathway are usually located next to each other on the bacterial chromosome (chapter 6). Genetic and molecular analysis shows that such genes are transcribed in a *single* mRNA (Figure 11). The mRNA consists of a **leader sequence**, then the **coding sequence** for the first gene. This is followed by a short **spacer sequence** and then the coding sequence for the second gene and so on. There is a final **trailer sequence** after the last gene. This mRNA structure is very important in the regulation of gene activity in prokaryotes (chapter 9).

In eukaryotes, transcription *and* RNA processing are required to produce a mRNA molecule. One of the first eukaryote genes to be compared with its mRNA was the β gobin gene (chapter 6). In an experiment, β globin mRNA was hybridised to β globin DNA. Electron microscopy of the hybrid molecule showed that there was a sequence in the middle of the DNA which was missing from the RNA (Figure 12). It was later shown that this was one of two

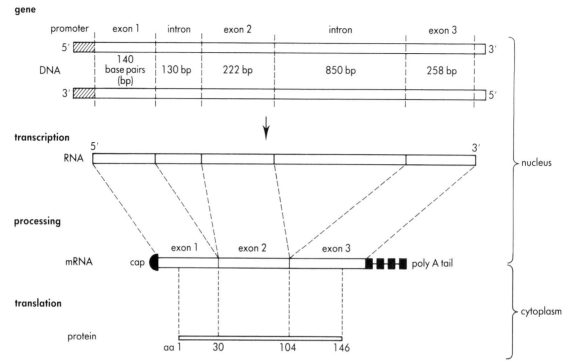

**Figure 13** *The structure of the human β globin gene. Transcription and processing are necessary to produce a mRNA from most eukaryote genes*

intervening sequences in the globin gene. One is much shorter than the other (Figure 13). The DNA coding sequence for the 146 amino acids of β globin is broken in two places in the gene. The two non-coding sequences are called **introns**; the three parts of the coding sequence are called **exons**. The number of introns varies between genes: there are two in all the human globin genes, but about 100 in the Duchenne muscular dystrophy gene.

The complete DNA sequence of a gene, including introns and exons, is transcribed into RNA (Figure 13). The introns in this RNA are then cut out while the RNA is still in the nucleus. The exons are **spliced** together to form a complete

coding sequence for the protein. There are two further modifications to the RNA in the nucleus. They are important in stabilising the mRNA for transport out of the nucleus to the ribosome and also for ribosome recognition: a nucleotide containing a modified base is added to the 5' end of the RNA molecule (**capping**) and several adenine nucleotides are added to the 3' end of the molecule (**poly A tailing**). The final product of transcription and RNA processing in the nucleus is a mRNA which is passed into the cytoplasm to be translated. Note that, unlike most prokaryote mRNAs, all eukaryote mRNAs code for a single protein.

# Translation

**Translation** is the process that converts a sequence of nucleotides in mRNA into a corresponding sequence of amino acids in a protein. The two major components of all protein synthesising systems are **ribosomes** and **transfer RNA (tRNA)** molecules.

**Ribosomes** are the 'translation factories' in all cells. For this reason a great deal of work has been done to discover what they are made of and how they function. Two sorts of gene contribute to the structure of ribosomes. One group makes **ribosomal RNA (rRNA)**, and another makes **ribosomal proteins**.

Ribosomes are small (2 nm) organelles. They are made up of two subunits, one large and one small (Figure 14). Both subunits consist of a skeleton of rRNA surrounded by a number of ribosomal

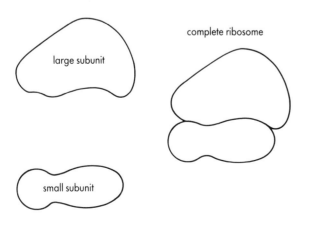

**Figure 14** *Ribosome structure*

proteins. Prokaryote ribosomes are smaller than eukaryote ones because the rRNA molecules are shorter and there are fewer proteins (Table 4).

Table 4   *Comparison of prokaryote and eukaryote ribosomes*

|  | PROKARYOTE | EUKARYOTE |
|---|---|---|
| SIZE* | | |
| Overall | 70 S | 80 S |
| Small unit | 30 S | 40 S |
| Large unit | 50 S | 60 S |
| | | |
| rRNA | | |
| Small unit | 16 S (1541 bases) | 18 S (1874 bases) |
| Large unit | 23 S (2904 bases) | 28 S (4718 bases) |
| | 5 S | 5.8 S |
| | | 5 S |
| | | |
| NUMBER OF PROTEINS | | |
| Small unit | 21 | 33 |
| Large unit | 31 | 49 |

* Size is estimated by rate of sedimentation in a centrifuge with units of S (Svedberg units)

There is good evidence that ribosomes exist in two states:

   (i) complete ribosomes which are synthesising proteins,

   (ii) ribosomes that are not synthesising proteins and have separated into large and small subunits.

Amino acids are the wrong size and shape to fit directly onto triplets of bases on a mRNA. Frances Crick suggested that there must be 'adaptor molecules', one for each amino acid. These ideas were supported by the discovery that amino acids are bound to small RNA molecules in the cytoplasm. These are **transfer RNA (tRNA)** molecules. They hold an amino acid ready to form a peptide bond, and also have a separate site to recognise the amino acid codon on the mRNA. Many of these tRNA molecules have been isolated from prokaryotes and eukaryotes. They are between 74 and 95 bases long and although there are some differences between the various tRNAs, they all have the same basic shape (Figure 15). Base sequences in different parts of a tRNA molecule base pair and help to fold the molecule. Unpaired bases between these base paired regions loop out. A particular loop (Figure 15) always contains a triplet (the **anticodon**) which is complementary to a codon on the mRNA. Each codon and anticodon will base pair like two complementary triplets in a DNA molecule.

Figure 15 shows that an amino acid binds to its tRNA more or less at the opposite end to the anticodon, at a CCA 3′ terminal sequence which is found on all tRNAs. All amino acids are loaded

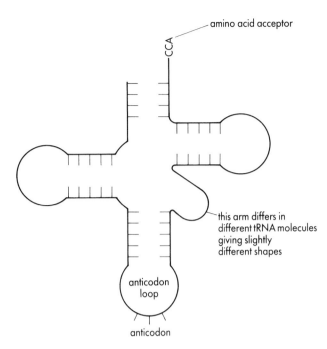

Figure 15   *A summary of the structure of all* E. coli *tRNA molecules. The anticodon sequence differs in the various tRNA molecules to match the triplet codon for the amino acid they carry*

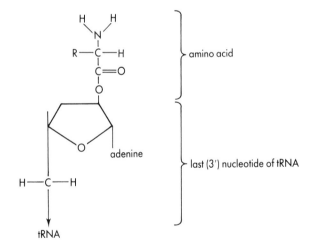

Figure 16   *Attachment of amino acid to its tRNA through the 3′ terminal adenosine nucleotide*

onto their respective tRNA by binding their COO⁻ terminus to the A of this sequence (Figure 16). An amino acid is bound to its proper tRNA because there is a different loading enzyme for each amino acid and its partner tRNA. Loading requires ATP. When attached to its tRNA, the amino acid is primed for peptide bond formation.

As there are 20 different amino acids, there must be at least 20 different tRNAs, one for each amino acid. In fact, many cells contain about *60* different tRNAs to deal with synonomous codons and other features of the genetic code, i.e. the same amino acid may be carried by more than one tRNA molecule.

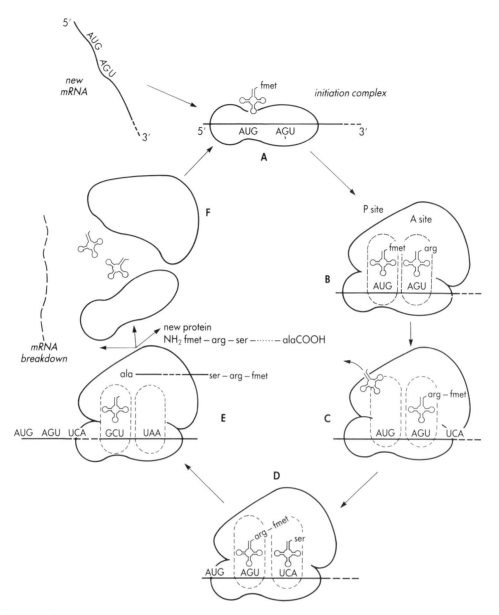

**Figure 17** *Stages of protein synthesis: A initiation; B, C, D, elongation; E termination; F recycling components*

There is one tRNA that behaves differently from all the others in both prokaryote and eukaryote cells. This is the **initiator tRNA** which carries the amino acid methionine. In *E. coli*, the amino ($N^+H_3$) terminal of the methionine is blocked. Only its $COO^-$ terminal is available to form a peptide bond. This blocked methionine is symbolised as fmet and the initiator tRNA is often called 'fmet tRNA'; fmet is the first amino acid in every newly synthesised *E. coli* protein.

## Protein synthesis

Protein synthesis is a continuous process but it can conveniently be divided into three stages:

(i) Initiation
(ii) Elongation
(iii) Termination.

The description that follows is based on

extensive biochemical analyses of *E. coli* protein synthesis.

(i) **Initiation**. Protein synthesis begins when a small ribosomal subunit binds at a recognition sequence on a mRNA molecule and loads an initiator tRNA to the nearby AUG codon (Figure 17a). The mRNA, small ribosomal subunit and initiator tRNA form an **initiation complex**. Several enzyme-like proteins (**initiation factors**) are needed to form the initiation complex. The formation of the complex requires the hydrolysis of energy-rich molecules; GTP (guanosine triphosphate) is used as the energy-rich molecule throughout protein synthesis and it is formed by interaction with ATP as follows:

$$ATP + GDP \rightarrow ADP + GTP$$

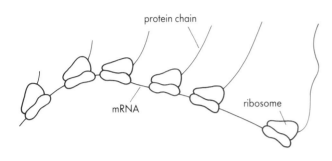

*Figure 18    Interpretative diagram of a polysome (see photograph)*

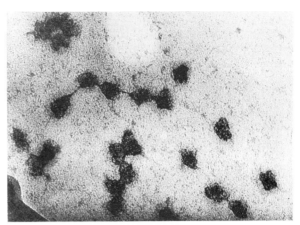

*This electron micrograph shows polysomes. The structure of a polysome is shown in Figure 18*

Once the initiation complex is formed, the large ribosomal subunit binds to it and the ribosome is ready for protein elongation.

(ii) **Elongation**. There are two sites on the completed ribosome which can carry tRNAs: the **peptide** or **P site** is now occupied by the initiator tRNA with its amino acid methionine, the **amino** or **A site** will now be filled by a second tRNA as determined by the second codon on the mRNA (Figure 17b). This is an energy-requiring step and GTP is hydrolysed. An enzyme (one of the proteins in the large subunit) now removes the f-methionine from the initiator tRNA and forms a peptide bond between the $COO^-$ terminal of this amino acid and the $N^+H_3$ terminal of the second amino acid. This second amino acid remains bound to its tRNA by its $COO^-$ terminus (Figure 17c). The initiator tRNA is removed from the P site so that the second tRNA, carrying two amino acids, can be moved into the P site from the A site (Figure 17d). This step also requires the hydrolysis of GTP. The mRNA normally shifts with the tRNA so that the A site is now ready for the third tRNA (Figure 17d).

A number of proteins called **elongation factors** are involved in the various rearrangements that take place on the ribosomal complex during the extension of the protein chain. The elongation steps are repeated and, each second, three amino acids are added to the growing protein each second at 37°C. e.g. it takes *E. coli* or one of your own cells about two minutes to synthesise an protein of average size.

(iii) **Termination** A stop codon eventually enters the A site. When this happens, the completed protein is cleaved from the last tRNA in the P site and released from the ribosome (Figure 17e). We know that, in normal cells there are no tRNAs that recognise stop codons. Termination is not yet fully understood but we know that, in *E. coli*, there are two protein **release factors** that are necesary to terminate protein synthesis and release the finished protein. When the protein is released, ribosomes split up so they are ready to form another initiation complex. In *E. coli*, used mRNA is rapidly broken down (Figure 17f).

Notice that the mRNA is translated from the 5′ end towards the 3′ end causing the protein to be synthesised from its amino ($N^+H_3$) terminal towards its carboxyl ($COO^-$) terminal. In both prokaryotes and eukaryotes, several ribosomes bind to the same mRNA (a **polysome**, Figure 18), several copies of a protein are therefore being synthesised at the same time from this polysome.

## The products of translation

An *E. coli* cell can make about 4000 different proteins and the average eukaryote cell makes even more than this. Many of these proteins are **enzymes** which catalyse the synthesis of smaller but essential molecules (including simple carbohydrates, amino acids, fatty acids and nucleotides) as well as larger and more complex molecules (such as polysaccharides and nucleic acids). However, proteins also have other roles in an organism: some are concerned with **support** (e.g. histones, the structural proteins of eukaryote chromosomes), others with **motility** (e.g. actin and myosin of muscle), or **communication** between cells (e.g. hormones such as insulin).

When translation on the ribosome is complete, proteins must be moved to the position where they are needed. This may be in the cytoplasm, in the nucleus or outside the cell. It has recently been discovered that many newly synthesised bacterial and eukaryote proteins include a sequence of amino acids which is not involved in their eventual function. Some of these short sequences are at the amino terminal of the protein, others are at the carboxy terminal. They are 'signal' sequences to assist the cell in 'posting' the protein to its correct position. Once this is achieved, the signal sequence is cleaved from the protein. e.g. a eukaryote 'import into nucleus' sequence is pro–pro–lys–lys–lys–arg–lys–val. Genetic engineers attached this sequence to a protein that is normally located in the cytoplasm and found that it was then transported into the nucleus.

This example shows that a gene not only carries the information which specifies a particular function, but also the necessary regulatory information. This ensures that genes act in the right place *and* at the right time. Gene regulation will be explored further in chapter 9.

# BIBLIOGRAPHY

Beebee, T and Burke, J (1988) *Gene Structure and Transcription* IRL Press, Oxford
Crick, F H C (1962) The Genetic Code *Scientific American* 207 (4), 66–74
Nirenberg, M W (1963) The Genetic Code II *Scientific American* 208 (3), 80–94
Crick, F H C (1966) The Genetic Code III *Scientific American* 215 (4), 55–62
Doolittle, R F (1985) The Proteins *Scientific American* 253 (4), 74–86.

# QUESTIONS

1 Two auxotrophic mutants (Arg1$^-$ and Arg2$^-$) of a haploid fungus were isolated. They both required arginine to be added to minimal medium for growth. Each one was crossed to a wild type strain of the fungus (Arg$^+$) and both crosses gave arginine auxotroph and wild type offspring in the proportion 1 : 1. Offspring phenotypes were tested by growing samples of each mycelium on both minimal medium and minimal supplemented with arginine. When the two arginine mutants were crossed, the offspring consisted of both arginine auxotrophs and wild types in the proportion 3Arg$^-$ : 1Arg$^+$. Are the two auxotrophs allelic mutants of a single gene, or mutations in two genes controlling different steps in the arginine biosynthetic pathway in this fungus? Explain your answer.

2 Compare the structures of DNA and protein and explain the biological significance of their similarities and differences.

3 Give one piece of evidence to support the idea that a gene must control the amino acid sequence of a protein and therefore determine the activity of that protein.

4 The DNA in the first part of the coding sequence of a gene has the following nucleotide pair sequence:

...5′ A T G T T A G C T G A T C C G C\* A A A T G A T G T T A...3′

promoter...3′ T A C A A T C G A C T A G G C G T T T A C T A C A A T...5′

a) Which is the coding strand of the DNA?
b) What is the nucleotide sequence of the mRNA?
c) Use the codon dictionary on page 102 to determine the amino acid sequence in this part of the protein.
d) What would be the effect of a nucleotide pair substitution changing C\*G into a TA pair?

5 What is the evidence that the genetic code is a triplet one?

# CELL DIVISION AND DEVELOPMENT

A cell grows and then divides into two cells. This is the usual method of reproduction in single cell organisms, e.g. *E. coli* or *Amoeba proteus*. Multicellular organisms such as *Drosophila melanogaster* consist of many millions of cells. These are formed from one original cell, the fertilised egg, by repeated divisions of one cell into two. This chapter discusses the mechanics of cell division and shows how each daughter cell inherits a complete set of genes. Three aspects of gene regulation are also presented in this chapter:

  (i) a mechanism for switching genes on or off,
  (ii) control of cell differentiation,
  (iii) correct positioning of tissues and organs in multicellular animals.

## 9.1 CELL GROWTH AND CELL DIVISION

Cells grow before they divide. This pattern is called the **cell cycle**.

**Prokaryotes**. The bacterium *E. coli* grows and divides into two equal-sized daughter cells about once every 20 minutes under optimum conditions. Two features distinguish these growing prokaryote cells from their eukaryote counterparts:

  (i) bacterial DNA is synthesised *throughout* cell growth,
  (ii) two copies of the bacterial chromosome which segregate towards opposite ends of the cell are often still synthesising DNA.

**Eukaryotes**. Eukaryote cells are larger than bacteria and most of them take several hours to divide, e.g. human kidney cells in culture take 27 hours. Each cell grows continuously until it reaches a fixed size and then divides (Figure 1). Daughter cells are often the same size, but in some organisms a small cell is budded off a larger one, e.g. the budding yeast *Saccharomyces cerevisiae*. In all eukaryote cells, DNA is synthesised in a *restricted* period of the cell cycle. This is called the **S (synthesis) phase** (Figure 1). The period of growth before DNA synthesis is called the $G_1$ (**1st gap**) **phase**; in this phase, each chromosome is a single unit. DNA synthesis in S phase splits each chromosome down its length into two chromatids. A second gap ($G_2$) comes between S and **mitosis** (or **M phase**). In mitosis, chromosomes condense and their chromatids segregate into two daughter nuclei. Cell division usually follows this nuclear division. Animal

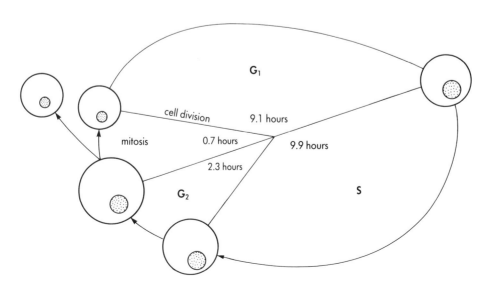

*Figure 1    Stages of the cell cycle. Times are for mouse fibroblast cells in culture*

cells are able to divide by constricting in the middle (Figure 2a). This is impossible in plant cells because they have a rigid wall outside their plasma membrane. When they divide, plant cells lay down new plasma membrane material between the two daughter nuclei and then secrete wall material between the two new plasma membranes (Figure 2b).

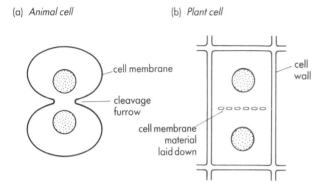

(a) *Animal cell*          (b) *Plant cell*

*Figure 2    Cell division in (a) an animal cell, and (b) a plant cell*

# DNA replication

**DNA replication** is synthesis of two new DNA molecules which are exact copies of one parent molecule. James Watson and Frances Crick pointed out that this would occur if the two strands of a DNA molecule separated and each one acted as a template for the synthesis of a complementary strand. This is called **semi-conservative replication**. Watson and Cricks' idea was mentioned in chapter 2 but is considered in more detail here. It explains how one copy of genetic information becomes two copies which can then be separated and passed to daughter cells.

## Semi-conservative replication

**Prokaryotes**. Matthew Meselson and Franklin Stahl provided the first evidence for semi-conservative replication. They grew a culture of *E. coli* in a medium containing a 'heavy' isotope of nitrogen, $^{15}N$, until the bacterial DNA contained almost all heavy bases. DNA was extracted from a sample of these bacteria ('sample 1'). The rest of the bacteria were placed in a medium containing the 'light' isotope, $^{14}N$. Two samples were taken from this culture after 20 minutes ('sample 2 and sample 3'), and a fourth one at 40 minutes ('sample 4').

DNA was extracted from all these samples and put through density gradient centrifugation (chapter 1). The results of this experiment are shown in Figure 3a. The DNA from the sample 1 sedimented far down the gradient (heavy band). After one round of DNA synthesis in the light $^{14}N$ medium (sample 2), all the DNA sedimented higher up the gradient (intermediate band). After two rounds of synthesis (sample 4), there were two bands in the gradient. One of these bands was in the intermediate position, the other was even higher in the gradient (light band). Sample 3, also taken after one round of synthesis, was heated to separate the strands of the DNA molecules. This produced two bands, one light and one heavy, instead of the single intermediate band in the untreated sample from the same cell generation.

The simplest interpretation of these results is given in Figure 3b. Both strands of the original DNA are heavy. When this DNA replicates, light nucleotides are made into new strands using the heavy ones as templates. These molecules are intermediate on the gradient (sample 2) and consist of 1 heavy and 1 light strand (sample 3). When this intermediate DNA replicates, one daughter molecule must contain two light strands and the other must contain one light and one heavy strand (sample 4).

**Eukaryotes**. Whole eukaryote chromosomes have also been shown to replicate semi-conservatively.

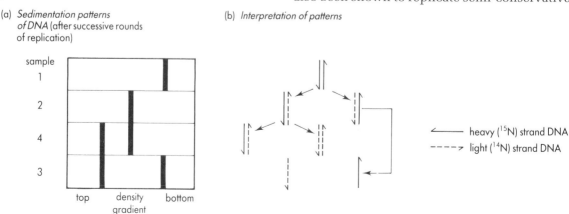

(a) *Sedimentation patterns of DNA* (after successive rounds of replication)

(b) *Interpretation of patterns*

⟵——— heavy ($^{15}N$) strand DNA

⟵- - - -> light ($^{14}N$) strand DNA

Conclusion: both strands of a DNA molecule must act as templates during replication

*Figure 3    Evidence for semi-conservative replication of bacterial DNA*

# Segregation of chromosomes

## Prokaryotes

When chromosomal DNA is isolated from *E. coli*, it is usually associated with cell membrane material. It is likely that the DNA is attached to membrane proteins involved in DNA replication. The suggested site of attachment is called the **R site**. New cell membrane material is laid down in the middle of a growing cell. It is thought that an R site divides and the two sites separate as cell membrane material is laid down between them. This would separate the newly replicated chromosome (Figure 4).

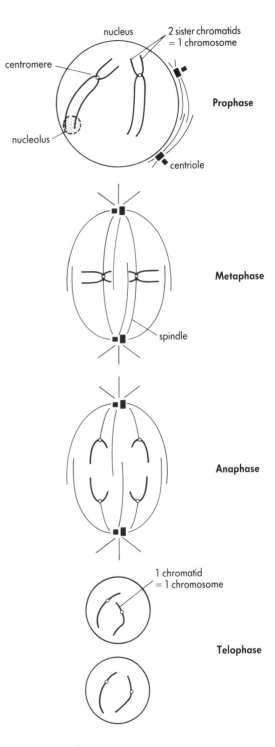

*Figure 5   Mitosis*

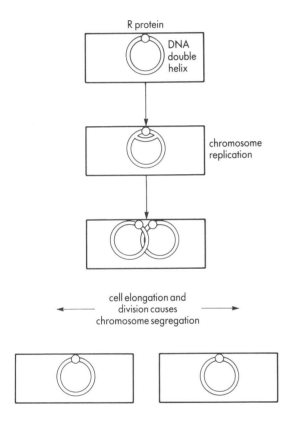

*Figure 4   Chromosome replication and segregation during growth and division of a bacterial cell*

## Eukaryotes

Mitosis is the name given to nuclear division in all eukaryote cells except those dividing for sexual reproduction. Chromosomes become condensed in mitosis so that they can easily be moved around the cell. Mitosis is a continuous process but, because chromosomes change their shape and position and the nuclear membrane disappears, various stages can be named (Figure 5). Mitosis as described here occurs in most eukaryotes. (It is a little modified in some fungi and protoctists where the nuclear membrane does not break down.)

A major feature of nuclear division is the separation of chromosomes on a **spindle** (Figure 5). It is formed in the cytoplasm in a series of changes that go on at the same time as changes in the nucleus. In $G_1$ there is a single **microtubule organising centre (MTOC)** present in the cytoplasm. An obvious feature of each MTOC in

111

most animal cells is a pair of **centrioles** (Figure 5). These are similar to basal bodies of cilia. Centrioles are absent from the MTOC of most plant cells. During S phase, the MTOC and centrioles divide. Early in mitosis, pairs of centrioles move to opposite sides of the nucleus and spindle fibres form between them. Centrioles and spindle fibres are made of **microtubules**; These are made up of the protein **tubulin**.

The first stage of mitosis is *prophase* (Figure 5). The chromosomes appear and become more condensed. This takes place within the nuclear membrane. The transition from extended $G_2$ chromosomes to condensed mitotic ones is gradual. From the beginning of prophase, each chromosome is divided lengthways into two chromatids, reflecting DNA replication in the previous S phase. Sister chromatids are joined at a **centromere**; A centromere may occur in the middle of a chromosome (**metacentric**) or towards one end (**acrocentric**), but its position is fixed for a particular chromosome. A centromere appears as a gap in a chromosome stained for DNA because it contains more protein and less DNA than chromatin on either side.

A **nucleolus** is visible in early prophase, attached to **nucleolar organisers** on one or more chromosomes. In the nucleus, ribosomes are put together from their component molecules. The **nucleolar organiser** regions of the chromosomes are the sites of the ribosomal RNA (rRNA) genes (chapter 8), e.g. in humans there are rRNA genes on the short arms of chromosomes 13, 14, 15, 21 and 22. During prophase the nucleolus disassembles and disappears. It is reassembled during the succeeding $G_1$.

The beginning of **metaphase** (Figure 5) is marked by the disappearance of the nuclear membrane and the movement of the chromosomes to the middle of the spindle. Some spindle fibres overlap in the middle of the spindle, others are attached to a face of a centromere (Figure 5). In metaphase, each chromosome sits in the middle of the spindle quite separate from all other chromosomes. Even if the cell is diploid and there are homologous chromosomes, they behave quite independently in mitosis. Contrast this with meiosis (chapter 5).

At **anaphase** (Figure 5), sister chromatids move away from each other towards opposite poles of the spindle, half-centromeres leading. Recent evidence suggests that spindle fibres act in two ways to separate chromatids once each centromere has split (Figure 6):

(i) Tubulin molecules are removed from the ends of the microtubules where they are attached to a half-centromere. This shortens these spindle fibres and pulls the half-centromere towards the spindle pole.

(ii) Tubulin molecules are added to the free ends of spindle fibres where they overlap in the middle of the spindle. These elongating fibres slide past each other and push the spindle poles apart. This requires energy from ATP hydrolysis.

By **telophase** (Figure 5), groups of chromatids have formed at each spindle pole. Each chromatid can now be called a chromosome. Membrane vesicles associate with each chromosome and eventually fuse to form a nuclear membrane. The chromsomes become more diffuse as the cell divides and the daughter cells move into $G_1$.

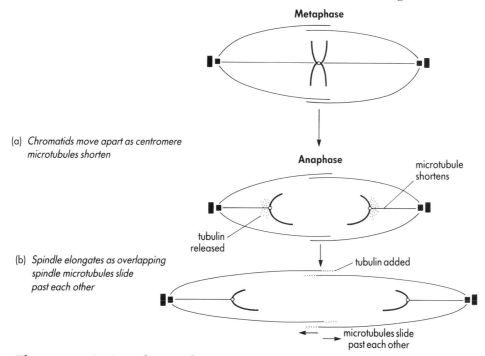

(a) *Chromatids move apart as centromere microtubules shorten*

(b) *Spindle elongates as overlapping spindle microtubules slide past each other*

*Figure 6   The two steps in sister chromatid separation during anaphase of mitosis*

# Cell division and cancer

Cell division and mitosis are under genetic control. This has been shown by isolating temperature-sensitive mutants in yeasts and mammalian cells in culture. These mutants will grow and divide normally at one temperature but, if moved to a higher temperature, they stop at some position in the cell cycle. Different mutants stop at different positions in the cycle, and some of them will restart the cycle if they are moved back to the lower temperature.

Cancer cells arise in many species. An important feature of these cells is that they no longer respond to the control systems in the body that regulate cell division. The cells divide continuously to form a mass of tissue called a **tumour**. They continue to divide in culture and form masses of cells several layers thick. In contrast, normal cells in culture form a layer one cell thick and then stop dividing. Some cancer cells also gain the ability to move away from their original tissue to other sites in the body and divide there. This is called **metastasis**.

There is evidence that a number of changes must take place in a cell before it becomes a cancer cell. Molecular genetic techniques have been used to isolate mutations in various cancer cells and it is found that the same genes are involved in different cancers in a variety of multicellular animals. Non-mutant alleles of these genes have been shown to be essential for normal cell growth and cell division. There are two main types of mutation:

(i) **micro mutation**, which alters the amino acid sequence of *the protein* produced by a cell cycle control gene.
(ii) **gene translocation** to another site, e.g. onto another of the organism's chromosomes, or into a viral chromosome. This alters the activity of the gene.

The proteins produced by some of the genes have been isolated and located in the cell. One group of proteins is active at the cell membrane, another group is located in the nucleus. Several of the proteins at the cell membrane are involved as receptors for hormones and growth factors which control various aspects of cell metabolism including cell division. Some of the proteins in the nucleus may be involved in regulation of cell division. The molecular connections between the membrane proteins and the nuclear group have yet to be discovered.

# Transfer of genetic information

DNA replication and mitotic cell division give every cell a complete set of chromosomes. The experiments below show that each cell must also get a complete set of genes.

Leaf tissue can be removed from a plant, e.g. a potato. By treating it with a mixture of hydrolytic enzymes, individual cells can be separated with their cell walls removed (Figure 7a). Such cells are called **protoplasts**. Protoplasts can be grown

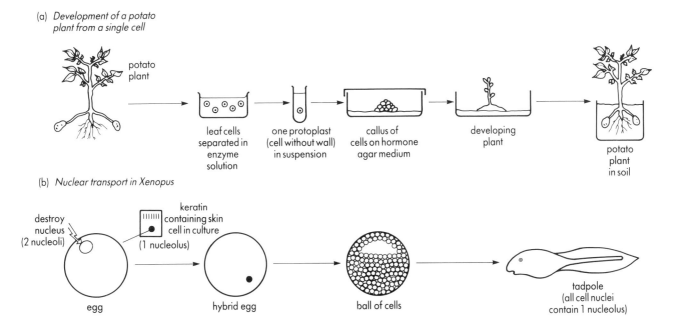

(a) *Development of a potato plant from a single cell*

potato plant → leaf cells separated in enzyme solution → one protoplast (cell without wall) in suspension → callus of cells on hormone agar medium → developing plant → potato plant in soil

(b) *Nuclear transport in Xenopus*

destroy nucleus (2 nucleoli) / keratin containing skin cell in culture (1 nucleolus) / egg → hybrid egg → ball of cells → tadpole (all cell nuclei contain 1 nucleolus)

*Figure 7    The nucleus from one cell of a multicellular plant or animal contains all the genetic information needed to form a complete organism*

on a solid medium containing osmotic stabilisers, growth factors and nutrient molecules. They regenerate cell walls, divide, and form a mass of undifferentiated cells called a **callus**. This callus will eventually give rise to one or more mature plants, each one with leaves, stems, stem tubers and roots. Only if it contained a complete set of genes could a leaf cell give rise to a complete plant.

Specialised cells from multicellular animals will divide in culture but it has not been possible to form a complete animal from them. In Figure 7b, a nucleus is removed from a skin cell of the toad *Xenopus laevis*. If it is transplanted into a toad egg without a nucleus, this 'hybrid' cell will form a complete tadpole. This means that the nucleus from a skin cell contained the genetic information needed to make all the different cells in a tadpole. As a control, the nucleus of the skin cell was taken from an animal whose cell nuclei always contained one nucleolus. The egg was from a toad strain with two nucleoli per cell. The tadpole cells all had nuclei with one nucleolus.

If all the cells in a multicellular organism contain the same genes, then only *differential activity* of those genes can account for cell specialisation. This implies *regulation of gene activity*.

# 9.2 REGULATION OF GENE ACTIVITY

Gene activity in the bacterium *E. coli* is better understood than in any other cell. The activity of some of the 4000 genes in *E. coli* has been studied in such great detail that the quantity of protein they produce is known. For example, under optimal conditions, there are about 20,000 copies of each ribosomal protein and about 100 000 copies of one of the elongation factors required for protein synthesis. If the carbohydrate lactose is the only energy source for bacterial growth there are about 3000 copies of the enzyme β galactosidase (which catalyses the breakdown of this disaccharide into glucose, Figure 8). A bacterial cell has only one copy of each of the genes that produce these different proteins so there must be some regulation of the quantity of protein produced by each gene.

It has also been discovered that the amount of β galactosidase enzyme *alters* with the amount of lactose present in the medium. If lactose is abundant, there are 3000 copies of the enzyme; but if lactose is absent there are less than three molecules of the enzyme per bacterium. A bacterium can regulate the activity of the gene that produces β galactosidase according to the

surrounding conditions. In general, for prokaryote and eukaryote cells: **A system is turned on when it is needed and turned off when it is not needed. This saves the cell a great deal of energy.**

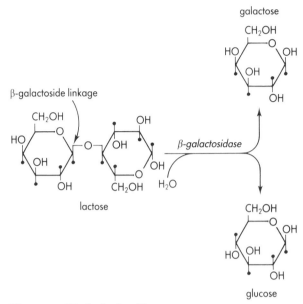

**Figure 8    Hydrolysis of lactose**

## The lactose operon

Gene regulation of lactose breakdown was first worked out by Francois Jacob and Jacques Monod. They shared a Nobel Prize with André Lwoff for their work. This work is important for two reasons:

(i)   many bacterial genes are regulated in a similar way,

(ii)  their model of gene regulation is the basis for today's research in eukaryote cells.

Two features of lactose metabolism in *E. coli* were the starting point for Jacob and Monod's **operon hypothesis**:

(i)   There are three enzymes involved in lactose breakdown (Figure 9a). The quantities of these enzymes in a cell are correlated: when lactose is added to the medium, the number of molecules of all three enzymes increases together. Equally, if lactose is removed, the number of molecules of all three enzymes falls away in parallel. This is **co-ordinate gene expression**.

(ii)  The three genes for the enzymes are linked next to each other on the bacterial chromosome (Figure 9a).

They are **structural genes** because they determine the structure of the enzyme protein.

(i) and (ii) suggest that all three genes might be turned on and off by a single switch. Jacob and Monod isolated a mutant bacterium whose lactose breakdown was not regulated: large quantities of all three enzymes were present in this mutant all the time, whether lactose was present in the medium or not. The mutation was located in a single gene separate from the three structural genes. This must be a **regulatory gene** (Figure 9b).

## Negative regulation

Jacob and Monod suggested that the normal protein produced by the regulatory gene *switched* off the structural genes by binding to the DNA just in front of the first structural gene (β galactosidase gene Z, Figure 10a). A protein which switches genes off by binding to a DNA sequence to prevent transcription acts as a **negative control**; the protein is called a **repressor**. Jacob and Monod called the site near the structural gene, where the repressor binds, the **operator**. They suggested that the protein from their mutant regulator gene was altered and could not bind to the operator. The structural genes were therefore permanently switched on. Normal repressor protein has now been isolated and it does bind to operator DNA just upstream of the β galactosidase sequence; mutant protein will not bind.

(a) *Structural genes and their protein products*

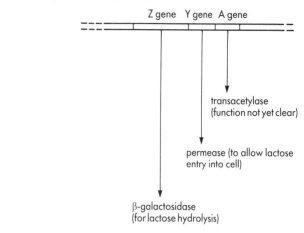

(b) *Regulatory gene position*

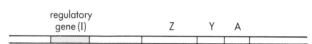

**Figure 9   The arrangement of genes involved in lactose breakdown in E. coli**

(a) *Repressor protein binds to operator DNA and prevents transcription of structural genes*

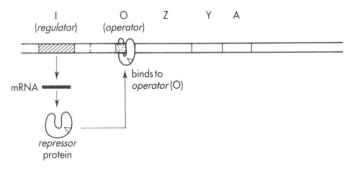

(b) *Lactose binds to repressor and deactivates it; RNA polymerase binds to promoter and transcribes structural genes*

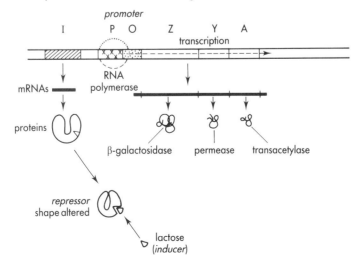

**Figure 10   Regulation of activity of genes involved in lactose breakdown in E. coli**

If normal repressor binds to operator DNA and prevents the lactose structural genes from being transcribed, how can they be switched on when needed? Jacob and Monod thought that lactose might *induce* the formation of the enzymes needed to break itself down as follows.

They suggested that the repressor protein is **allosteric**, i.e. it has separate sites which bind different molecules (Figure 11). The lactose repressor has one site to bind to DNA and a second site to bind a form of lactose, allolactose. When this lactose binds, it alters the shape of the protein so that the DNA binding site is closed and the repressor is prevented from binding to the operator. This means that when lactose binds to repressor, the three lactose metabolising genes are free to be transcribed by RNA polymerase. Later

work has shown that all three genes are transcribed on the same mRNA (Figure 10b). This helps to explain co-ordinate expression of these genes which form an **operon**.

The activation of the structural genes by the inducer is not permanent. As soon as bacteria use up the lactose in the medium, the repressor is freed to bind to the operator and inhibit transcription. Bacterial mRNAs are broken down soon after synthesis so, once mRNA synthesis is stopped, the enzymes for lactose utilisation disappear from the cell.

The DNA between the regulator gene and the β galactosidase gene has now been isolated and sequenced to study how the repressor prevents transcription. Purified repressor binds to a particular base pair sequence in the operator (figure 12a); RNA polymerase binds to a different sequence in the promoter. In this and all other promoter-operator systems, the two nucleotide pair sequences overlap (Figure 12b). This means that when repressor is bound to the DNA, RNA polymerase cannot bind.

*E. coli* is able to switch the genes for lactose breakdown on and off throughout its life. The regulator gene is always expressed at the same low level whether lactose is present or absent and a constant amount of repressor (about 10 molecules) is always available to bind either DNA or lactose. Continued synthesis of a small amount of repressor is a very efficient way to regulate the activity of a set of enzymes or other proteins which are needed in quite large quantities, but only in certain environmental conditions.

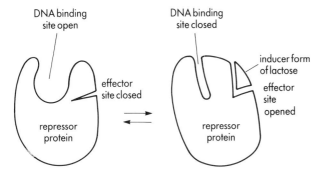

The DNA binding site and the effector site are separate. When the inducer binds to the effector site, the DNA binding site is closed. It opens in absence of inducer

**Figure 11   Lac repressor is an allosteric protein**

(a) *The lac operator sequence*
Arrows indicate that the sequence is almost a complete mirror image round the central G ≡ C pair; mirror imaging is found in many DNA regions that bind regulatory protein

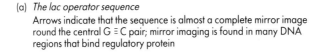

(b) *Overlap of the lac promotor and operator sequences*

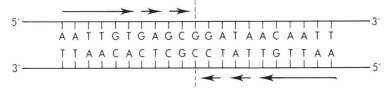

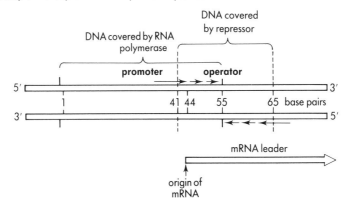

**Figure 12   The lac operator sequence overlaps with the promoter**

## Positive control

Although lactose and other disaccharides can act as an energy source for bacteria, all of them have to be hydrolysed into glucose and other monosaccharides. This is the role of the lac operon. Glucose is always used first if it is already present in the medium in addition to lactose or any other disaccharide. Thus lactose does not induce the lactose operon if glucose is present. How is this achieved?

Jacob and Monod showed that the lactose operon is negatively controlled by the repressor; later work has shown that it is also **positively controlled** by a different protein. In positive control, a protein must bind to DNA to activate genes. In the lactose operon, this protein is called **catabolite activator protein (CAP)** because it activates genes that are concerned with the

breakdown (catabolism) of various complex sugars. The protein binds to the DNA of the lactose operon just ahead of the promoter sequence (Figure 13a) at the CAP site. CAP binding is necessary for loading RNA polymerase onto the promoter. Glucose indirectly inactivates CAP protein; inactivated CAP does not bind to DNA (Figures 13b, c). This greatly reduces RNA polymerase binding at the lactose promoter. Even if the repressor is missing from the operator, almost no RNA polymerase binding means almost no transcription and therefore almost no lactose catabolising enzymes. Therefore, if glucose and lactose are both present in the medium, glucose will be used first (Figure 13b). If both glucose and lactose are absent, the lactose operon is completely switched off (Figure 13c).

(a) *No glucose, lactose present* → abundant lac mRNA

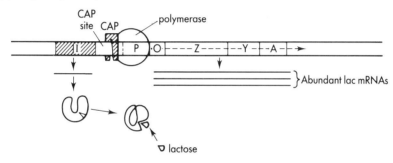

(b) *Glucose present, lactose present* → almost no lac mRNA

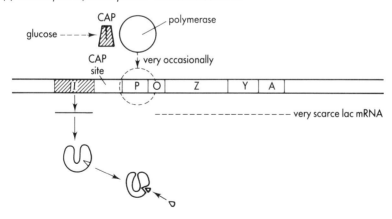

(c) *Glucose present, lactose absent* → no lac mRNA

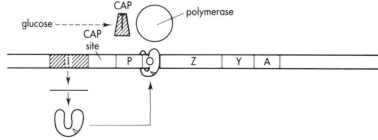

*Figure 13    The regulation of the lactose operon under various conditions*

# General features of gene regulation

The regulation of several other genes in viruses, bacteria and eukaryote cells is under investigation. Some of them show detailed differences from the regulation of the lactose catabolising genes outlined above, but the main features of the lactose system do seem to be widely applicable:

  (i) Many genes are switched on and off by allowing transcription or preventing it.

 (ii) Transcription is regulated by protein product(s) of one or more control genes. Some proteins exert positive control of transcription, others exert negative control.

(iii) A control protein binds to a particular sequence of nucleotide pairs – the **target sequence**. Target sequences have to be near the beginning of the structural gene whose activity they control. It has recently been discovered that some target sequences are many thousands of base pairs along the chromosome from their gene. They are brought close to their gene by DNA folding.

(iv) Control proteins have one site which can bind to the target DNA sequence. In another part of the protein, there is a site which can bind and release effector molecule(s). These effectors alter the shape of the protein so that it will bind/not bind to the target DNA.

# Hormones and genes

**Hormones** are **chemical messengers** which circulate round the body of a multicellular animal. Physiologists have shown that different hormones control the activity of particular target tissues. More recently it has been shown that hormones will activate genes in these tissues. Evidence for hormone activation of genes came from studies on a small fly, *Chironomus tentans*. The synthesis of its new cuticle during larval moults, pupation and adult metamorphosis is regulated by the moulting hormone **ecdysone**. Like other flies, *C. tentans* has polytene chromosomes in several of its cells (see photograph). Unlike the fruit fly *D. melanogaster*, the centromeres of these chromosomes are not fused.

*Chironomus* chromosomes have large 'puffs' involving particular bands on each chromosome; the chromatin in these puffs is much less condensed than in the rest of the chromosomes. Radiolabelled RNA precursors have shown that the puffs are the sites of RNA synthesis (see photographs). (This is thought to be mRNA synthesised from DNA.) Inhibitors of RNA synthesis prevent radiolabelling of puffs. If

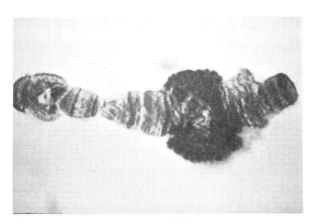

*The polytene chromosomes of* Chironomus tentans

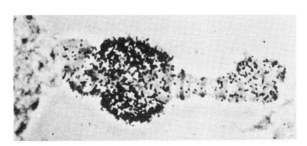

Chironomus tentans *polytene chromosomes: radiolabelled uridine is incorporated into RNA in the puffed regions*

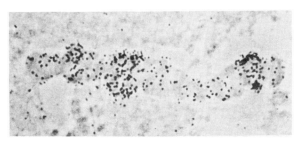

Chironomus tentans *polytene chromosomes: if RNA synthesis is inhibited, no radiolabelled uridine is incorporated into RNA in the puffed regions*

ecdysone is injected into *Chironomus* larvae, a band on chromosome 1 puffs within 30 minutes and another band on chromosome 4 puffs within an hour. It is now known that every hormone acts by binding to a specific receptor protein on the cell surface or in the cytoplasm (depending on the hormone). The hormone receptor complex activates specific genes in the nucleus.

# 9.3 DIFFERENTIATION AND DEVELOPMENT

All the cells in a multicellular organism contain the same genes. But there are many different cell types: muscle, nerve, skin, etc. These cells express many of the same genes. Some of the genes produce 'housekeeping' proteins including

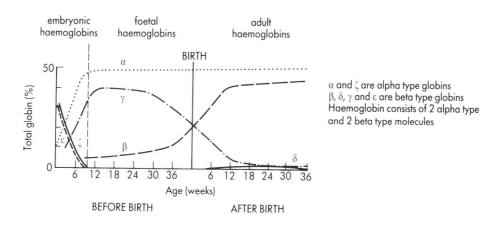

**Figure 14   Changes in synthesis of globins in the human foetus and infant**

enzymes which catalyse essential biochemical pathways (e.g. glycolysis and the Krebs' cycle) to provide the cell with energy. Others help to maintain cell structure, e.g. histones in chromosomes (chapter 2) and tubulins in the cytoskeleton and spindle. Different amounts of 'housekeeping' proteins lead to differences in cell size.

Differentiated cells also contain specialist proteins. e.g. human haemoglobin is found only in human red blood cells. The various types of human globin were described in chapter 7. Figure 14 shows the concentrations of different globins in red blood cells during development. Embryonic haemoglobin ($2\zeta$, $2\epsilon$), foetal haemoglobin ($2\alpha$, $2\gamma$) and adult haemoglobins ($2\alpha$, $2\beta$, or $2\alpha$, $2\delta$) are present in different cells at different times in development. The different haemoglobins are never present in the same cell. thus, not only are red blood cells differentiated from every other type of cell by the presence of haemoglobin, but they differ from each other at different stages of development too.

Globin genes appear to be permanently switched off in the majority of human cells because they are located in tightly condensed chromatin (chapter 2). It is thought that the genes are inaccessible to regulatory molecules in this condensed state. In red blood cells (before they lose their nucleus), the chromatin in the region of the globin genes seems to be uncoiled. The idea of gene inactivation by chromatin condensation is supported out by other examples, e.g. inactivated genes on the heterochromatic X chromosome (chapter 7); and chromatin decondensation during RNA synthesis in chromosome puffs. The molecular details of this control of gene activity are still to be discovered.

# Animal development

It has long puzzled biologists how all the components of an animal are fitted together

correctly. One of the most exciting discoveries in the last 20 years has been how genes control the development of the fruit fly *Drosophila melanogaster.*

At 25°C, a fruit fly takes 9-10 days to reach maturity. The stages are summarised in Figure 15. A day after fertilisation, the egg hatches as a larva, consisting of the head and 12 segments. The larva

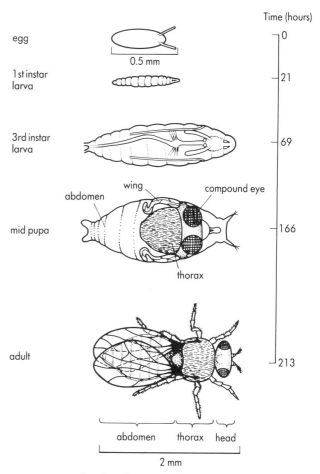

**Figure 15   The development of Drosophila melanogaster**

grows, shedding its exoskeleton twice, but otherwise changes very little. Five days after fertilisation, the larva pupates. In the pupa radical changes occur: larval tissues are reshaped into an adult which hatches on day 9. The adult fly has the same segmental organisation as the larva but segments are more obviously differentiated. The head carries well developed compound eyes, sensory antennae and complex mouthparts. The three thoracic segments each carry a pair of legs. The middle segment also carries a pair of wings, and the third one carries a pair of balancing organs (**halteres**). The nine abdominal segments form a unit which is clearly distinct from the head and thorax.

Early experiments showed that many adult tissues are formed from 17 groups of unspecialised cells present in the larva. These cells are formed early in development before the larva hatches from the egg case and they all appear identical. The groups of cells are called **imaginal discs**; they are arranged in eight pairs and one terminal group down the larva (Figure 16). Transplantation experiments showed that the cells in the different discs must be very different from each other, although they look alike. Thus, cells transplanted from an eye disc to an abdominal position will form an eye there. Cells transplanted from a wing disc will form wing tissue, and so on. This suggests that the pattern of the adult must be laid down very early in the egg. None of the imaginal disc cells appear specialised, but as they are formed in the early embryo, their developmental potential must be restricted.

Genes that regulate development appear to act in two ways:

(i) They add molecular 'labels' to cells as they are formed. Groups of cells in different parts of the embryo are given different labels.

(ii) A nucleus in a labelled cell is activated to produce a second label. In this way, the product of one regulatory gene activates the next one to form a branching series of labelling steps.

*A non-mutant fly (*Drosophila melanogaster*)*

*A bithorax mutant fly (*Drosophila melanogaster*). The bithorax gene controls normal wing and haltere development. Mutation in this gene causes the development of a second pair of wings in place of halteres*

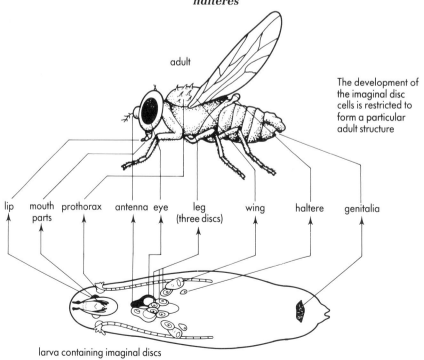

adult

The development of the imaginal disc cells is restricted to form a particular adult structure

lip    mouth    prothorax    antenna    eye    leg    wing    haltere    genitalia
       parts                                   (three discs)

larva containing imaginal discs

*Figure 16    Adult tissues in* Drosophila melanogaster *are formed from groups of undifferentiated cells laid down early in larval development*

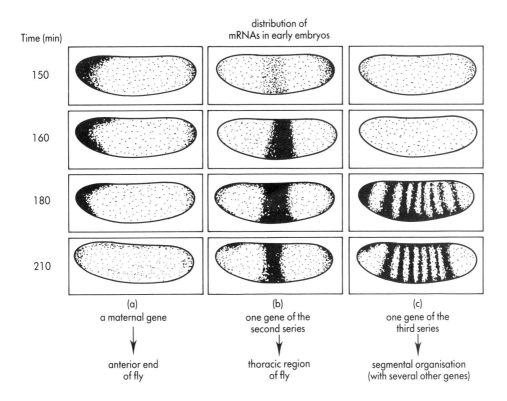

Time (min)

distribution of
mRNAs in early embryos

150

160

180

210

(a)
a maternal gene

↓

anterior end
of fly

(b)
one gene of the
second series

↓

thoracic region
of fly

(c)
one gene of the
third series

↓

segmental organisation
(with several other genes)

**Figure 17    Distribution of mRNAs of three genes which form part of the cascade which controls the pattern of development of** Drosophila. *(Based on in situ hybridisation studies using radiolabelled probes for the three types of mRNA)*

A cascade of gene activity gives cells in different positions in the embryo a particular set of proteins which make up the bars of their 'bar code'. The analogy is a good one: gene on/off → protein present/absent → bar present/absent. The final bar code determines how a cell will differentiate, and how it will interact with other cells. If any of the regulatory genes mutates, the cascade is broken and the fly will develop abnormally.

The analysis of gene control of development has depended on the isolation of two sorts of mutant. the first group are recessive lethal mutations which alter development and halt it, usually before the larva hatches from the egg. These mutants are severely deformed. They either lack segments or parts of segments or have them duplicated. In the second group, development continues into adulthood but the fly develops organs in unusual parts of the body, e.g. the antennapedia mutation (which replaces the fly's antennae with legs) and the bithorax mutation (which replaces halteres with a second pair of wings). This mutation is shown in the photographs. Genetic engineering techniques have been used to develop molecular probes for the mRNA and proteins produced by several of these genes, and the genes themselves have been sequenced.

Molecular studies have shown that the basic pattern of the fly is set out very early in its life. The antero-posterior and dorso-ventral axes of the embryo are determined by the deposition of mRNA and protein from a few genes into the cytoplasm of the developing egg. This happens while the egg is still inside its mother and *before* it is fertilised. The genes are called **maternally active genes**. The mRNA and proteins produced by maternal genes are laid down in different parts of the egg.

Fertilisation of the egg initiates nuclear division, cell division and development of the embryo. The maternal genes are active (Figure 17a). Soon after fertilisation, a second set of pattern genes is activated by the maternal gene products. Some of these genes are active towards the front of the embryo, others in the middle (Figure 17b) and others at the rear. Their action divides embryonic cells into three groups which will eventually become head, thorax and abdomen. Third and fourth tiers of genes are activated by the products and interactions of the second set; these allocate the embryonic cells into segmental units. Their gene products appear as stripes on an otherwise perfectly uniform embryo (Figure 17c). Different genes are activated in the different stripes and they determine what type of structures will be formed when the segments eventually separate and differentiate later in development, and finally in tissue reorganisation in the pupa.

This cascade of gene activity labels about 5000 cells present in the early embryo. This means that all the millions of cells derived from them will differentiate along particular pathways. As often happens in such work, similar genes are now being found in many other segmented animals including humans.

# BIBLIOGRAPHY

Mazia, D (1974) The Cell Cycle *Scientific American* 230 (1) 54–69

McIntosh, J R and McDonald, K L (1989) The Mitotic Spindle *Scientific American* 261 (4) 26–36

Bishop, J M (1982) Oncogenes *Scientific American* 246 (3) 68–80

Beebee, T and Burke, J (1988) *Gene Structure and Transcription* IRL Press, Oxford

Gehring, W J (1985) The Molecular Basis of Development *Scientific American* 253 (4) 136–148.

# QUESTIONS

**1** Show the pattern of radiolabelled DNA that Meselson and Stahl would have obtained if DNA replication was 'conservative', i.e. one daughter molecule consisted of the two strands of the parent molecule, and the other daughter molecule consisted of two new strands.

**2** Draw two columns on a piece of paper with headings: a) mitosis, b) meiosis. Compare the two types of division by writing *yes* or *no* under each heading in answer to the following statements. Justify your answers.
  (i) Involves two successive divisions.
  (ii) Chromosomes replicate before this division.
  (iii) Occurs in a haploid cell.
  (iv) Chiasmata form.
  (v) Homologous chromsomes segregate.
  (vi) Different chromosomes assort independently and randomly.
  (vii) Sister chromatids separate.
  (ix) Occurs in prokaryotes.
  (x) Occurs in asexual reproduction.
  (xi) Occurs during embryonic growth of a female mammal.

**3** Explain the following terms: operator, promoter, structural gene, regulator gene.

**4** Give two reasons why the three *E. coli* enzymes in lactose breakdown increase and decrease together. Explain if eukaryote enzymes could be regulated in both these ways.

**5** Each cell in a multicellular organism can be considered as having a 'bar code'. How is this bar code formed and what is its significance?

# POPULATION GENETICS AND EVOLUTION

Some species are quite similar. For example, a chimpanzee does not seem very different from a gorilla. However they are both somewhat different from other species such as baboons, and much more different from species such as giraffes or lions.

It is probable that very similar organisms are closely related and stem from a recent common ancestor. In contrast, organisms with only a few similar characters are likely to be more distantly related; they might have a common ancestor much further back in the earth's history. This divergence of organisms from a common ancestor is called **evolution**.

In 1858, Charles Darwin and Alfred Wallace put forward an idea to show how evolution can occur. In that year, they published their theory of evolution by **natural selection**. In his book, Darwin emphasised the differences beteen individuals, and suggested the preferential survival of individuals with advantageous characters when competing for limited environmental resources. However, he did not understand how advantageous characters could be *transmitted* from parents to offspring. When Mendel's discovery of genes and their inheritance was fully appreciated at the beginning of this century, experimental investigations of genetic changes in populations were begun to test for evolution in progress.

This chapter considers how evolution occurs, and the evidence to support it.

## 10.1 THEORIES OF EVOLUTION

During the early part of the nineteenth century, various people suggested that animals and plants might gradually change and evolve. This would explain why some species are similar: they have a common ancestor.

In 1809, Jean Baptiste Lamarck explained *why* evolution should occur. He suggested that an environment provides an opportunity for a particular way of life. Organisms and their progeny living in this environment gradually develop characters that adapt them to it. For example, the giraffe inhabits the African savannah and feeds mostly on the foliage of tall trees. Lamarckists have argued that the giraffe's ancestors had short necks and responded to this specialist food supply by gradually developing long necks to reach the food (Figure 1).

Lamarck's ideas are often called **the inheritance of acquired characters.** It is suggested that the environment actually induces the particular inheritable change in the organism which *adapts* it to that environment. Even with our

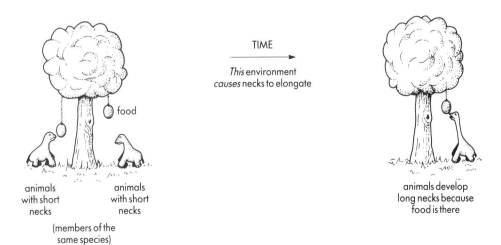

*Figure 1   Evolution by inheritance of acquired characters (discredited)*

understanding of molecular genetics, it is not at all clear how an environment could cause changes in particular genes so that the organism containing them is specifically fitted to that environment. Most biologists believe that mutations occur at random and, until very recently, the experimental evidence has entirely supported this view.

# Darwin and evolution

In 1858, Darwin and Wallace published the theory of the origin of species by **natural selection**. This theory explained *how* evolution could occur; it is widely accepted today, supported by a large body of evidence.

Charles Darwin developed his ideas on evolution between 1836 and 1858 after he had returned from a five-year voyage as a naturalist aboard the survey ship HMS *Beagle.* He put these ideas on paper in 1839 but, although he showed the manuscript to various colleagues, he did not publish it. By 1858, Darwin had worked out the theory in considerable detail. In that year Alfred Russell Wallace, who had been working independently in the Far East, sent Darwin a manuscript on evolution which mirrored his own views. Their ideas were presented jointly at a meeting of the Linnaean Society in London July 1 1858. Darwin's detailed arguments were published the following year in his book *The Origin of Species.*

# Natural selection

Darwin and Wallace's theory rest on three important observations:

(i) Animal and plant species form local breeding groups called **populations**. The individuals within these populations are often different from one another in a number of ways, i.e. they show **variation**.

(ii) Parents produce many more young than they need to replace themselves. This means that numbers in a population tend to increase.

(iii) An environment is **limited** so there is only enough food, shelter, breeding space, etc. to support a population of a particular size.

Darwin and Wallace used these three observations to create the following theory, the theory of natural selection:

(i) As any environment is limited, members of a population will **compete** with each other to obtain the necessary resources (food, space, etc.) to stay alive and reproduce.

(ii) Among all the various types of individuals in the population, there will be some individuals with characters better suited to the environment than other individuals in the population.

(iii) The individuals that are best adapted will be more likely to **survive** and **reproduce**.

(iv) If the advantageous characters are **inheritable** (genetic), they can be passed on to the next generation. Individuals with these characters will therefore increase in the population at the expense of the individuals that are less well adapted.

This theory is very different from the Lamarckian theory. It suggests that there is an *independent* mechanism which causes organisms to vary. The environment merely acts as a sieve, only allowing some types of variation to survive (Figure 2).

TIME

*competition* for food

animals of the same species show variation in neck length; some can reach food and survive, others cannot and so they die

variations in neck length; low food eaten out by all members of the species, only those with the longest necks can reach highest food and survive

**Figure 2   *Evolution by natural selection (accepted)***

Darwin observed that the variation within several domesticated animal and plant species strongly supported the theory. He quoted the diversity within domestic species as examples. Unfortunately, genetics and inheritance were not understood at that time and it was difficult to see how a particular character could be passed unchanged from parent to offspring. Early in this century, Mendel's genetic explanations of variation and inheritance were rediscovered. It was then clear that:

(i) different genes could account for a lot of the variation between organisms,

(ii) these genes could be transmitted in a regular way between generations.

Hardy and Weinberg extended Mendel's discoveries to cover inheritance of a pair of contrasting characters in a large population of individuals mating at random. Their idea formed the starting point for all subsequent explanations of how gene frequencies change during evolution. The following sections review the sources of genetic variation and describe the effects that the environment has on this variation.

# 10.2 GENETIC VARIATION

## The origin of genetic variation

Evolution could not occur unless there was genetic variation in a population. If individuals containing certain genes tend to survive and reproduce, but individuals containing other genes tend not to, then this is a small step in the process of evolution. Chapter 7 showed how changes can occur in genes. These changes are mutations and they may be micromutations (changes in a single gene) or macromutations (changes involving several linked genes).

Mutations are stable changes. They are passed on from parents to offspring if they occur in reproductive cells as well as the cells in the body where they are expressed. Mutation is the origin of all genetic variation.

## Genetic variation in populations

As discussed in chapter 7, a mutation is a rare event and many mutations are disadvantageous to the organism. This suggests that most organisms should show little genetic variation. If so, how can populations contain sufficient genetic variation to respond to the environment in the way Darwin suggested? It is thought that relatively simple haploid organisms are less variable than more complex diploid organisms. The two sorts of organism respond to changes in the environment in rather different ways.

### Haploid organisms

Haploid organisms rely mostly on very large populations and new mutations in each generation to respond to changed environmental conditions. Many simple organisms, such as some single celled eukaryotes (e.g. *Chlamydomonas*) and all prokaryotes (e.g. bacteria) are haploid. This means that they have only one gene for each character (except for a very few gene duplications). If any one gene mutates, the character it controls will alter. If the alteration is disadvantageous, the organism will probably die before it can reproduce and the mutant gene will be lost from the population. Therefore, populations of haploid organisms have no way of storing disadvantageous mutations. However, single celled organisms reproduce very rapidly by repeated cell divisions to produce very large populations. Even if the mutation rate is low, some of the individuals in a large population will be mutant although they may soon die. Any gene can mutate at a low frequency every generation. If the environment changes and one or a few individuals contain an altered gene which helps them survive under new conditions, then more and more individuals will contain the gene as the cells divide.

### Plasmid transfer

Many bacteria also have a mechanism which can distribute an advantageous gene through a population and between species very rapidly by conjugation and plasmid transfer. The gene is passed from one individual to another without the bacteria reproducing. A good example of this system is the transfer of genes which allow bacteria to survive antibiotic treatment. These 'antibiotic resistance' genes have become widespread in many different bacteria since antibiotics have been widely used in agriculture and medicine.

Several antibiotic resistance genes are carried on plasmids. These are **resistance transfer factors**, or **R plasmids**. R plamids acquire resistance genes by transposition (chapter 7). Plasmids are small, usually extrachromosomal, DNA molecules (chapters 2 and 6). R plasmids are like F plasmids; they carry the genes to replicate themselves and make a conjugation tube. A plasmid contains relatively little DNA and when it is free of the chromosome it can replicate several times during the life of a bacterial cell. The copied plasmids are passed between bacteria by conjugation (Figure 3). R plasmids can therefore transfer resistance genes to several other bacteria during the life of the donor cell. This means that whole groups of bacteria can acquire resistance to an antibiotic very quickly. As plasmid transfer

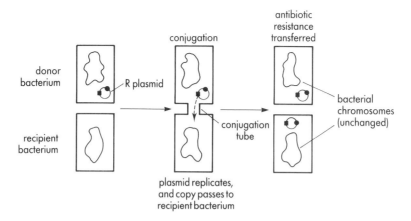

donor
bacterium

R plasmid

recipient
bacterium

conjugation

conjugation
tube

plasmid replicates,
and copy passes to
recipient bacterium

antibiotic
resistance
transferred

bacterial
chromosomes
(unchanged)

2 different antibiotic resistance genes carried
on an R plasmid

**Figure 3   *Spread of resistance genes between bacteria by plasmid replication during conjugation***

can occur between different bacterial species, resistance may develop in a non-pathogen but then transfer to a pathogen. Antibiotic resistance genes will give their carriers a tremendous survival advantage where there is widespread use of antibiotics, e.g. in hospitals and on farms.

R plasmids that carry up to 14 different antibiotics resistance genes have been discovered. They are a cause of great concern to the medical profession because many populations of bacteria which are human pathogens are now resistant to a large number of antibiotics. It seems likely that plasmid transfer is an important way to spread useful genes through a whole range of different bacteria.

Uptake of naked DNA and transfer by viruses (chapter 5) may also be mechanisms for gene transfer between bacteria in their natural environment.

## Variation in diploid organisms

The populations of diploid organisms are generally smaller than those of most haploid organisms. Since the populations are relatively small, only a few new mutations are likely to occur in each generation. If they depended entirely on new mutations, higher animals and plants would be unlikely to survive changes in the environment.

Diploid organisms carry two copies of every gene although often only one needs to be functional. Therefore animals and plants can carry two different copies of many of their genes. This means that these organisms can *store* mutant genes. If the organisms reproduce sexually and mate among each other, their population contains a large amount of genetic variation called a **gene pool**. Each organism contains just one of the many possible sets of genes that can be formed from the pool.

The genes making up the gene pool are of two types:

(i) **Major genes**. Some characters are switched between alternatives by different alleles of a single gene. These alleles can substitute for each other at the gene locus. Many examples of this sort of gene were given in chapters 3 and 4. Major gene loci with a number of alleles are common in many natural populations of diploid organisms. The alleles of the human ABO blood group (chapter 3) are just one example. Characters determined by a major gene locus with more than one allele show a **genetic polymorphism**.

(ii) **Polygenes**. Many quantitative characters, like human size and weight, are determined by several different gene loci acting together. Each gene locus makes a small contribution to the character and is one of a series of *polygenes*. In most populations there are different alleles at many of the polygene loci, so these characters are continuously variable. The genetics of this type of character were considered in chapter 4.

Genetic variation is obvious in humans and many domesticated species, but less so in most wild organisms, e.g. all wild rabbits look similar. However, various biochemical and molecular techniques have shown that there is a lot of genetic variation in most species. This variation often gives rise to different forms of the same protein which can be demonstrated using electrophoresis. e.g. in several human populations in Africa there is more than one form of haemoglobin A. In several East African populations, haemoglobin S (sickle cell haemoglobin) is a common alternative to normal haemoglobin A (chapter 8).

Table 1 summarises the results of a large number of morphological and biochemical studies. it shows that many animals and plants have a large number of polymorphic genes. Thus, in many populations, there is a great deal of genetic variation. i.e. these populations have extensive gene pools.

**Table 1   The average amount of genetic variation in major groups of animals and plants**

| | NUMER OF SPECIES TESTED | PROPORTION OF GENES WHICH ARE POLYMORPHIC |
|---|---|---|
| Vertebrates | 68 | 24.7% |
| Invertebrates | 57 | 46.9% |
| Higher plants | 8 | 46.4% |

# Release of genetic variation

Mendel discovered two genetic processes:—
   (i) **genetic segregation** of alleles at each locus,
   (ii) **random recombination** between alleles at different loci.
The two processes were dealt with in detail in chapters 3 and 4 but they are summarised in Figure 4. They release variation in natural populations of sexually reproducing diploid organisms. Mutation produces different alleles, but segregation and recombination break down existing combinations of alleles and form new ones in each generation. They will produce a variety of combinations of both polymorphic genes and polygenes. In this way, many different individuals can be produced in each generation.

# Genetic segregation

The effect of genetic segregation is easiest to study in those characters switched by major genes because each gene locus can be considered separately. The alleles have clear cut effects. However segregation is also an important mechanism for releasing variation in characters controlled by polygenes.

If a particular character is polymorphic, with two alleles 'A' and 'a', then a population will contain both homozygotes (AA and aa) and heterozygotes (Aa). The **Hardy Weinberg calculations** (see below) show the basic rules which determine the proportions of these different genotypes in a random mating population.

# Hardy Weinberg calculations

In this section, a semi-natural garden population of *Antirrhinums* is used as an example because the genetic composition of the starting population can then be stated. This means that the various calculations can be set out in order. It is important to remember that the calculations also apply to natural populations, given the same assumptions.

Red (**AA**), white (**aa**) and pink (**Aa**) flowered *Antirrhinums* often occur together in a garden. In nature, they will cross fertilise and produce seed. A random sample of this seed can be collected each year and resewn the following year to produce generation after generation of plants. In the garden situation there is not likely to be any restriction on which plants mate together because insects move from flower to flower. However, the genotype frequencies in succeeding generations can be predicted, even in this uncontrolled mating situation. All we need to know is the numbers of the three genotypes planted out in the first generation. We assume that there are no restrictions on mating and that plants of all three flower colours survive and produce seed equally well.

(i) *Genetic segregation*

Two heterozygotes for one gene (Aa) produce 3 types of progeny as a result of A segregation from a

A or a combines with A or a

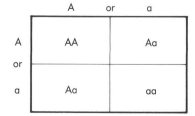

1 parent type (Aa) gives 3 progeny types
(if one or both parents is homozygous then progeny are less variable)

(ii) *Random recombination*

Two heterozygotes for two genes (AaBb) produce 9 types of progeny

AA or Aa or aa possibilities combine with BB or Bb or bb possibilities

| | AA or | Aa or | aa |
|---|---|---|---|
| BB or | AA BB | Aa BB | aa BB |
| Bb or | AA Bb | Aa Bb | aa Bb |
| bb | AA bb | Aa bb | aa bb |

1 parent type (AaBb) gives 9 progeny types

*Figure 4   Segregation and recombination produce genetic variation in polymorphic populations*

Suppose 300 red (**AA**), 450 pink (**Aa**) and 250 white (**aa**) *Antirrhinums* were planted. Between them, they can produce only two types of gametes, either 'A' or 'a'. Red plants will produce only **A** gametes, pink plants will produce half **A** and half **a** gametes, and white plants will produce only **a** gametes. If we assume that every plant (red, pink or white) produces an identical number of gametes, then the frequency of the two types of gamete is directly related to the numbers of each type of plant and can easily be calculated:

p = frequency of **A** gametes

$$= \frac{\text{no. of AA} + \frac{1}{2}\text{ no. of Aa}}{\text{total plants}}$$

$$= \frac{300 + (\frac{1}{2} \times 450)}{1000} = 0.525, \text{ or } 52.5\%$$

q = frequency of **a** gametes

$$= \frac{\text{no. of aa} + \frac{1}{2}\text{ no. of Aa}}{\text{total plants}}$$

$$= \frac{250 + (\frac{1}{2} \times 450)}{1000} = 0.475, \text{ or } 47.5\%$$

*Half* the number of heterozygotes is included in the calculations of both p and q because these plants produce half **A** and half **a** gametes. p and q are also the frequencies of the **A** and **a** alleles in the plants of this first generation planted out by the gardener. There are only these two alleles present, so:

$$p + q = 0.525 + 0.465 = 1 \text{ or } 100\%$$

Because there are more **AA** plants than **aa**, the frequency of the **A** gene and the proportion of **A** gametes produced is greater than **a**. Male and female gametes must fuse to produce the next generation. We can use Mendel's method to calculate the genotype frequencies in the next generation. The only modification is that the gamete frequencies are *not* p = ½ = 0.5**A** : q = ½ = 0.5**a**, which *is* true in controlled matings when both parents are heterozygote. Here they are p = 0.525**A** : q = 0.475**a** in the population as a whole. So the following fusion table (Table 2) can be laid out.

The frequencies of the three genotypes in the second generation are therefore predicted as:

| **AA** | **Aa** | **aa** |
|---|---|---|
| $p^2 = 0.276$ | $2pq = 0.498$ | $q^2 = 0.226$ |

Suppose 1000 seeds were collected at random from the original plants and sewn to produce the plants in this generation. There should be 276 red ones, 498 pink ones and 226 white ones. Note that the number of each type of plant has changed from the first generation. What will happen when these plants reproduce to give rise to a third generation? Calculating the frequencies of the gametes produced by the second generation gives:

$$p = \frac{276 + (\frac{1}{2} \times 498)}{1000} = 0.525,$$

$$q = \frac{226 + (\frac{1}{2} \times 498)}{1000} = 0.475$$

These are the same gamete frequencies as in the first generation. When the gametes fuse they will give rise to a third generation with genotype frequencies of:

$$0.276 \text{ } \textbf{AA} : 0.498 \text{ } \textbf{Aa} : 0.226 \text{ } \textbf{aa}$$

So once random mating takes place, the three genotypes will continue in the proportions: $p^2 : 2pq : q^2$, in all further generations. However the numerical values of these three proportions are not absolutely fixed. They depend on allele frequencies:

if p = 0.5 and q = 0.5, then $p^2 = 0.25$, $2pq = 0.50$ and $q^2 = 0.25$,
but if p = 0.75 and q = 0.25, then $p^2 = 0.56$, $2pq = 0.38$ and $q^2 = 0.06$.

There are a number of factors which can alter gene frequencies in any generation, e.g. death of a larger number of one genotype than another, or uneven production of gametes by different genotypes, or influx of seed of one genotype from another garden. If any of these differential or selective events occurs, gene frequencies in that generation will change. If the altered population continues to mate at random, then the genotype frequencies will continue in the proportions $p^2 : 2pq : q^2$, but these will have new numerical values. These values will remain the same until gene frequencies change again. Factors which alter gene frequencies are considered in more detail on page 130.

**Table 2** *Effect of gamete fusion in a randomly mating population*

| MALE GAMETES | frequencies | FEMALE GAMETES | | |
| | | **A**<br>p = 0.525 | and | **a**<br>q = 0.475 |
|---|---|---|---|---|
| **A** | p = 0.525 | **AA**<br>$p^2 = 0.276$ | | **aa**<br>pq = 0.249 |
| and | | | | |
| **a** | q = 0.475 | **Aa**<br>pq = 0.249 | | **aa**<br>$q^2 = 0.226$ |

## Hardy Weinberg in natural populations

(i) **Gene locus with dominance**. Note that it is only possible to calculate unambiguous gene and gamete frequencies if all three genotypes have distinct phenotypes. Only then can the numbers of alleles **A** and **a** be counted. If there is dominance, the gene frequencies can only be estimated on the assumption that the three genotypes are in the proportions $p^2 : 2pq : q^2$. Suppose that a particular population of *Cepaea nemoralis* (chapter 3) contains 500 snails with pink shells and 500 snails with yellow shells. There are two phenotypes but three genotypes: $\mathbf{C^P C^P}$, $\mathbf{C^P C^Y}$ and $\mathbf{C^Y C^Y}$. If the genotypes are assumed to be distributed in Hardy Weinberg proportions then:

$$500/1000 \text{ pink} = p^2 + 2pq, \text{ and}$$
$$500/1000 \text{ yellow} = q^2$$

Gene frequencies can be estimated as:

$$q = \text{frequency of } \mathbf{C^Y} = \sqrt{q^2} = \frac{500}{1000} = 0.707$$

Since there are only two alleles in this population, and $p + q = 1$, the frequency of $\mathbf{C^P} = p - 1 - q = 0.293$.

The numbers of the $\mathbf{C^P C^P}$ genotype would be expected to be $(p^2 \times 1000) = 86$, and $\mathbf{C^P C^Y}$ should be $2pq \times 1000) = 2 \times 0.293 \times 0.707 \times 1000 = 414$. However, there is no way to test that these are the *actual* number of the two genotypes.

(ii) **Locus with co-dominant alleles.** For genes with no dominance, it can be established whether or not different individuals are in the expected Hardy Weinberg proportions. An example is the human MN blood group. There are two alleles and both are expressed in the heterozygote. A sample from a Japanese population gave 406 MM individuals, 744 MN individuals and 332 NN individuals. Genes can be counted so gene frequencies are:

$$p = \frac{(406 + 372)}{1482} = 0.52$$

and

$$q = \frac{(332 + 372)}{1482} = 0.48$$

Therefore, if the humans were in the proportions $p^2 : 2pq : q^2$, there should have been 400 MM : 740MN : 342NN aa. A Chi-squared test (chapter 2) can be carried out to discover if the observed and expected numbers are significantly different:

|  | MM | MN | NN | TOTAL |
|---|---|---|---|---|
| Obs. no. | 406 | 744 | 332 | 1482 |
| Exp. no | 400 | 740 | 342 | 1482 |
| Dev.$^2$/Exp. | 0.09 | 0.02 | 0.29 | |

$$\chi^2_{(1)} = 0.09 + 0.02 + 0.29 = 0.40$$
$$P \gg 0.05$$

The three genotypes are therefore in the expected Hardy Weinberg proportions. This means that there cannot be any mate selection or differential mortality with respect to these alleles. The individuals in this population are mating at random with respect to this gene locus.

# Random recombination

Eukaryote individuals contain many thousands of genes and many of these are polymorphic (Table 1). Recombination between many polymorphic loci can produce large numbers of different combinations of genes. This can be explained by considering a simple two locus system as follows.

An organism is polymorphic at two loci with **A/a** and **B/b** alleles. The two loci are not linked so they recombine at random. The frequency of the **A** and **a** alleles in a large, randomly mating population are p and q. The **B** and **b** allele frequencies are r and s. This means that the three genotypes at the **A/a** locus have frequencies of $p^2$ (**AA**) : $2pq$ (**Aa**) : $q^2$ (**aa**). The three **B/b** genotype frequencies are $r^2$ (**BB**) : $2rs$ (**Bb**) : $s^2$ (**bb**). Every individual contains *both* an **A/a** genotype *and* a **B/b** genotype. The different genotypes and their frequencies are therefore obtained by *multiplying* the two sets of genotype frequencies (probability rule 2, chapter 3):

| Genotypes | AA | Aa | aa | BB | Bb | bb |
|---|---|---|---|---|---|---|
| Frequencies | $(p^2$ | $+ 2pq$ | $+ q^2)$ | $\times (r^2$ | $+ 2rs$ | $+ s^2)$ |

This calculation has been done in Figure 5 to give both algebraic and numerical results for $p = q = r = s = 0.5$, i.e. where the two alleles are equally frequent at both loci. In this case, individuals with at least one heterozygous locus are by far the most frequent members of the population. The exact frequency of heterozygote individuals depends on gene frequencies. If alleles A and B were at high frequencies, there would be more homozygotes. Nevertheless, random recombination will maintain some variation in a population as long as different loci have more than one allele.

There is another way to look at the effect of random recombination. The following calculations use the same method as the one used to demonstrate the amount of variation in a character controlled by polygenes (chapter 4). If two human parents were heterozygote for a

| locus | alleles | | | genotypes at each locus | | |
|---|---|---|---|---|---|---|
| A/a | A | | a | AA | Aa | aa |
| frequency | $p = 0.5$ | | $q = 0.5$ | $p^2 = 0.25$ | $2pq = 0.5$ | $q^2 = 0.25$ |
| B/b | B | | b | BB | Bb | bb |
| frequency | $r = 0.5$ | | $s = 0.5$ | $r^2 = 0.25$ | $2rs = 0.5$ | $s^2 = 0.5$ |

combined genotypes
and frequencies

| | AA $p^2 = 0.25$ | Aa $2pq = 0.5$ | aa $q^2 = 0.25$ |
|---|---|---|---|
| **BB** $r^2 = 0.25$ | AABB $p^2r^2$ 0.0625 | AaBB $2pqr^2$ 0.125 | aaBB $q^2r^2$ 0.0625 |
| **Bb** $2rs = 0.5$ | AABb $p^2 2rs$ 0.125 | AaBb $2pq2rs$ 0.25 | aaBb $q^2 2rs$ 0.125 |
| **bb** $s^2 = 0.25$ | AAbb $p^2s^2$ 0.0625 | Aabb $2pqs^2$ 0.125 | aabb $q^2s^2$ 0.0625 |

*Figure 5* **Method to calculate genotype frequencies for two unlinked polymorphic gene loci in a random mating population**

particular gene on each of their chromosomes, they would be heterozygous for 23 different genes. These can segregate three genotypes at each locus so they have the potential to produce $3^{23}$ or more than 94 billion ($94 \times 10^9$) different genotypes in their offspring. They would have a chance of only 1 in 8.4 million of reproducing exactly their own genotype. The probability of producing a different genotype from their own is therefore very high indeed. Most of these would be similar to themselves but extreme genotypes are possible, although unlikely (see chapter 4).

Recombination is therefore a source of variation for both polymorphic genes and polygenes. It gives the population considerable evolutionary potential in a changing environment. In a stable environment however, recombination can be a disadvantage. This is because a favourable genotype, if heterozygous, is unlikely to produce exact copies of itself.

If genes are linked on the same chromosome, the chances of their recombining is reduced and special mechanisms like chromosome inversion are even more likely to hold advantageous groups of alleles together (chapter 7).

# 10.3 ALTERING GENE FREQUENCIES

Various processes act on natural populations so gene and genotype frequencies are altered in each generation. These processes fall into two categories:

(i) random events.
(ii) ordered or selective processes.

## Genetic drift

Genetic drift is a random event. Once Mendel had shown how genes are inherited, and Hardy and Weinberg had demonstrated how these genes are expected to behave in populations, biologists realised that evolution might occur by chance as well as being directed by natural selection.

The term **genetic drift** is used to describe changes in gene frequency which happen by *chance*. For example, the fruit fly *Drosophila* can have red or brown eyes, determined by a pair of genes: **A** (red eyes) and **a** (brown eyes). Figure 6 shows the effect of genetic drift in two small populations of *Drosophila*, both of which start with 50% red genes and 50% brown genes. The frequency of the red gene moves up or down at random in both populations. After 20 generations, one population accumulated 100 per cent red genes by chance and the other population has drifted to 10% red genes.

These random changes happen because only some of the flies in each generation reproduce. Sometimes there are more red eyed flies among the parents than in the population as a whole. On the other hand there are sometimes more brown eyed parents. A small sample of parents is chosen just like tossing a coin a few times. If a coin is tossed six times, the expected result would be three heads and three tails. By chance however, it might be five heads and one tail. Chance variations are more likely in small samples so genetic drift is likely to have most effect when populations are small, or when only a few individuals reproduce.

If, by chance, red eyed flies are more often parents, in the next generation there will be a new Hardy Weinberg equilibrium and there will be more red eyed flies in the population. A lack of red eyed parents mean fewer red eyed flies in the next generation. Genetic drift therefore tends to increase the numbers of one gene or the other but it is never possible to predict which one will become common. In the two populations which started with the same numbers of red and brown eyed flies, one became entirely red by chance, the other mostly brown (Figure 6).

An important case of genetic drift is when a few individuals become isolated from the rest of the species and start a new population (see below). These founder members of the new population are a small sample of the population from which they came. By chance, they may have a very different gene frequency. While the founder population remains small, it may undergo genetic drift and become even more different from the large parental population. This process is called the **Founder Principle**.

# Natural selection

The best evidence for evolution by **natural selection** comes from studies of present day populations. This is because only on these populations can the various theories be tested and the mechanisms of evolution be invstigated by experiment.

Various populations, either in the laboratory or in their natural environment, have been studied over the last 50 years. Natural selection and small scale evolutionary changes have often been observed in these studies. However, living organisms first appeared on Earth several thousand million years ago. It is hardly surprising that the changes that have been observed over 50 years or less, are small compared with those that have happened in the time span of evolution. Biologists therefore, have to look for other kinds of evidence to support the theory of evolution in addition to the experimental studies. In this account some experimental evidence is considered first, followed by evidence from living and fossil species.

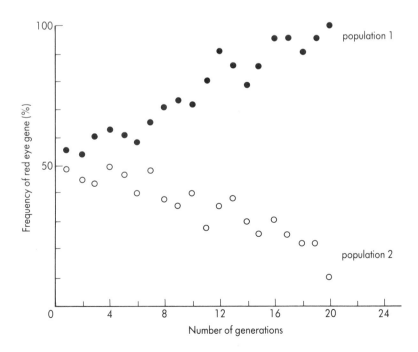

*Figure 6    Genetic drift: the changes in frequency of the red eye gene in two small laboratory populations of* Drosophila melanogaster. *These changes occurred by chance*

melanic form

speckled form

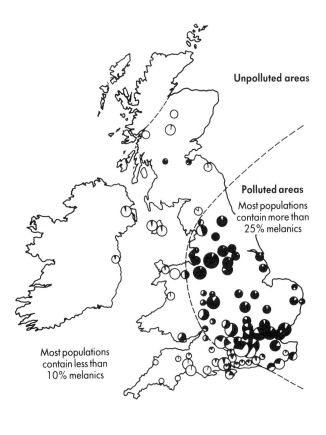

Unpolluted areas

Polluted areas
Most populations
contain more than
25% melanics

Most populations
contain less than
10% melanics

black segment of circle = melanic moths
white segment of circle = speckled moths

0%

(size of circle reflects sample size)

50%

*Figure 7 The frequencies of melanic and speckled forms of the peppered moth* Biston betularia *in various British populations*

Darwin proposed natural selection as the force that causes changes in populations. More recently biologists have realised that natural selection can also maintain variation and therefore stabilise a population. These two types of selection are:

    (i) **directional selection** (which changes gene frequencies),

    (ii) **stabilising selection** (which maintains gene frequencies).

The effect of selection on genes at a single locus can be described by algebra applied to the Hardy Weinberg equilibrium. These are called **deterministic models** because gene frequencies are predicted with certainty. More realistic models, which include an element of chance are called **stochastic models**. Both types of model population are demonstrated most effectively if programmed into a computer. In this book, evidence for selection is provided from natural populations.

## Directional selection

**Directional selection** happens when an environment favours all the individuals carrying one gene (e.g. **a**) at the expense of individuals carrying an alternative (e.g. **A**). It is most easily investigated in a natural population when the environment changes. Changes have occured in populations of the peppered moth *Biston betularia*. These changes are related to industrial pollution and they have been studied in some detail.

The peppered moth is found throughout the United Kingdom. It now has **speckled** and **black (melanic)** colour forms in many populations (Figure 7). This is a genetic polymorphism. The usual melanic form is determined by a dominant gene (**A**), the speckled form by its alternative (**a**).

Until the mid-nineteenth century, almost every captured individual had speckled wings. For the next 100 years, melanic individuals increased in some populations. This shift towards the melanic form in response to industrial pollution is called **industrial melanism**. By the late 1950s, biologists had built up a picture of the proportions of speckled and melanic forms in different populations. Speckled moths predominated in rural areas such as Cornwall and Scotland; melanic forms were common in industrialised regions such as the Midlands and London (Figure 7).

The following explanation accounts for these changes. Industrial pollution kills lichens on tree bark, and soot makes the bark uniformly black. In non-polluted areas, tree bark is covered in lichen and speckled grey-green. Peppered moths rest on the bark of trees during the day, with their wings outspread. To human eyes, melanic moths are better camouflaged than speckled ones against black bark; the opposite is true on lichen covered bark. In 1955, H B D Kettlewell suggested that, because birds hunt by sight, they might miss camouflaged moths and take the more conspicuous ones. This idea has been tested by direct observation and experiment.

(i) Field studies led by Kettlewell showed that several species of birds, including nuthatches, robins and song thrushes took and ate the resting moths.

(ii) Speckled and melanic moths were collected and put out on polluted (blackened) and unpolluted (speckled) areas of bark on several trees in a wood near Liverpool. In an experiment carried out over several weeks, the moths taken by birds from the two types of bark were counted (Table 3). These data show that moths were taken most often on backgrounds from which they stood out.

Evidence (i) and (ii) strongly support the hypothesis that the melanic form of the peppered moth has become more common in industrial areas because speckled forms have been 'visually selected against by bird predators'. The Clean Air Act has reduced industrial pollution and, since 1965, there has been a corresponding sharp decrease in the proportion of melanic peppered moths in many populations in industrial areas, probably because the trees are becoming less blackened by soot.

## Economically important species

There are several other examples of changes in natural populations as a result of man-made changes in the environment, and some of them are of importance to human beings. Many animal and fungal species feed or grow on agriculturally important plants or animals, or on their stored products. Weeds grow in close proximity to crop plants and often outcompete them. All these organisms are called **pests**; they do great damage and can reduce food availability to human communities as well as causing great economic losses. Various chemicals (**pesticides**) have been used to kill pest species. Their use has applied directional selection to the pest populations and this has resulted in the development of resistant populations. Where a single pesticide has been widely and continuously used, many populations now have a high proportion of resistant individuals. Recent control methods have therefore used lower concentrations of a particular pesticide, and applications of *mixed* pesticides. This reduces the selection pressure for a particular resistance gene, and resistance evolves more slowly. A few examples follow.

(i) **Blow flies**. The blow fly, *Calliphora*, quickly became resistant to 'DDT'. This insecticide is very stable and was withdrawn in the 1950s when it was found to spread to natural food chains. It accumulated in, and severely reduced the fecundity of several predators. Many insect species are becoming resistant to **pyrethroids**, but they remain the favoured insecticides of the moment since they are broken down by soil bacteria and so do not spread to natural food chains.

(ii) **Rats and mice**. Rats (*Rattus norvegicus*) and mice (*Mus musculus*) are resistant to the anticoagulant 'warfarin' which has been used on a large scale to control their populations. A dominant allele (**R**) at a single locus in rats confers resistance. However, this allele also confers a requirement for vitamin K. Heterozygotes (**Rr**) are resistant to warfarin and have only a small requirement for vitamin K; homozygotes (**RR**) are resistant to warfarin but have a massive requirement for vitamin

**Table 3** *The proportions of speckled and melanic moths taken by birds from unpolluted and polluted tree bark in a Liverpool park*

| COLOUR OF MOTH | NUMBERS USED | % MOTHS TAKEN AND TYPE OF BARK | |
| | | Unpolluted | Polluted |
| --- | --- | --- | --- |
| speckled | 218* | 20% | 44% |
| melanic | 218† | 40% | 15% |

\* 148 put on unpolluted bark; 70 put on polluted bark
† 40 put on unpolluted bark; 178 put on polluted bark

GENETICS AND EVOLUTION

K which is difficult to meet. Although **rr** homozygotes are killed by warfarin, they have a much better chance of survival than **RR** rats *if* warfarin is absent from the environment. It is interesting that rats and mice appear to have evolved resistance by different genetic mechanisms; in mice, the resistance seems to be polygenic.

(iii) **Fungi**. Some economically important fungi are developing fungicide resistance, e.g. various *Botrytis* species parasitise soft fruit crops and many of them are resistant to **benomyl** fungicides.

(iv) **Weeds**. The groundsel (*Senecio vulgaris*) is just one weed species that has developed resistance to **triazine** herbicides.

Not all human-directed evolution of resistance causes such problems. An example of useful change is the evolution of **heavy metal tolerance** (resistance) in several grass species. Populations with a high proportion of heavy metal tolerant plants are found on spoil heaps associated with various mining activities. Now that industrial activity is altering, many sites that are polluted with heavy metal are being landscaped for different use and can be planted with tolerant plants.

### Stabilising selection

**Stabilising selection** results in several different types of individual being maintained in a population so that genetic variation is maintained. One type of stabilising selection is **heterozygote advantage**: if heterozygotes (e.g. **Rr**) are favoured by selection then both alleles **R** and **r** will be maintained in the population and all three genotypes (**RR**, **Rr** and **rr**) will be produced in each generation (Figure 4a). One example of this form of stabilising selection maintains both warfarin-sensitive and warfarin-resistant alleles in rat populations in areas where warfarin is used as a selective agent (see above). The sensitive homozygotes tend to be killed by warfarin, the resistant homozygotes often die because of their massive vitamin K requirement. Heterozygotes tend to survive both these selective pressures; their offspring will include homozygotes as well as heterozygotes and so both alleles are maintained in such populations.

## Evolution of dominance

It benefits an organism if a disadvantageous mutation is not expressed. Before the Industrial Revolution, the melanic form of the peppered moth, *Biston betularia*, was very rare and probably appeared sporadically by mutation. It made the individual carrying it stand out in the non-industrialised countryside, and was therefore

selected *against*. When the gene became advantageous in industrial populations, the heterozygote was intermediate between the melanic homozygote and the speckled, homozygote; the intermediates were less well camouflaged than the melanics in sooty backgrounds. A heterozygote now looks the *same* as the melanic homozygote, i.e. the melanic form is **dominant**. Both the homozygote and the heterozygote now gain an advantage because they are well camouflaged against blackened tree trunks.

Dominance is a genetic modification. This was established by crossing a dominant individual from a Birmingham population to a recessive individual from a Cornish population. Dominant offspring were then back crossed to the Cornish population. Within three generations, dominance had broken down and there were many intermediates. Offspring receive half of their genes from each parent, so the first generation got 50% of its genes from each population. After one back cross of the hybrid to the Cornish strain, the moths contained 25% 'Birmingham' genes and 75% 'Cornish' ones. After the second back cross, the moths were 87.5% Cornish genes. The breakdown of dominance can therefore be attributed to the 'diluting out' of the background genotype which caused dominance in the Birmingham population.

Dominance suppresses the effects of a disadvantageous gene in a heterozygote and by doing so helps to maintain the gene in the population. Even if the recessive homozygotes die, the gene may be maintained in the heterozygote. This means that the gene is only very slowly removed from the population. Selection for dominance is therefore a stabilising factor in evolution because it helps to maintain variability. By chance, this was valuable for *Biston betularia*: the speckled gene of the moth was maintained at a low frequency in industrial populations (less than 2%) so these populations were able to respond rapidly to the changed conditions brought about by the Clean Air Act.

## 10.4 COMPARISON OF SPECIES

Individuals belonging to different species tend to have different characters which adapt them to different ecological niches. For example, blackbirds (*Turdus merula*) hold slugs in their beak and wipe away their slime cover before eating them; song thrushes (*Turdus philomelos*), a different species, have modified this behaviour. They can crack open a snail shell against a

134

convenient stone and eat the snail inside. Thrushes therefore have a source of food that is not available to blackbirds. This aspect of feeding behaviour is **innate** ('built in') and genetically determined. Because the two species do not interbreed, they cannot exchange genes and so they cannot share this character.

The species is an important unit in evolution because it is a unit of reproduction. This has two important effects:

  (i) An advantageous mutation or combination of genes which arises in one individual can be passed on to the whole species by interbreeding.

  (ii) An advantageous mutation in one species cannot be swamped by genes from other species because they cannot interbreed. This means that different species can adapt to different environments.

Biologists studying evolution need to obtain evidence about how new species form but there has not been time for new species to form during experiments with populations. Charles Darwin was one of the first people to realise that new species must be formed by splitting old ones. He reached this conclusion after studying the finches which inhabited the Galapagos Islands in the Pacific Ocean. He visited the islands towards the end of his voyage aboard HMS *Beagle* (1831–1836).

# The Galapagos finches

The Galapagos Islands lie 960 km west of Ecuador. They are a group of volcanic islands separated from each other by several miles of open sea. The largest, Albemarle, is 128 km long. Several of the larger islands rise more than 2000 ft above sea level. These islands have three different environments: arid lowland, humid forest, and humid upland. The smaller islands tend to be low lying and arid with some coastal mangrove swamps. The birds inhabit lowland and woodland habitats.

Apart from one species, all the Galapagos finches are restricted to the Galapagos Islands. The distant species is on Cocos Island, 960 km to the north. There are 14 species of finch arranged in four genera. They are all about the same size as a sparrow and have dull black or brown plumage. They share similar courtship displays, nests and eggs. The main *difference* between the species is in the size and shape of their *beaks* (Figure 8). The finches can be broadly divided into three ecologically distinct groups:

**The groundfinches** are mostly confined to arid lowlands. They include: three seed-eating species; two cactus-eating species; and one species that eats mostly leaves. The three seed-eating species have beaks of similar shape but different size. They live together on the arid coastal regions of several of the main islands (Figure 9). They often feed on the same plants, but they avoid competition because they usually eat different sized seeds. Some of the islands (e.g. Wenman, Tower and Hood) have only one of these species, others have two. Where one or more species is missing, the remaining ones often have a more variable beak size and also a more variable diet.

**The treefinches** are mostly found in the humid woodlands. They include: three species that search leaves and twigs for insects; one species that strips bark in its search for insects; a woodpecker finch using small twigs and cactus spines to probe for insects in decaying wood; and one vegetarian species rather like a bullfinch. Several of these species show small differences in beak shape on different islands.

**The warbler finches** behave like European Warblers. They include two species, both of which eat insects. (One of these is the Cocos Island species.)

The Galapagos finches are so similar, except for their beaks, that it is generally agreed that they had a common ancestor. It seems likely that a few ancestral finches were accidentally blown from the South American mainland, and the

| food | seeds | seeds, cactus flowers and fruit | small soft insects | insects in wood (uses cactus spines) |
|---|---|---|---|---|
| species | *Geospiza magnirostris* | *Geospiza scandens* | *Certhidea olivacea* | *Camarhyncus pallidus* |

*Figure 8   The beak shape of four species of Galapagos finch*

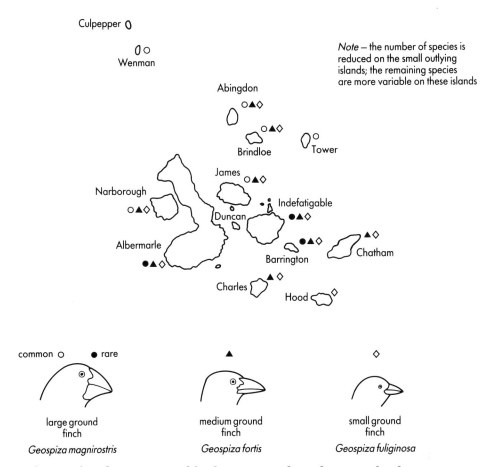

**Figure 9   Distribution of seed-eating ground finch species on the Galapagos Islands**

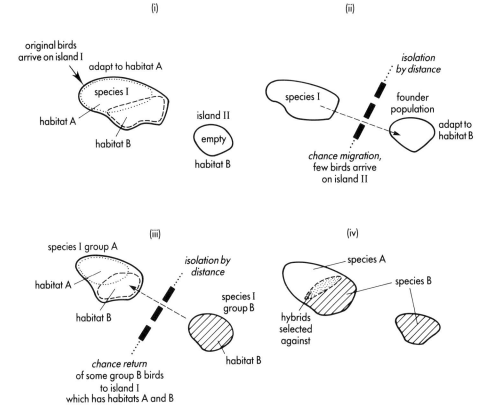

**Figure 10   The roles of isolation and adaptation to different habitats in genetic divergence between populations. New species are formed when populations are reproductively isolated**

hypothesis shown in Figure 10 would account for the subsequent formation of different species. It can be set out as follows:

(i) The original birds arrived on an empty island (Island 'I') and occupied a particular habitat. Their progeny adapted to this habitat by natural selection and formed species 'I'.

(ii) On a rare occasion, a few birds were carried to another island (Island II) with a different empty habitat. The new population was small and isolated, so the Founder Principle operated and the birds evolved rapidly by genetic drift and directional selection to become adapted to the new habitat. This meant that the populations on the separate islands diverged genetically from each other, particularly for beak shape (to become species I, group A and species I, group B).

(iii) On another rare occasion, a group of birds (e.g. from group B) reinvaded an island (e.g. island I) which was already occupied (by group A). This island contained both habitats.

(iv) The two groups of birds, adapted to different habitats and therefore genetically different, would now meet. Hybrids between the two groups might be inviable, or sterile, because of the parents' genetic differences. Alternatively, the hybrids might have an intermediate beak shape which would put them at a disadvantage when feeding in competition with pure bred members of either group. In this situation, birds which mated *within* groups would be more likely to produce offspring which themselves survived to reproduce. Any genetic-based behaviour patterns preventing individuals from mating between groups would be at a selective *advantage*. When these behaviours became fixed, the birds would only mate *within* groups. These groups are now separate species (species A and species B), each one adapted to a different habitat and reproductively isolated.

The pattern of divergence and reproductive isolation seen among the Galapagos finches is common among many other species. In general, all the available evidence supports the hypothesis that new species are formed by **isolation** and **genetic divergence**.

# 10.5 FOSSILS AND EVOLUTION

**Fossils** are remains of organisms preserved (usually in stone) during the history of the earth.

# Fossil records

The fossil record for elephants is more complete than that of many other organisms. It is summarised in Figure 11 which shows how various elephant species may be related to each other. Each vertical line represents the distribution of one species. Fossils are put into separate species if they are so different that they are unlikely to have been members of the same breeding group. Where a vertical line is dotted in figure 11, the species is missing from the fossil record (although it reappears later). Where a vertical line is crossed, present evidence suggests the species has become extinct. Horizontal dashed lines show the likely derivation of new species.

The fossil remains suggest that there were once several species of elephant, although only two of them have survived to the present. The African elephants (*Loxodonta africana*) and Indian elephants (*Elephas maximus*) of today have such marked skeletal differences that the two species

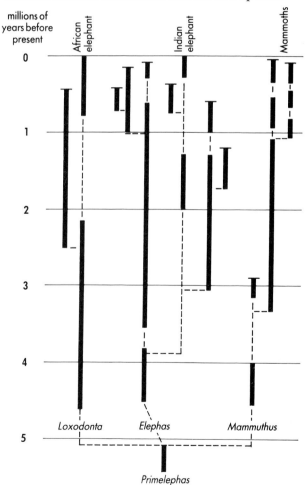

**Figure 11    Distribution of fossil elephant species (sub-family Elephantinae) over the last 5 million years**

are thought to be relatively distantly related and so are placed in different 'genera'. A **genus** (plural **genera**) is a group of similar species. The elephants are arranged in three genera: two of them are *Loxodonta* and *Elephas*. They are both different from the mammoths (genus *Mammuthus*) which became extinct about 10,000 years ago, although human cave paintings and deep frozen specimens from Siberia show us that they looked similar.

A fossil form, *Primelephas*, which could have given rise to all three genera was last found in rocks laid down, over 5 million years ago. There is then a gap of several hundred thousand years before three types of fossil are found almost simultaneously (Figure 11). They are so different that it is impossible to derive any of the three from each other and so it seems very likely that they are separate species which must have descended independently from *Primelephas*.

The fossil histories of many organisms are like this. There are lengthy periods when species show little change but, occasionally, a distinct new species appears. This pattern of stability and sudden change is called a **punctuated equilibrium**. In other cases, one species may have separated more **gradually** into two (Figure 12).

There are at least two genetic events that could contribute to the *sudden* appearance of species in the fossil record:

(i) Studies of living populations suggest that new species could be formed by the Founder Principle over a relatively short period (perhaps a few hundred years for organisms of short generation time). The originators of the new species would be small populations isolated in new environments. A small number of individuals would therefore form a new species almost instantaneously *compared with* the time span of the fossil record. It is unlikely that the species would be detected as fossils until its numbers had built up.

(ii) Analysis of *Drosophila* developmental mutants (chapter 9) suggests that one such mutation might have such far-reaching effects on an organism that its descendants could give rise to a whole new array of species. If it initially depended on one or a few mutations, such species diversification could happen quite rapidly. An example of such a mutation would be the bithorax gene which affects wing number in Diptera (flies). Most insects have two pairs of wings, but the dipteran species have a single pair of wings; their hind wings are much reduced and are converted to organs for balance, called halteres. We know from mutation studies (chapter 9) that this major switch in development is largely controlled by the bithorax gene.

As well as showing the rapid appearance of new species, the fossil histories of the elephants and many other groups show that many different species were formed but then died out. There are many species of animals and plants alive today and some of them are very ancient but it is important to realise that they are only a tiny fraction of the species which have appeared but later become extinct during the history of the earth.

# BIBLIOGRAPHY

Arthur, W (1987) *Theories of Life* Penguin,
Berry, R J (1977) *Inheritance and Natural History* Collins
Bradshaw, A D and McNeilly, T (1981) *Evolution and Pollution* (Studies in Biology) Edward Arnold
Sheppard, P M (1975) *Natural Selection and Heredity* 4th Edn. Hutchinson.

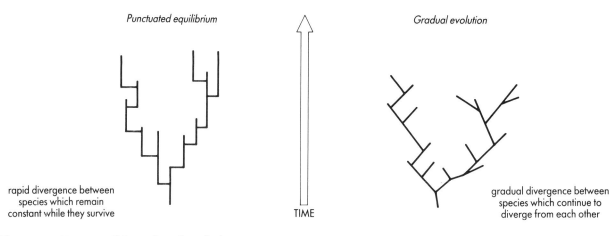

*Punctuated equilibrium*

rapid divergence between species which remain constant while they survive

TIME

*Gradual evolution*

gradual divergence between species which continue to diverge from each other

**Figure 12    *Two possible modes of evolution***

# QUESTIONS

**1** Wild rabbit populations are reappearing in Britain a few years after their decimation by a viral disease. Some of these rabbit populations are polymorphic for coat colour. Several populations are polymorphic for agouti/non-agouti (black) phenotypes. In one such population, 12% of the rabbits are non-agouti.
   a) What are the frequencies of the agouti and non-agouti alleles in this population?
   b) What proportion of the agouti rabbits would be expected to be heterozygous at the agouti locus?
   c) Assuming random mating, and in the absence of disturbing factors, what will be the frequency of non-agouti rabbits in the next generation? How do you explain this result?
   d) List the possible disturbing factors and briefly explain what their effect might be.

**2** Protein polymorphisms are particularly useful in the study of gene frequencies in populations because a heterozygote can be distinguished from either homozygote by electrophoresis of the protein. Some leaves were removed from a sample of 35 *Phlox* plants growing in the wild and the enzyme phosophoglucose isomerase was extracted from them. Electrophoresis showed that two plants were homozygous AA, 13 plants were heterozygous AA′ and 20 plants were homozygous A′A′.
   a) What are the allele frequencies among these plants?
   b) Test the genotype frequencies to see if they fit Hardy Weinberg expectations.
   c) How would you account for the results of your test?
   d) The plants were left to mate at random and were not disturbed in any way. How many generations would pass before you would obtain a sample of plants that conformed to the expectations of a population which were mating at random? How could you tell that mating was at random?

**3** Alleles B and b affect the colour pattern of a particular species of butterfly. The phenotype produced by the B allele is dominant. The patterns determine the visibility of a butterfly and its risk of predation by birds. Observations on predation in a natural environment suggest that the butterflies with a B phenotype have a greater probability of survival (65%) than individuals with a b phenotype (45%). What type of selection is operating on this butterly population and what is its likely effect?

**4** Explain why the frequency of warfarin-resistant rats is only likely to continue to increase in a population with the continued use of warfarin. Which genotype is most likely to be favoured under this selection?

**5** Summarise the theory of evolution put forward by Darwin. Does this theory need to be altered as a result of more recent work? (Explain your answer.)

# 11 APPLIED GENETICS

Applied genetics brings about short term evolution of particular species. Humans rely on other organisms for food and other essentials. Scientists have taken useful species and have improved them in different ways by genetic manipulations.

This chapter concentrates on two aspects of applied genetics:

(i) The modification of agriculturally important species by **breeding**.

(ii) The alteration of an organism's genotype by **inserting DNA** from a different species.

Breeding from selected parents and DNA manipulations are forms of '**genetic engineering**'. Since the beginning of this century, scientists have used genetic principles to modify the genotypes of plants, animals and micro-organisms. DNA manipulation is more recent. Both methods require genetic variation to be effective.

## 11.1 THE APPLICATION OF GENETICS

The aim of the applied geneticist is to create individuals which have an optimum set of characters so that yields are maximised. This is beneficial to the consumer and also to farmers or industrialists who get the greatest return for their investment. The first part of this chapter will concentrate on the methods used to increase productivity in agriculturally important species, especially crop plants. The reason for this emphasis is that crop plants are the primary source of food for all humans, and almost the only source for many millions of people. However, applied genetics has also contributed to great increases in animal productivity.

There has been an immense change in the genetics of crop plants. Wheat, rice, maize and barley are now the predominant cereal crops making up some 90 per cent of the world's supply of grain. A few years ago, when local cereal varieties were grown, different plants growing in a single field were likely to show genetic variation. The varieties of one cereal species growing in different parts of the country would certainly have contained quite different sets of genes. The plants would have adapted to local conditions as a result of local selection. This would have been a combination of **artificial selection** by the farmer, as he chose the seed for each succeeding crop, and **natural selection** due to the local environment acting on the plants in the field. The situation is now very different from this. Seed from a few plant breeding stations is sewn over wide geographical areas so all the individuals in one field of cereals are likely to have a similar genotype. In addition, this genotype is likely to be distributed over a wide geographical range. Combined with development of fertilisers and pesticides, these genetic changes have produced substantial increases in crop productivity, worldwide. This is the '**green revolution**'. The improvements in productivities of some British crops and farm animals is summarised in Table 1.

There are still many problems in agriculture, including the evolution of resistance in pests (chapter 10). There is concern that the genetic uniformity of modern cereals may lead to

*Table 1    Increases in animal and plant productivity in Britain in the period 1939–1963*

| PRODUCT | PRE-WAR YEARLY AVERAGE | YEARLY AVERAGE 1960–1963 | % INCREASE |
|---------|------------------------|--------------------------|------------|
| Wheat | 17.8 cwt/acre | 31.3 cwt/acre | 76 |
| Sugar beet | 8.2 tons/acre | 13.0 tons/acre | 63 |
| Potatoes | 6.7 tons/acre | 8.9 tons/acre | 33 |
| Milk | 560 gallons/cow | 777 gallons/cow | 39 |
| Eggs | 149 eggs/hen | 191 eggs/hen | 28 |

widespread damage by a single virulent pest or pathogen (see below). The cost and long term supply of fertilisers may be a problem and the accumulation of pesticides and fertilisers in the environment could be damaging.

All these difficulties and many others concerned with the supply of food, chemicals and energy, can be helped by DNA manipulation of various organisms combined with suitable breeding programmes. Applied genetics will surely have a continuing role to maintain and improve agriculturally and industrially important organisms in the future.

# Agriculturally important characters

Major genes *and* polygenes are important in agriculture. Here, we consider three different aspects of major gene activity, followed by some examples of quantitative characters.

## Major genes

(i) **Genes and enzymes in oil seed rape**. Chapter 8 introduced the discovery that many major genes act by producing enzymes which control metabolic pathways. Some major gene mutations which alter biochemical pathways have been important in converting a plant species into a major crop. Seeds which have a high oil content are an important source of edible oil. Most oil-producing species cannot yet be grown commercially as far north as Britain. However, oil seed rape grows well in our climate and produces seed with approximately 40 per cent oil.

The original varieties of this plant contained erucic acid (a fatty acid) which has poor digestability and accumulates in muscle and liver cells to cause irreversible pathological changes. A mutant was discovered which blocks a step in the synthesis of this molecule (Figure 1) so that it was reduced from 50% of the seed's fatty acid content to less than 0.3%. Rape seed has therefore become important in cattle feed. The plant also contains linolenic acid which is unstable with a rancid-tasting oxidation product. A mutation blocking its formation in rape seed oil has meant that this is now an important component of margarine and cooking oil. These two mutants have contributed to the widespread use of this plant as a crop.

(ii) **Genes and proteins in maize kernels**. Humans and other mammals cannot make the amino acids lysine and tryptophan so they obtain them from their food. In maize

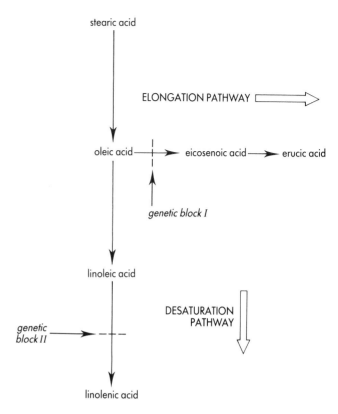

**Figure 1    Stages in fatty acid biosynthesis**

endosperm for example, there are four groups of proteins. They all have different solubilities. One group, the **prolamines**, are usually most abundant (40–55% of maize kernel proteins). A second group of proteins (**glutelins**) account for 30–35% *but* glutelins are the main source of lysine and tryptophan. Two maize mutants, opaque-2 and floury-2 reduce prolamines and increase glutelins: opaque-2 raises lysine from 2 gm lysine per 100 g protein to 3.39 g per 100 g. This mutant has been bred into a modern productive strain of maize, thereby increasing its nutritive value for pigs and humans.

(iii) **Plant resistance to fungal parasites**. Many different micro-organisms (viruses, bacteria and fungi) infect living plants. Fungal infections have caused widespread damage to crops. e.g. the catastrophic spread of the fungus *Helminthosporium maydis* across much of the maize crop of the USA in 1970, causing losses of millions of dollars. The fungus causes 'southern cornleaf blight' which severely damages sensitive plants. The disease spread so widely because a highly productive variety of maize had recently been introduced and was extensively grown across the country and this variety happened to be sensitive to the fungal pathogen.

**Table 2    The genetics of flax resistance to a fungal parasite, flax rust. Data from Flor (1954).** Sens: *sensitive,* Res: *resistant,* st: *strain*

(a)    *The inheritance of resistance in a cross between two varieties of flax*

| Tester | $P_1$ | $P_2$ | Flax varieties, generations, genotypes and numbers | | | |
| --- | --- | --- | --- | --- | --- | --- |
| | | | | $F_1$ | | $F_2$ | |
| Rust | Ottawa | Bombay | | | | | |
| | rr | RR | Rr | | RR | Rr | rr |
| 22 | Sens. | Res. | Res. | | Res. | Res. | Sens. |
| Observed nos. | | | | | 153 | | 41 |
| Expected nos. | (3 : 1) | | | | 145.5 | | 48.5 |

$$\chi^2_{(1)} = 1.55 \quad P \gg 0.05$$

(b)    *The inheritance of virulence in a cross between two isolates of the flax rust*

| Tester | $P_1$ | $P_2$ | Rust isolates, generations, genotypes and numbers | | | |
| --- | --- | --- | --- | --- | --- | --- |
| | | | | $F_1$ | | $F_2$ | |
| Flax | st 22 | st 24 | | | | | |
| | AA | aa | Aa | | AA | Aa | aa |
| Bombay | Avirulent | Virulent | Avirulent | | Avirulent | Avirulent | Virulent |
| Observed nos. | | | | | 105 | | 28 |
| Expected nos. | (3 : 1) | | | | 99.75 | | 33.25 |

$$\chi^2_{(1)} = 1.11 \quad P \gg 0.05$$

Many plant species show genetic variation for resistance to fungal infection, giving resistant and sensitive individuals. An example is the resistance of flax (*Linum usitatissimum*) to flax rust (*Melampsora lini*), a basidiomycete fungus. The infective stage of this fungus on flax is effectively diploid; other fungal pathogens tend to be haploid.

The results of crossing two varieties of flax (Ottawa and Bombay) and testing the plants in each generation with a particular rust strain (strain 22) are shown in Table 2a. In the $F_2$ generation, there are 153 resistant plants and 41 plants which are sensitive to strain 22. This is not significantly different from a '3 resistant : 1 sensitive' ratio. This suggests that the two flax varieties are homozygous for different alleles of a single gene and that a resistance allele from Bombay flax is dominant over the sensitivity allele from Ottawa flax.

As indicated in the above experiment, rust strain 22 will not infect Bombay flax but a different isolate (rust strain 24) will do so. The two rusts were crossed (Table 2b) and the parents, $F_1$ and $F_2$ were all tested on Bombay flax leaves for infectivity. In the $F_2$, 105 rusts were non-infective and 28 were infective. This is not significantly different from a 3 : 1 ratio and it suggests that the two rust strains are homozygous for different alleles of an infectivity gene. In this case, the rust 24 infective (virulent) allele is recessive to the rust 22 non-infective (avirulent) allele.

These results mean that a fungus which expresses an allele of one particular gene can infect a particular host plant. However, a host plant which contains a resistance allele will not be infected by that fungus. Further analysis has shown that different flax varieties are resistant to different rust strains because they contain resistance alleles at different gene loci. The idea that a particular fungal infectivity gene is countered by a matching plant resistance gene is called the **'gene for gene' concept**.

A single natural plant population may contain a number of different individuals each one resistant to a different strain of a pathogenic fungus. This will prevent the destruction of the whole population by a particular pathogen. For this reason, plant breeders are introducing several *different* resistance genes into commonly grown varieties of cereals.

The molecular mechanisms of infectivity and resistance are of great interest. The virulence of southern cornleaf blight fungus to sugar cane (*Saccharum*) and the mechanism of resistance in this plant is well understood: when the fungus infects sugar cane leaves it is quite restricted and forms a small lesion, but lines of browning leaf cells spread out from the fungal site and the leaf eventually dies. Cell browning is due to a soluble fungal toxin.

The fungal toxin is an $\alpha$ galactoside (Figure 2), similar to two common plant $\alpha$ galactoside sugars, melibiose and raffinose. Purified toxin placed on sugar cane leaves at very low concentrations ($10^{-15}$g) causes cell browning typical of fungal infection. Radiolabelled toxin was used to probe various cell fractions from sugar cane leaves; it was found that toxin binds specifically to the cell membrane fraction. Chromatography and gel electrophoresis were

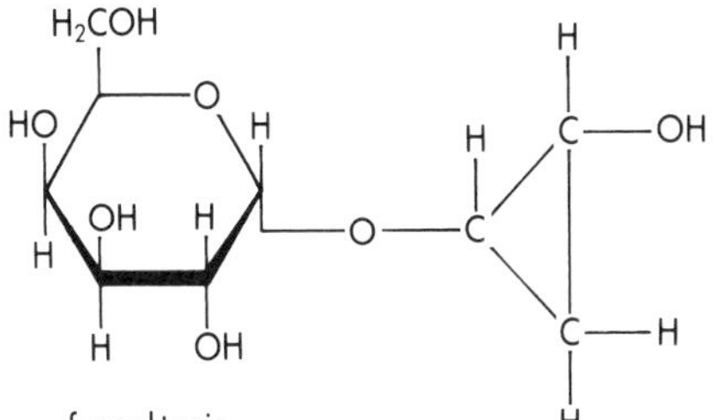

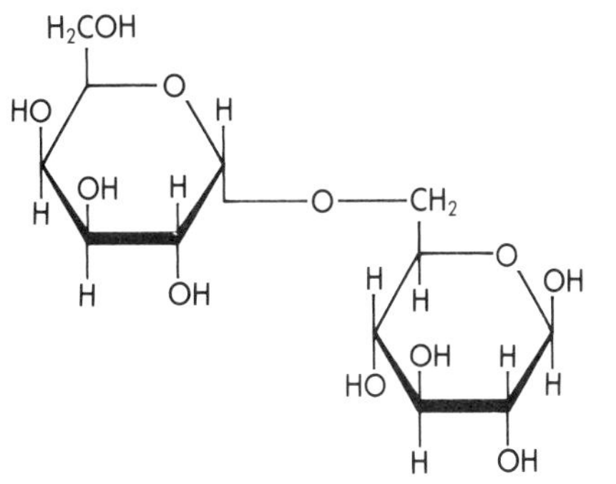

*Figure 2    The structure of the fungal toxin involved in Southern corn leaf blight (compared to the structure of the plant sugar melibiose)*

used to separate proteins from the membrane, and a receptor protein was identified which bound labelled toxin. When toxin binds to the receptor in the sensitive plants, it disturbs a leaf cell's ionic balance, thus interfering with respiration and photosynthesis. Sugar cane plants resistant to infection by the fungus were found to contain a membrane protein that *differed* from the receptor in sensitive plants by four amino acids in 110. This protein would not bind the toxin.

## Polygenes

Many characters that are of economic importance in plants and animals are determined by polygenes (chapter 4). Table 3 gives narrow heritability ($h^2$) estimates for a few of them. As mentioned in chapter 4, narrow heritability shows how much of the variation in a character is caused by the additive action of different genes.

*Table 3    Narrow heritability ($h^2$) estimates of some agriculturally important characters*

| CHARACTER | $h^2$ (%) |
|---|---|
| Maize plant height | 70 |
| Pig back fat thickness | 70 |
| Cattle body weight | 65 |
| Poultry body weight | 55 |
| Poultry egg weight | 50 |
| Cattle milk yield | 35 |
| Maize yield | 25 |

# 11.2 BREEDING METHODS

If any character is to be modified by **breeding**, there has to be genetic variation for that character. Breeding **programmes** are designed to increase the frequency of a particular genotype in the crop population. There are three features which have to be considered when altering the characteristics of a species:

(i) **A source of variation**. A genetically variable population is needed to initiate a breeding programme. The variation may already be present in the founding population or it may have to be introduced from elsewhere.

(ii) **The original breeding system of the species**. Some agriculturally important organisms such as wheat are normally self-fertilising; others, like maize, normally cross-fertilise. This affects the outcome of a breeding programme to improve the crop.

(iii) **Breeding**. This usually involves three steps.

    (a) *Inbreeding*: closely related individuals showing the desired characters are chosen as the parents of the next generation.

    (b) *Selection*: viable individuals with the most useful set of characters are chosen as parents in each generation.

    (c) *Crossing*: useful characters are combined by crossing different inbred and selected lines.

# Sources of variation

(i) **Induced mutations**. Plant geneticists have used ionising radiations and mutagenic chemicals to generate variation. Although these techniques have had problems, they have made a significant contribution to the improvement of crop plants. At the Institute of Radiation Breeding in Japan, growing rice plants have been exposed to ionising radiations from a cobalt-60 source. Many of the induced mutations were found to be lethal, but a rice strain developed from a mutant seed produced like this reached maturity about two months more quickly than the 'Norin 8' strain from which it was derived. This mutation could be combined by breeding and selection with other radiation-induced mutants which have rice grains with up to 16%

more protein. (Induced mutations have also provided valuable sources of genetic variation in several other crop plants including wheat.)

(ii) **Spontaneous mutations and gene banks**. Plant breeders rely extensively on mutations that have arisen spontaneously. These mutations are found in locally adapted populations around the world. For example, a mutation producing short wheat stems in almost all modern wheats was introduced by American plant breeders from Japanese wheat populations. Short stem varieties were also found in Korea and China.

Several genes have been introduced into crop plants from related wild species, e.g. a wild barley *Hordeum spontaneum* was the source of genes for resistance to the downy mildew fungus bred into UK barley strains such as Maris Badger.

Plant breeders are concerned that the widespread use of a few successful crop varieties and the alteration of many natural environments will mean that many potentially useful genes will be lost as local varieties and wild species disappear. This could be very serious because today's successful crop may not be so successful tomorrow. Newly evolved pest strains, or other changes in the environment, can reduce the value of a particular variety of crop plant very quickly. For example, the widespread planting of barley varieties like Maris Badger has selected for virulent downy mildew strains so that the *Hordeum spontaneum* (wild barley) genes no longer offer protection from infection.

Plant improvement must be an ongoing process. To try and prevent the loss of genes that may be valuable, various centres have been set up to form seed or plant collections for particular crop plants and their relatives. There is a great need for such '**gene banks**' to include many species that are currently under the threat of extinction as more and more land is modified for use by man. Some of these species may contain valuable genes which could be transferred into crop plants by DNA manipulation techniques.

# Natural breeding systems

Many plants and some animals are **hermaphrodite**, i.e a single individual produces both male and female gametes; but most animals and a few plants are **dioecious** with single sex individuals, either male or female. Hermaphrodites may self-fertilise, and several plant species and a few animal species do so. In some single sex species, closely related individuals regularly mate and reproduce. Self-fertilisation, or mating between closely related individuals, are forms of **inbreeding**.

Whatever their sexual system, many animals and plants are **outbreeding**. This means that the male and female gametes which fuse are produced by different, usually unrelated, individuals. Single sex individuals cannot self-fertilise, and inbreeding is often discouraged by behaviours which disperse offspring and therefore separate relatives. For example, in humans, outbreeding is encouraged by social and legal conditions. In many hermaphrodite animals and plants, self-fertilisation is impossible because of the structure of their reproductive organs. In some hermaphrodite plants, there are genetic systems that ensure outbreeding (chapter 3).

Outbreeding species mate at random and populations contain many heterozygotes (chapter 10). Inbreeding tends to *reduce* the number of heterozygotes in a population. R W Allard showed that the Hardy Weinberg genotype frequencies are modified when self-fertilisation and random mating both occur in a population. Instead of the three genotype frequencies being:

| | | | |
|---|---|---|---|
| AA | $p^2$ | they become: | $p^2 + 2pq[i/(4 - 2i)]$ |
| Aa | $2pq$ | | $2pq[2c/2(2 - i)]$ |
| aa | $q^2$ | | $q^2 + 2pq[i/(4 - 2i)]$ |

where p is the frequency of A, q is the frequency of a, i = the proportion of individuals self-fertilising, and c = the proportion of individuals random mating. The genotype frequencies are modified in this way because self-fertilising heterozygotes produce half their offspring as homozygotes (Figure 3). These are a loss to the heterozygote genotypes and a gain to the homozygote genotypes. This is why Allard's modified homozygote frequencies include an added proportion from the heterozygotes, and this

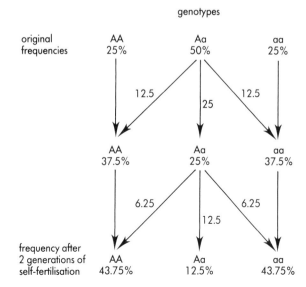

*Figure 3   Effect of self-fertilisation among a group of individuals (of whom 50% are heterozygous at the start)*

proportion depends on the amount of self-fertilisation. Allard's modified genotype frequencies are easily converted to numerical values and this shows the general effect of inbreeding more easily.

Suppose that two populations have gene frequencies for a pair of alleles of p = q = 0.5, but one population is random mating and the other is completely self-fertilising. In the random mating population, c = 1 and i = 0. This is reversed in the inbreeding population, i = 1 and c = 0. Substituting these numbers in the modified Hardy Weinberg proportions gives a random mating population with genotype frequencies: AA 0.25, Aa 0.50, and aa 0.25 as expected (chapter 10). In the self-fertilising population, the frequencies are: AA 0.5, Aa 0.0, and aa 0.5.

Theoretically, in a completely self-fertilising population, there should be no heterozygotes. However, mutation and stabilising selection will tend to maintain heterozygotes. Populations which *sometimes* self-fertilise and *sometimes* cross-fertilise will have intermediate genotype frequencies between complete outbreeders and complete inbreeders. In populations which go from outbreeding to inbreeding, it will take several generations to reach the appropriate genotype frequencies because the heterozygotes are only gradually lost (Figure 4).

Plant species, such as maize, with separate male and female flowers, tend to *out*breed. Their populations tend to contain *hetero*zygotes. In contrast, hermaphrodite species such as wheat, which often self-fertilise, tend to have populations with higher frequencies of *homo*zygotes. This difference has marked effects on the response of these two species to selective breeding.

# Breeding methods

### Inbreeding

Inbreeding is the production of young by related individuals. In self-fertilisation, one individual is both mother *and* father, and this is the closest form of inbreeding. Brother-sister matings or crosses between cousins are progressively less close forms of inbreeding.

Figure 4a emphasises that inbreeding happens when one ancestor contributes through both the male and female gametes which form an individual. This ancestor is called a **common ancestor**. The solid arrows in Figure 4a show the routes along which genes could pass to an individual from a common ancestor. If an individual (I) and its common ancestor (A) are closely related (self-fertilisation), there are few solid arrows between them and this is close inbreeding with a high probability that I will be homozygous for an allele present in A. When I is

distantly related to A, many solid arrows connect them, there is little inbreeding and there is only a small chance that I will be homozygous for A's alleles (half first cousin mating, Figure 4a). In some cases, an individual may inherit genes from more than one common ancestor, e.g. if its parents were brother and sister (Figure 4a), then both grandparents (A and B) are common ancestors. Several common ancestors increase the likelihood that an individual will be homozygous because there is more than one route by which it can become so.

Sewall Wright worked out a method for predicting the rate at which individuals would progress to homozygosity at one locus under various systems of inbreeding. The results of his calculations, for the types of mating just considered, are shown as a set of graphs in Figure 4b. Homozygosity is achieved most rapidly by self-fertilisation; it is never achieved by matings between half first cousins.

(a) *How an individual (I) receives its genes from a common ancestor (A or B)*

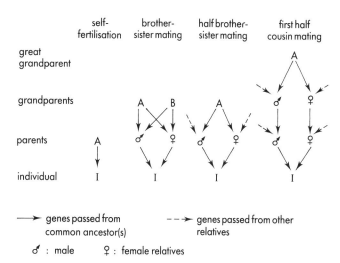

(b) *Progress towards homozygosity using different breeding methods*

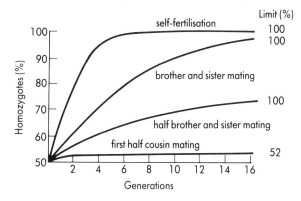

***Figure 4    Forms of inbreeding and how they affect progression towards homozygosity***

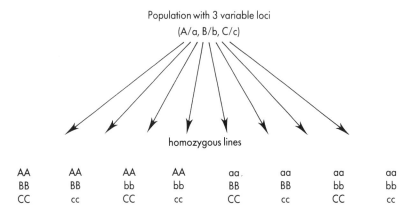

Population with 3 variable loci
(A/a, B/b, C/c)

homozygous lines

| AA | AA | AA | AA | aa | aa | aa | aa |
|----|----|----|----|----|----|----|----|
| BB | BB | bb | bb | BB | BB | bb | bb |
| CC | cc | CC | cc | CC | cc | CC | cc |

At one locus there are 2 possible homozygotes, with 'n' loci there are '$2^n$' possible homozygous combinations

**Figure 5** *The number of different homozygous lines produced from a variable population depends on the number of variable loci*

Suppose ten different plants from the same population are self-fertilised and, in each case, one offspring is grown and self-fertilised, and this is continued for a number of generations. This produces ten different **inbred lines**. If the original population was variable at a number of loci, it is very likely that the ten lines will be homozygous for different alleles at different loci (Figure 5) because there is no reason why all the lines should become homozygous for the same alleles; this is a matter of chance. It means that inbreeding produces homozygosity and uniformity within every line, but different lines may be uniform for *different* characters, or different forms of the same character.

## Inbreeding depression

All forms of inbreeding will tend to produce homozygous individuals. It is therefore potentially useful to the applied geneticist as a method for producing genetic uniformity. All the offspring derived from two identical homozygous parents will have their genotype and show their characters. Applied geneticists regularly use inbreeding to produce genetic uniformity for desirable characters but there are problems with the method so no crop plants or domesticated animals are homozygous for many of their loci.

Regular inbreeding to produce genetically uniform individuals showed that species such as maize, sugar beet or poultry (which are normally outbreeders) become much less 'vigorous' and also less fertile as they move towards homozygosity. This is **inbreeding depression**. In contrast, when two individuals from different inbred lines are crossed, the offspring are heterozygous at many of their loci and are often much more vigorous and more fertile than the parents. This is **heterosis**, or **hybrid vigour**. Both phenomena are illustrated in Figure 6. The problems of inbreeding depression are less pronounced in species such as wheat or tomatoes which inbreed regularly in their 'natural' field or glasshouse populations. Many different inbred lines have therefore been produced in these species; some hybrids between these inbred lines

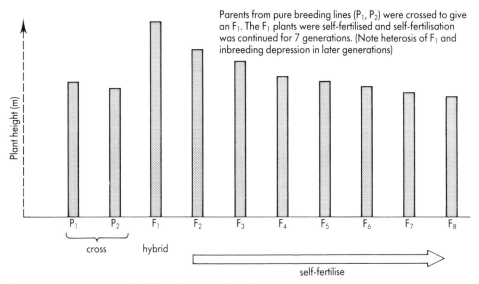

Parents from pure breeding lines ($P_1$, $P_2$) were crossed to give an $F_1$. The $F_1$ plants were self-fertilised and self-fertilisation was continued for 7 generations. (Note heterosis of $F_1$ and inbreeding depression in later generations)

**Figure 6** *Bar diagrams to represent heights of maize plants*

Variation among parental population

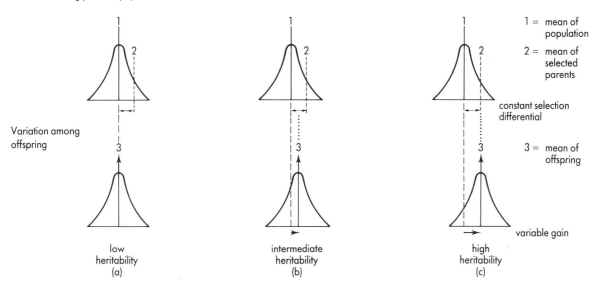

Variation among offspring

low heritability (a)

intermediate heritability (b)

high heritability (c)

1 = mean of population

2 = mean of selected parents

constant selection differential

3 = mean of offspring

variable gain

**Figure 7**  *Effect of selection for characters with different heritabilities*

are more vigorous than their parents, but this is not always the case.

## Artificial selection

Selection for animal or plant improvement is directional (chapter 10); the breeder wishes to enhance one aspect of a character to increase productivity. Many characters concerned with productivity are **quantitative** (Table 3), so the effect of directional selection on additive variation is considered here.

Chapter 4 showed that quantitative characters tend to follow a normal distribution: most individuals are intermediate and heterozygous, a few individuals are homozygous and extreme. To alter the expression of the character in a population, a breeder selects the more extreme forms in the founding population and breeds from them. The results of this selection depend on the extent to which the character is determined by the additive effect of polygenes. If the narrow heritability ($h^2$) is low, and variation is mostly environmental, then there is no reason why offspring should be like their parents and they will vary like the general population (Figure 7a). If the character has high $h^2$, the selected parents will have similar genotypes. Many of their offspring will have these genotypes too (Figure 7c). The mean of the character in the offspring will be close to the mean of the selected parents. With intermediate $h^2$, there will be some response to selection (Figure 7b).

The breeder can use different selection intensities to move the mean expression of the character towards the extreme. If he uses the most extreme individuals which are all similar, then breeds from their most extreme offspring and goes on repeating this procedure, he is practising very **intense** selection (Figure 8a). If $h^2$ is high, this

form of selection means that only very similar genotypes reproduce in every generation, and this should produce a rapid increase in homozygosity. If the breeder uses a group with greater variation for the character, there will be a greater range of genotypes; this is less intense selection (Figure 8b) and the shift to homozygosity will take many more generations of selective breeding.

The breeder can *combine* inbreeding with selection, either voluntarily or involuntarily. The breeder can voluntarily choose similar phenotypes among related individuals to be the parents. The involuntary case arises when only a few individuals are available for selection: the curves in Figures 7 and 8 show that the number of extreme individuals available for intense directional selection is likely to be small. In a small population the individuals in each generation are likely to be related. By breeding from a small number of similar individuals and keeping the populations small, intense selection

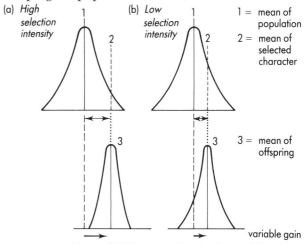

(a) *High selection intensity*

(b) *Low selection intensity*

1 = mean of population

2 = mean of selected character

3 = mean of offspring

variable gain

**Figure 8**  *Effects of different selection intensities for a character with a high heritability*

will be accompanied by inbreeding. Both directional selection and inbreeding increase the frequency of homozygotes. Thus, intense selection and inbreeding combined are likely to give a rapid increase in homozygosity. However, in a normally outbreeding species, this will be accompanied by a rapid loss of vigour and fecundity.

# Plant breeding programmes

A number of detailed breeding programmes have been worked out depending on whether the plant is an inbreeder or an outbreeder.

In both outbreeders and inbreeders, loss of vigour due to increased homozygosity is overcome by balancing artificial and natural selection. Artificial selection is imposed when similar individuals from a variable population are chosen by the breeder as parents; they are used to produce as many offspring as possible and these are all grown on under field conditions. Under these conditions, natural (environmental) selection will operate to remove the less vigorous offspring. Some of the more vigorous individuals

which also show the character of interest are then selected as parents for the next generation.

However, there are differences in the breeding programmes for inbreeders and outbreeders:

(i) **Inbreeders.** In species that usually self-fertilise, (e.g. wheat) each original parent gives rise to a separate line. The balanced selection discussed above can be continued within each line for successive generations (Figure 9a). The members of each line are eventually homozygous for many of their gene loci, including those controlling the character of interest.

(ii) **Outbreeders.** Species such as maize usually outbreed. Selected parents are self-fertilised by man to produce a number of lines and the offspring in these lines are exposed to natural selection. The best of them are then crossed between lines (Figure 9b). This alternation of selfing and crossing is repeated as long as necessary. It means that the lines are eventually homozygous for the genes controlling the character of interest, but heterozygous for many other gene loci.

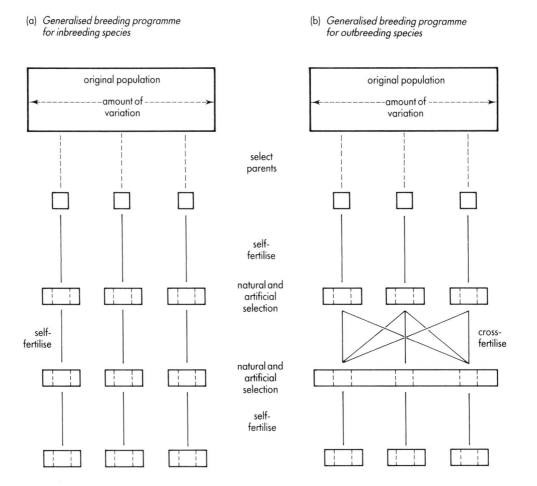

(a) *Generalised breeding programme for inbreeding species*

(b) *Generalised breeding programme for outbreeding species*

*Figure 9   Generalised breeding programmes for producing pure lines in crop plants*

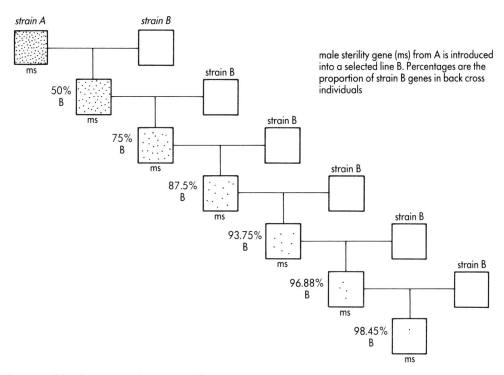

strain A

strain B

male sterility gene (ms) from A is introduced into a selected line B. Percentages are the proportion of strain B genes in back cross individuals

ms

50%
B

strain B

ms

75%
B

strain B

ms

87.5%
B

strain B

ms

93.75%
B

strain B

ms

96.88%
B

strain B

ms

98.45%
B

ms

*Figure 10    Repeated back crossing increases the proportion of genes from one strain*

(iii) **Introducing genes by repeated backcrossing**. Inbreeding and selection produce a number of lines homozygous for various useful characters. It may be necessary to introduce a new allele into these selected lines. e.g. a gene for dwarfism, or pathogen resistance. This is done by crossing a member of the line to an individual with the new gene; the offspring of this cross will contain a mixture of the genes of the two parents and will no longer be true breeding for the favourable characteristics of the original selected line. In general, parents contribute half their genes to their offspring. The new character can be integrated into the original line by several generations of backcrossing individuals showing the new character to individuals from the original selected line (Figure 10).

(iv) **$F_1$ hybrids**. Selected lines often differ in the combination of characters they possess. They can be crossed to produce heterozygotes which combine the advantageous characteristics of their parents. All the heterozygote, or '$F_1$ hybrid', individuals produced by a cross will have a similar genotype and therefore similar characters. They may also show hybrid vigour. This is why so many agricultural and horticultural crops are grown from hybrid seed; it maximises the probability of a uniform and highly productive crop. To produce hybrid seed commercially, controlled crossing must be carried out on a massive scale. One method of achieving this is to incorporate genes for male sterility into one of the parental lines, e.g. DNA manipulation in oilseed rape (chapter 3). Male sterility genes have been isolated in maize and wheat and introduced into various strains by breeding. If individuals from two parental lines are grown in alternating rows, the individuals from the male sterile line which produce seed must have been pollinated by an individual from the other line. These seed are guaranteed to be hybrid.

# In vitro methods

Various techniques to manipulate genetic material in plants, other than by breeding, have been developed. One method involves manipulating chromosomes in cultured cells, e.g. the formation of a new fertile crop plant called *Triticale*, an artificial alloploid between wheat (genus *Triticum*) and rye (genus *Secale*). Alloploidy is explained in chapter 4. In 1974, it was estimated that over 1 000 000 acres of *Triticale* was grown, spread over 52 different countries. *Triticale* can be formed using tetraploid or hexaploid wheat (chapter 7); the best *triticale* combines 42 chromosomes of hexaploid wheat with 14 chromosomes of diploid rye.

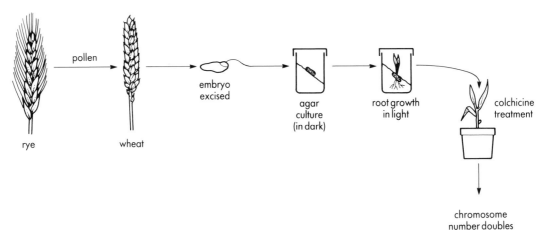

*Figure 11   Methods used to produce* Triticale, *an artificial hybrid between rye and wheat*

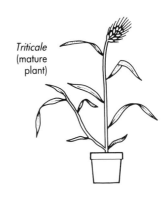

The methods used to produce *Triticale* are summarised in Figure 11. Wheat and rye genomes are relatively incompatible so hybrid embryos often develop abnormally. However, many immature embryos develop normally if they are excised from hybrid seed and grown on a defined cell culture medium. The embryos are cultured in the dark until roots form. Each of their cells contains 28 chromosomes (21 + 7). Young plants are treated with colchicine to prevent spindle formation (chapter 7) and to double the chromosome number in many cell nuclei: 2 ( 21 + 7) = (42 + 14) = 56 chromosomes. With two sets of wheat chromosomes and two sets of rye chromosomes, meiosis is normal and male and female gametes contain 28 chromosomes. Gamete fusion produces fertile *Triticale* plants; the initial plants had some disadvantages, but most of these have now been removed by selective breeding.

# 11.3 DNA MANIPULATION
## Gene transfer

An understanding of DNA and RNA is of the greatest significance in applied genetics. The enzymes and methods used to study nucleic acids (chapter 2) can be used to isolate genes from one organism and insert them in a completely different one. The kind of transfers that are being carried out at present are considered here. The next sections outline the basic techniques of gene isolation and gene transfer. Such molecular genetic engineering has applications in medicine, agriculture and industry, as well as in forensic science.

### Genes introduced into bacteria
Different genes have been transferred into *E. coli* from other micro-organisms, animals and plants. *E. coli* can be grown in large quantities and their genetics are well understood so the bacterium is used extensively in genetic engineering. e.g. in the synthesis of human insulin (important for the relief of diabetes) and human growth hormone (important for children carrying gene mutations giving them a requirement for this hormone).

Genes for viral coat proteins can also be inserted into bacteria. The value of producing large quantities of a single coat protein, or even part of a protein, is that these can be used safely in human vaccines to induce **antibodies** against certain viral diseases. Until now, these vaccines have been produced using attenuated (e.g. heat modified) forms of a whole virus but it is less hazardous to use part of one protein rather than the complete virus.

Many pharmaceutical materials are not proteins but small organic molecules synthesised by enzyme-controlled metabolic pathways. Their production requires the introduction of several genes to produce the necessary enzymes of the pathway. This approach has been already been used to modify an antibiotic called **actinorhodin** in streptomycete bacteria (a group of filamentous soil bacteria used in antibiotic production).

Bacteria are not ideal for all aspects of genetic engineering. There are two problems in expressing a *eukaryote* gene in bacteria.

(i) Bacterial promoter sequences (chapter 8) are different from eukaryote ones so the eukaryote sequence coding for the protein must be joined to a bacterial promoter.

(ii) Most eukaryote genes contain one or more introns (chapter 8). Prokaryote genes do not contain introns so there is no enzyme system in *E. coli* for their removal. Introns must therefore be removed *before* the eukaryote DNA is inserted into the bacterium, otherwise the protein produced will be quite different from the usual protein.

## Genes introduced into eukaryote cells

It has proved impossible to express some foreign genes in *E. coli*. The bacterium is useful for producing many copies of any eukaryote gene for DNA analysis but geneticists are turning to yeasts, plant and animal cells *in culture* to express genes from higher organisms as proteins. Yeasts are eukaryote cells and their transcription and translation systems are closer to those of humans than the systems in bacteria. This means that fewer modifications are needed for gene expression. A gene from the medicinal leech (*Hirudo medicinalis*) has recently been successfully inserted into yeast. It produces a leech salivary protein (hirudin) which prevents the formation of blood clots and will undoubtedly be useful in the treatment of thrombosis.

## Genes inserted into animals

It has been found that cells in the early embryos of animals will take up DNA and integrate it at various sites in their chromosomes. The genes carried on this DNA are expressed in the mature animal. An example is the introduction of a rat growth hormone gene into mice. The gene was expressed and the mice grew to be much larger than normal (see photograph). These sorts of techniques are currently being applied to the development of more productive farm animals. Techniques are developing so fast that it seems likely that corrective genes will eventually be transferred into humans known to be suffering from severely debilitating or lethal genetic diseases. Repair of genetic diseases of blood cells is likely to be attempted first. Blood cells are continually replaced from the bone marrow. A sample of bone marrow cells could be manipulated in culture and then returned to the patient.

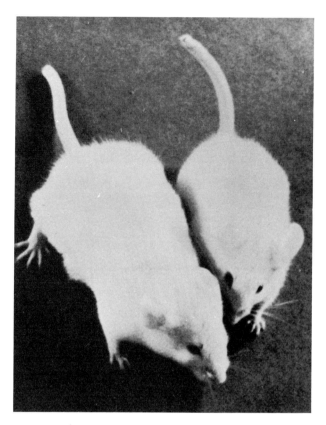

*The transgenic mouse (the larger of the two) has a rat growth hormone gene fused to a mouse promoter. It weighs 44 g compared to its brother (the smaller of the two) which does not carry the rat gene and weighs 29 g*

## Gene transfer into plants

Gene manipulation of plants is of great significance because of the importance of plants as food. Methods have been developed to transfer genes into dicot plants, and crop plants such as sugar beet have had genes for herbicide resistance (chapter 8) introduced into them. This may allow continued use of herbicides in weed control. A second example is a gene for the glycoprotein 'lectin'; normally expressed in pea seeds, this gene has been transferred to potato plants. It is advantageous because it inhibits the development of colorado beetle and tuber moth, which are potato crop pests in many parts of the world. A genetically engineered potato crop is currently undergoing field trials, to find out if the gene affects the growth of the potato plants and they will later be tested for pest resistance.

There have been problems finding a method to insert genes into monocot plants but several large companies have recently announced that they have sucessfully introduced a gene into maize. This is a very important advance because monocot plants are the most important crop plants all over the world.

# DNA manipulation methods

The procedure for transferring a gene from one organism to another can be summarised as follows:

(i) Extract DNA from the organism of interest and cut it into shorter lengths.
(ii) Insert these DNA molecules into carrier DNAs (**vectors**) *in vitro*.
(iii) Transfer modified vectors into cells (one per cell).
(iv) Let each cell produce many copies of its vector.
(v) Identify vectors carrying particular foreign genes and isolate them from the other vectors.

Enzymes, vectors and methods of selection are considered below.

## Enzymes

All the enzymes used in DNA manipulation are extracted from cells grown in culture. The main types are as follows:

(i) Restriction endonucleases
(ii) DNA ligases
(iii) DNA polymerases

Each restriction endonuclease used in DNA manipulation recognises a short sequence of nucleotide pairs and cuts the DNA there (chapter 2). Some restriction enzymes cut both strands of the DNA molecule in exactly the same position; Others make staggered cuts within the recognition site (Figure 12a). The latter enzymes form DNA molecules with 'sticky ends'. DNA molecules from two different organisms, cut with the same enzyme, have the same complementary nucleotide sequence at their cut ends. If the cut molecules are mixed, their 'sticky ends' will base pair.

Different DNA molecules, base paired by 'sticky ends', can be properly joined into a single DNA molecule by the DNA ligase enzyme (Figure 12b). DNA polymerases are used *in vitro* to repair DNA molecules and also to synthesise new molecules. One DNA polymerase (reverse transcriptase) is used to synthesise double stranded DNA copies of single stranded mRNA molecules. This DNA is called **cDNA**.

Eukaryote cells have already removed introns from mRNAs. Copying mRNA into cDNA *in vitro* is one way to *remove* introns from eukaryote genes. If the cDNA is inserted into bacteria, the gene on it can then be properly expressed.

(a) *Restriction enzymes cut DNA molecules to form 'blunt ends' or 'sticky ends'*

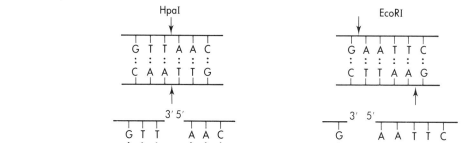

(b) *DNA ligase joins DNA molecules*

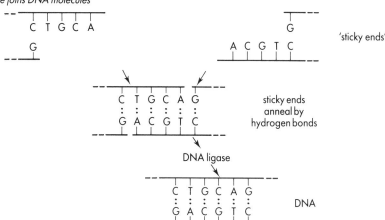

*Figure 12   The role on two enzyme types in DNA manipulations*

## Vectors

**Vectors** are carrier DNA molecules. Foreign DNA can be inserted into them *in vitro* to form a **recombinant vector** and this vector can then be taken up by a host cell. The vector replicates inside the cell and produces many copies of the foreign DNA. Some vectors also contain promoter and other control sequences to ensure the proper expression of the foreign gene in the host cell. We will consider two kinds of vectors:

(i) **Plasmid vectors**. These are mostly used to transfer a short length of foreign DNA (one gene) into a cell. The cell is often *E. coli*, but plasmids are also used to transfer foreign genes into yeast, or even a plant cell in culture (see below). There are several different plasmid vectors which can be used in genetic engineering. Some of these plasmids will allow the cell to express the foreign gene as protein. Plasmids are used for producing many copies of a piece of foreign DNA as follows (Figure 13):

(a) The plasmids are free in the bacterial cytoplasm. They are isolated by breaking open the cells followed by density gradient centrifugation (chapter 2).

(b) The plasmids usually carry a single recognition site for each restriction enzyme that cuts them (Figure 14). Foreign DNA cut with one restriction endonuclease (e.g. PstI) can be inserted in a plasmid (e.g. pBR322) cut with the same enzyme. This is a recombinant plasmid.

(c) Recombinant plasmids are reinserted into other cells by DNA transformation (chapter 5).

(d) Some plasmids replicate until there are many copies per cell. This means that

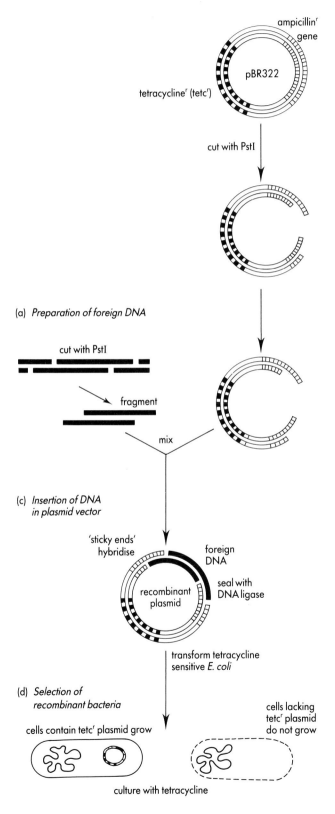

*Figure 13 Method for introducing foreign DNA into a plasmid vector and selecting for the recombinant plasmid in a bacterium*

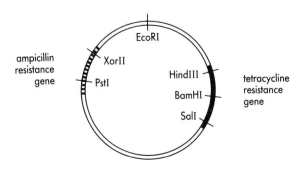

*Figure 14 The plasmid BR322, showing selectable genes and cloning sites for different restriction enzymes*

there will be a large number of copies of the introduced gene in each bacterium. The replicated plasmids containing foreign DNA are also copied from parent to daughter cells.

(e) The plasmids carry genes which mean that bacteria containing them will survive on a selective medium. For example, plasmid pBR322 contains two antibiotic resistance genes (Figure 14). Suppose a culture of antibiotic sensitive bacteria are transformed by pBR322 with foreign DNA inserted using PstI: the inserted fragment disrupts the coding sequence of the ampicillin resistance gene (Figure 14). Bacteria which have taken up the recombinant plasmid will survive on a medium containing tetracycline.

Gene transfer into bacteria is very useful for producing many copies of a particular gene. *E. coli* will replicate foreign DNA as if it were its own. The foreign gene may be expressed as a protein. In other cases, the DNA can be purified by reisolating the plasmid and cutting out the foreign DNA with the restriction endonuclease used to insert it. This provides a large quantity of a particular sequence of DNA which can be used in various ways, including nucleotide sequence analysis (chapter 2).

(ii) **Virus vectors.** Several different viruses are used as vectors; one is the bacteriophage lambda (λ). It is useful because it will carry a large fragment of foreign DNA without altering it. (Often, a large fragment of DNA inserted in a plasmid tends to have sections deleted when the plasmid replicates.)

The lambda strain used as a vector is modified by removal of a 25 000 nucleotide pair segment of its DNA. There are two convenient EcoRI sites that can be used for this (Figure 15). The chromosome fragment removed is not essential, it contains genes for the temperate life history. The virus survives as a virulent phage. DNA is extracted from virus particles and cut; the missing segment can be replaced *in vitro* by the same amount of foreign DNA (Figure 15). The engineered chromosome is then added to viral proteins in a test tube. Under certain conditions, the DNA and proteins will combine to form mature virus particles. These viruses will infect *E. coli*, go through their virulent life cycle and produce many viral progeny, all of them containing a copy of the introduced DNA.

A whole eukaryote genome can be cut into suitable lengths by EcoRI. If all the fragments are inserted into different λ viruses, they will contain the complete eukaryote genome in 25 000

nucleotide pair lengths. This is called a **genomic library**. Genomic libraries have been prepared for a number of eukaryote species and are the source from which a particular gene can be selected.

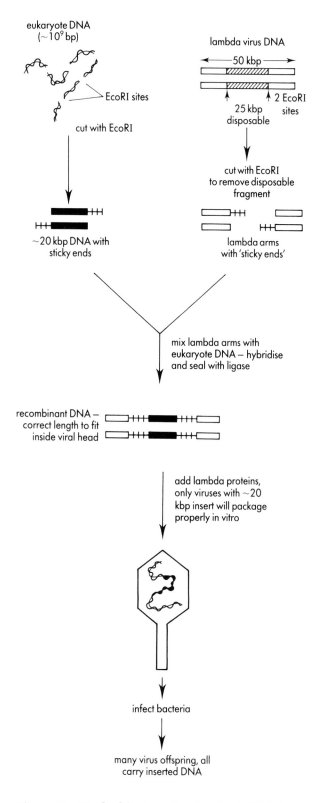

*Figure 15    Method for inserting foreign DNA into virus vectors*

## Methods of selection

Long molecules of chromosomal DNA are isolated from cells. Many different fragments are produced when this DNA is cut. Each recombinant vector may therefore contain a different fragment of foreign DNA, or a different foreign gene. One of the main problems in genetic engineering is to find out which bacterium or which virus contains a particular gene. The methods fall into two main groups:

(i) **Identification of the gene by its product**

(ii) **Identification of a particular sequence of nucleotide pairs.**

(i) For example, some genes can be identified simply through their gene product. Suppose you wish to isolate a gene which determines one enzyme involved in the synthesis of a particular biochemical, e.g. the amino acid tryptophan. This gene would be present in any yeast or bacterium which grows on minimal medium and is therefore Trp$^+$ (chapter 5). Suppose DNA is extracted from such an organism and inserted in a plasmid. The recombinant plasmid could be used to transform a bacterial strain that is mutant for that particular gene (Trp$^-$). This strain will not grow on minimal medium unless it contains a recombinant plasmid carrying the normal *trp$^+$* gene. Any bacterium which produces a colony on minimal medium must therefore contain a *trp$^+$* recombinant plasmid. This technique is

marker rescue and it is used in the isolation of genes involved in the synthesis of antibiotics.

(ii) For example, if a radiolabelled mRNA or cDNA for a particular gene has been isolated, the bacterium or virus carrying that gene can be identified by nucleic acid hybridisation (chapter 8). The method used to identify a bacterial colony carrying a particular gene in a recombinant plasmid is summarised in Figure 16. Bacteria are transformed and those carrying recombinant plasmids are identified (see plasmid vectors above). These bacteria are spread on an agar plate and each one forms a colony; the plate is called the **master plate**. A filter is lightly pressed onto the master plate and some bacteria from each colony adhere to it. The filter and plate are separated and the plate is put to one side. The bacteria on the filter are burst in situ to release their DNA. This DNA is baked onto the filter to keep it in its original position. It is made single stranded. The labelled probe is added to the filter and will only hybridise with DNA from the colony which contains the recombinant plasmid with the appropriate gene. The position of the bound probe on the filter is compared with the positions of the colonies on the master plate. In this way, the colony containing the DNA of interest can be located and grown as required.

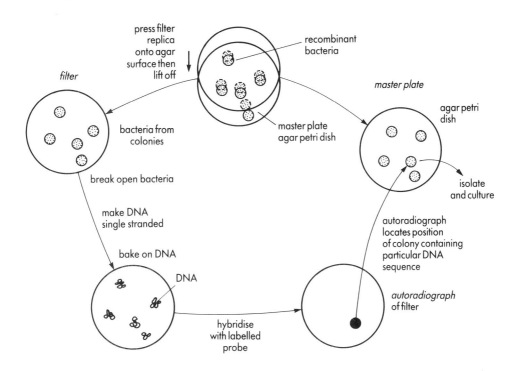

*Figure 16   Outline method for selecting bacterial colony containing a particular sequence of introduced DNA*

# 11.4 TRANSGENIC PLANTS

This chapter has mostly concentrated on modifications to plants. This section gives an account of gene transfer into plants using a DNA vector. The technique uses a genetically modified form of the soil bacterium *Agrobacterium tumefaciens*.

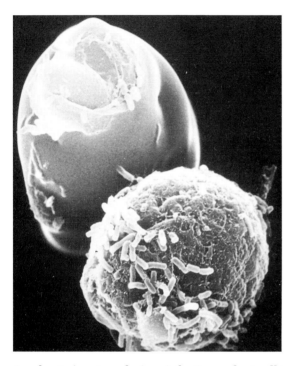

**Agrobacterium tumefaciens** *infecting a plant cell in culture. Rod-like bacteria can be seen on the surface of the plant cells in this photograph*

In nature, this bacterium (see photograph) will infect a wound in many plants and cause uncontrolled plant cell division. It has been shown that the ability of the bacterium to induce a tumour depends on the presence of a large plasmid in the bacterial cytoplasm. This is called the 'Ti' (**t**umour **i**nducing) plasmid. The Ti plasmid carries a group of closely linked T (toxin) genes. The bacterium produces a DNA copy of the T genes and injects it into the plant cell nucleus. This DNA inserts into a plant chromosome and the T genes cause the cells to divide in an uncontrolled way, forming a tumour. Injection and integration of the T segment is controlled by a second set of genes, the 'vir' (virulence) genes located on a different part of the Ti plasmid which does not enter the plant nucleus.

Ti plasmids have been modified to transfer foreign genes into plants (Figure 17). Two plasmids are needed as follows.

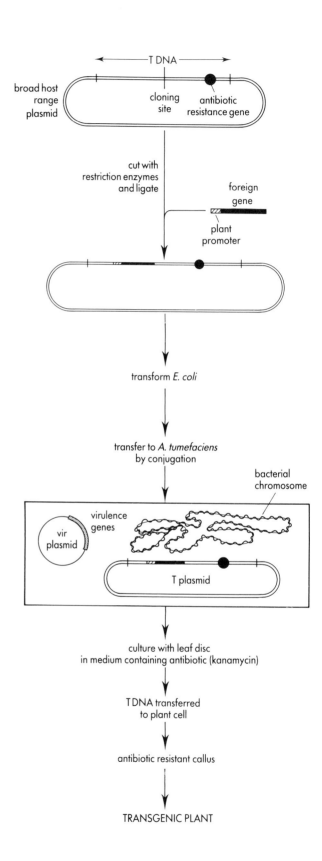

**Figure 17   Outline method for producing transgenic plants**

(i) **The T plasmid**. A T segment has been transferred to a plasmid which can replicate in a number of different hosts; it is a **broad host range plasmid**. This is maintained in *E. coli* but can be transferred to *A. tumefaciens*. The T segment has been modified in three ways:
   (a) tumour-forming genes have been deleted,
   (b) a gene for resistance to the antibiotic kanamycin has been inserted,
   (c) it has a restriction site for the introduction of foreign genes.
(ii) **The vir plasmid**. A second Ti plasmid has had all the T genes deleted but this plasmid contains the virulence genes.

Figure 17 shows that foreign genes are introduced into the T plasmid *in vitro*. This is then transformed into *E. coli*, and then transferred to *A. tumefaciens* by conjugation. After this, *A. tumefaciens* is cultured with plant leaf disc under appropriate conditions. The modified T segment is inserted in the plant cells driven by the vir genes on the second plasmid. Plant cells containing an integrated T segment are selected by their resistance to kanamycin. Under the correct growth conditions, the cells form a **callus** (chapter 9) and, eventually, new plants containing the foreign gene develop. These techniques were used to insert a lectin gene from peas into potatoes.

# BIBLIOGRAPHY

Brown, T A (1990) *Gene Cloning, An Introduction* 2nd Edn. Chapman Hall

Curtis, B C and Johnston, D R (1969). Hybrid wheat *Scientific American* 220 (5), 21–30

Hulse, J H and Spurgeon (1974) *Triticale. Scientific American*, 231 (2), 72–82

Prestcott-Allen, R and Prescott-Allen, C (1988) *Genes from the Wild* Earthscan Publications Ltd London

Strobel, G A (1975) A mechanism of disease resistance in plants *Scientific American* 232 (1), 80-90

Sigurbjornsson, B (1971) Induced mutations in plants *Scientific American* 224 (1), 86-96.

# QUESTIONS

1 There are three inbred varieties of wheat:
   variety X is resistant to a pathogenic strain of fungus,
   variety M is resistant to the same fungal strain,
   variety Y is sensitive to this fungal strain.
Three sets of crosses are set up to establish the genetic basis of resistance:

X × Y → $F_1$ all resistant, $F_1$ (X × Y) backcrossed to Y → ½ resistant : ½ sensitive plants.

M × Y → $F_1$ all resistant, $F_1$ (M × Y) backcrossed to Y → ½ resistant : ½ sensitive plants.

X × M → $F_1$ all resistant, $F_1$ (X × M) self-fertilised → $^{15}/_{16}$ resistant : $^1/_{16}$ sensitive plants.

   Is resistance governed by one gene locus or two gene loci? Explain your reasoning.

2 It is thought that inbreeding depression is due to the expression of harmful recessive alleles. Explain how this may happen. Account for the observation that inbreeding depression is much less acute in wheat than in maize.

3 Explain what breeding technique could be used to introduce new genes into an established crop plant variety. What advantage would there be in using induced mutants from the variety as the source of new genes, rather than a plant from a gene bank or a different part of the geographical range of the species.

4 Suggest why plant tissue culture techniques are useful in applied genetics.

5 If you were offered a plasmid vector or a λ virus vector to produce a genomic library of the organism you are interested in, which would you choose? Give your reasons.

   If your organism has a genome size of $5 \times 10^8$ nucleotide pairs and you could cut the DNA into fragments of 25 000 nucleotide pairs (average length), how many different recombinant vectors would there be in a complete genomic library?

# INDEX